Which Phase Were You Supposed to Do That?

Phase	What Needs to Be Done?
Phase 1: Gather Requirements	Collect Marketing Data
	Survey Customer Requirements & Proposed Solutions
	Justify the Project & Prioritize the Project Ideas
	Submit and Approve Request for Proposal (RFP)
	Write Requirements Document (RD)
	Write Beta Test Plan
	Identify Project Sponsor & Project Manager
	Get Project Team in Place
	Build Work Breakdown Structure (WBS) in Excel Spreadsheet
	Build Preliminary Project Plan (Schedule, Critical Path, PERT Chart & Gantt Chart)
	Estimate, Optimize & Finalize Project Plan
	Create Baseline Plan in Microsoft Project
Phase 2: Analysis	Write Project Scope Document (PSD)
	Create Entity Relationship Diagram (ERD)
	Create Data Flow Diagram (DFD)
	Define Data Dictionary
	Perform Object-Oriented Analysis
Phase 3: Design	Design Data Model
	Write Functional Specifications
	Design Storyboards (Prototypes)
	Write Detailed Design Specifications
	Write Documentation Plan
	Write Beta and SQA Test Plans and Test Cases
	Write Customer Support Plan
	Write Training Plan
	Write Change/Risk Management Plan
Phase 4: Develop	Develop Application
	Develop Data Model
	Unit and Integration Test
	Develop SQA System Test Plan and Test Cases
	Write Documentation
Phase 5: Test	Test System
	Track Defects and Enhancements
	Regression Test Fixes

(continued)

Software Project Management Kit For Dummies®

Which Phase Were You Suppose to Do That? (continued)

Phase	What Needs to Be Done?
Phase 6: Manage Release and Change	Perform Configuration Management Functions
	Create Change Control Processes and Select Board to Address Proposed Software Changes
Phase 7: Implement (At Customer Site)	Install and Test Beta Test System at Customer Site
	Beta Test Software and Report Defects to Customer Support
	Gather Requirements for Customizations
	Analyze Gap Between Customizations and Delivered Software
	Install Development System
	Implement/Adapt Software
	Perform Unit and Integration Tests
	Perform Customer Acceptance Test Procedure
	Cut-over Development System into Production as Pilot

Tips for Software Project Managers

- ✔ Gather the customer's requirements
- ✔ Organize a winning project team
- ✔ Become an effective liaison
- ✔ Develop a project plan
- ✔ Write a Statement of Scope
- ✔ Create detailed design specifications
- ✔ Optimize your schedule with Microsoft Project
- ✔ Focus on software quality assurance (SQA) at all times
- ✔ Control risks, changes, and scope creep
- ✔ Manage solid code baseline, builds, and releases
- ✔ Provide world-class documentation and training to your customers

Wiley, the Wiley Publishing logo, For Dummies, the Dummies Man logo, the For Dummies Bestselling Book Series logo and related trade dress are trademarks or registered trademarks of John Wiley & Sons, Inc. and/or its affiliates in the United States and other countries and may not be used without written permission. All other trademarks are the property of their respective owners. Wiley Publishing, Inc., is not associated with any product or vendor mentioned in this book.

Copyright © 2000 Wiley Publishing, Inc. All rights reserved.

Item 0634-X.

For more information about Wiley Publishing, call 1-800-762-2974.

For Dummies: Bestselling Book Series for Beginners

 ™

References for the Rest of Us!®

BESTSELLING BOOK SERIES

Are you intimidated and confused by computers? Do you find that traditional manuals are overloaded with technical details you'll never use? Do your friends and family always call you to fix simple problems on their PCs? Then the For Dummies® computer book series from Wiley Publishing, Inc. is for you.

For Dummies books are written for those frustrated computer users who know they aren't really dumb but find that PC hardware, software, and indeed the unique vocabulary of computing make them feel helpless. For Dummies books use a lighthearted approach, a down-to-earth style, and even cartoons and humorous icons to dispel computer novices' fears and build their confidence. Lighthearted but not lightweight, these books are a perfect survival guide for anyone forced to use a computer.

> *"I like my copy so much I told friends; now they bought copies."*
> — *Irene C., Orwell, Ohio*

> *"Quick, concise, nontechnical, and humorous."*
> — *Jay A., Elburn, Illinois*

> *"Thanks, I needed this book. Now I can sleep at night."*
> — *Robin F., British Columbia, Canada*

Already, millions of satisfied readers agree. They have made For Dummies books the #1 introductory level computer book series and have written asking for more. So, if you're looking for the most fun and easy way to learn about computers, look to For Dummies books to give you a helping hand.

Wiley Publishing, Inc.

5/09

Software Project Management Kit

FOR

DUMMIES®

Software Project Management Kit

FOR DUMMIES®

by Greg Mandanis with Allen Wyatt

WILEY

Wiley Publishing, Inc.

Software Project Management Kit For Dummies®

Published by
Wiley Publishing, Inc.
111 River Street
Hoboken, NJ 07030
www.wiley.com

Copyright © 2000 Wiley Publishing, Inc., Indianapolis, Indiana

Published simultaneously in Canada

No part of this publication may be reproduced, stored in a retrieval system or transmitted in any form or by any means, electronic, mechanical, photocopying, recording, scanning or otherwise, except as permitted under Sections 107 or 108 of the 1976 United States Copyright Act, without either the prior written permission of the Publisher, or authorization through payment of the appropriate per-copy fee to the Copyright Clearance Center, 222 Rosewood Drive, Danvers, MA 01923, (978) 750-8400, fax (978) 646-8700. Requests to the Publisher for permission should be addressed to the Legal Department, Wiley Publishing, Inc., 10475 Crosspoint Blvd., Indianapolis, IN 46256, (317) 572-3447, fax (317) 572-4447, e-mail: permcoordinator@wiley.com.

Trademarks: Wiley, the Wiley Publishing logo, For Dummies, the Dummies Man logo, A Reference for the Rest of Us!, The Dummies Way, Dummies Daily, The Fun and Easy Way, Dummies.com, and related trade dress are trademarks or registered trademarks of John Wiley & Sons, Inc. and/or its affiliates in the United States and other countries and may not be used without written permission. All other trademarks are the property of their respective owners. Wiley Publishing, Inc., is not associated with any product or vendor mentioned in this book.

LIMIT OF LIABILITY/DISCLAIMER OF WARRANTY: WHILE THE PUBLISHER AND AUTHOR HAVE USED THEIR BEST EFFORTS IN PREPARING THIS BOOK, THEY MAKE NO REPRESENTATIONS OR WARRANTIES WITH RESPECT TO THE ACCURACY OR COMPLETENESS OF THE CONTENTS OF THIS BOOK AND SPECIFICALLY DISCLAIM ANY IMPLIED WARRANTIES OF MERCHANTABILITY OR FITNESS FOR A PARTICULAR PURPOSE. NO WARRANTY MAY BE CREATED OR EXTENDED BY SALES REPRESENTATIVES OR WRITTEN SALES MATERIALS. THE ADVICE AND STRATEGIES CONTAINED HEREIN MAY NOT BE SUITABLE FOR YOUR SITUATION. YOU SHOULD CONSULT WITH A PROFESSIONAL WHERE APPROPRIATE. NEITHER THE PUBLISHER NOR AUTHOR SHALL BE LIABLE FOR ANY LOSS OF PROFIT OR ANY OTHER COMMERCIAL DAMAGES, INCLUDING BUT NOT LIMITED TO SPECIAL, INCIDENTAL, CONSEQUENTIAL, OR OTHER DAMAGES.

For general information on our other products and services or to obtain technical support, please contact our Customer Care Department within the U.S. at 800-762-2974, outside the U.S. at 317-572-3993, or fax 317-572-4002.

Wiley also publishes its books in a variety of electronic formats. Some content that appears in print may not be available in electronic books.

Library of Congress Cataloging-in-Publication Data:

Library of Congress Control Number: 99-66491

ISBN: 0-7645-0634-X

Manufactured in the United States of America

10 9 8 7 6 5

1O/QV/QS/QU/IN

About the Authors

Greg Mandanis is a software quality assurance (SQA) project manager at Concur Technologies, a premier business to business *eCommerce* ASP and application provider. He has taught computer applications courses at Heald Business College. He also was the project manager of the California State Board of Education's pilot Adult ESL Computer Assisted Instruction (CAI) program at South San Francisco's Adult Education. Over the past ten years, he has worked on a number of other software project teams and project management implementations. He is the author of the humorous sci-fi trilogy, *The Man From V.E.N.U.S.*, soon to be published by *Dry Bones Press*.

Greg has a Bachelor of Science degree in Management Information Systems from California Polytechnic State University at San Luis Obispo, California, where he was first introduced to software project management tools and programming beginning in 1977.

Greg can be contacted via e-mail at gman@eprojectschedulers.com. For additional software project management online resources and for software project management training for your team, please go to www.eProjectSchedulers.com.

Allen Wyatt is a veteran technology author and consultant. He is the president of Discovery Computing, Inc. in Cincinnati, Ohio.

Dedication

To my beautiful and supportive wife Christina and wonderful son Paul.

To software project managers and teams everywhere — wishing for all your success in the brave new eWorld.

Acknowledgments

I am very grateful to everyone at IDG Books Worldwide, Inc. who helped produce this kit. They collaborated to make this a truly simplified kit and "Reference for the Rest of Us," which gets the software project managers and their teams to dive in using Microsoft Project and other software tools beginning on Page 1.

I am particularly grateful to Sherry Morningstar and Greg Croy for sharing the initial vision for this project.

My hat's off to Kyle Looper, who suggested changing the scope of this project from a mere guide to a full-fledged CD-ROM kit. His superhuman effort made this kit readable, technically sound, and even funny at times.

I am also very grateful to Bill Barton of IDG Books for all his efforts to edit and provide invaluable feedback. Thanks to Allen Wyatt and Namir Shammas, who provided significant technical edits and invaluable feedback.

Publisher's Acknowledgments

We're proud of this book; please send us your comments through our online registration form located at www.dummies.com/register/.

Some of the people who helped bring this book to market include the following:

Acquisitions, Editorial, and Media Development

Senior Project Editor: Kyle Looper

Acquisitions Editors: Greg Croy, Sherri Morningstar

Senior Copy Editor: William A. Barton

Proof Editor: Teresa Artman

Technical Editor: Namir Shammas

Permissions Editor: Carmen Krikorian

Associate Media Development Specialist: Megan Decraene

Editorial Manager: Leah P. Cameron

Media Development Manager: Heather Heath Dismore

Editorial Assistant: Beth Parlon

Production

Project Coordinator: Regina Snyder

Layout and Graphics: Amy Adrian, Brian Massey, Tracy K. Oliver, Jill Piscitelli, Brent Savage, Brian Torwelle

Proofreaders: Laura Albert, Corey Bowen, John Greenough, Joanne Keaton, Marianne Santy, Ethel M. Winslow

Indexer: Steve Rath

Publishing and Editorial for Technology Dummies

Richard Swadley, Vice President and Executive Group Publisher

Andy Cummings, Vice President and Publisher

Mary C. Corder, Editorial Director

Publishing for Consumer Dummies

Diane Graves Steele, Vice President and Publisher

Joyce Pepple, Acquisitions Director

Composition Services

Gerry Fahey, Vice President of Production Services

Debbie Stailey, Director of Composition Services

Contents at a Glance

Cartoons at a Glance

By Rich Tennant

page 7

page 285

page 245

page 73

page 201

page 309

page 137

Cartoon Information:
Fax: 978-546-7747
E-Mail: richtennant@the5thwave.com
World Wide Web: www.the5thwave.com

Table of Contents

Introduction

You've probably heard all the media hype concerning e-Commerce and software start-ups. You know — tales of overnight billionaire success stories. You may be wondering how you can work on a software project so you can cash in on your stock options and get rich, too.

However, the alarming reality is that about one-half of the estimated 300,000 software projects in the United States will fail due to poor planning, inexperienced project managers, or inept project teams.

If you are a new or experienced project manager, or team member of a new software project, but you don't have the tools, or know where to begin, don't worry, be happy! (Woo hoo hoo hoo... Everybody sing along!) With the *Software Project Management Kit For Dummies* as your toolkit and your handy reference, you will find step-by-step instructions that will show you how to create successful software projects that stand the best chance of staying on schedule and under budget.

Who Should Read This Book?

Software Project Management Kit For Dummies is a toolkit for anyone who manages or participates as a member of any software project team. Effectively managing software projects is a team sport, which depends on the expertise and effort of every player big or small. As project manager, you get to be the team coach, deciding who plays where and calling the shots.

Typical software project teams include everyone in the software development cycle. Start-up entrepreneurs, project managers and sponsors, marketing mangers, functional architects, database administrators, systems analysts, developers, engineers, software quality assurance engineers, technical writers, customer-support engineers, and students all have a part in the mix.

About This Book

Whether you are managing or participating on a small, medium, or large software project, *Software Project Management Kit For Dummies* is for you. It doesn't matter if you are developing Internet/intranet applications, client-server monsters, or performing legacy conversions, *Software Project*

Management Kit For Dummies is for you. If you are developing a large mainframe application or cranking out a top-notch video game, *Software Project Management Kit For Dummies* is for you. Even if you are working on developing the greatest chicken soup recipe ever, *Software Project Management...* Well, on second thought, maybe you need a different *For Dummies* book.

Software Project Management Kit For Dummies is organized into a number of stand-alone modules, so you don't have to begin reading from page one to the end. You are free to pick and choose the modules that are appropriate for the software project tasks you happen to be working on at a given moment.

For example, suppose you are trying to find out how to manage the testing effort of your software project. To locate this information, you could search the topics and page references either in the table of contents or in the index.

Inside the back cover of this book, you will find a CD-ROM. It includes a wealth of templates that you and your project team are free to customize for your specific software project. Also on the CD-ROM you will find several project management software tools including: Microsoft Project 98, Soffront help desk, defect, knowledge base TRACK suite, and Marotz's Cost Xpert and Strategy Xpert software project cost schedule estimating tools.

How To Use This Book

Software Project Management Kit For Dummies has two primary features:

- ✔ Simple hands-on approach to software project management throughout the software development cycle
- ✔ CD-ROM containing the templates and tools necessary for managing any software project

You may ask, how do you read this book, and use the accompanying CD-ROM toolkit? There are a number of recommended approaches to using this kit. One approach is to read the book from cover to cover, using the templates on the CD-ROM sequentially referenced in each of the chapters. This approach follows the software development life cycle from beginning to end.

Another approach is to use the book as a reference tool, referring to any topic or CD-ROM template or tool that is applicable to your particular task at hand.

As you use this kit, please be aware of warnings to not skip certain steps critical to the software development life cycle. The kit is designed in a modular format to help you master each software project management skill to produce the deliverables for your project's success.

What You Don't Need To Read

Depending upon your role on a software project, you may be able to skip to the chapter, modules, and CD-ROM templates and tools which are applicable to the particular tasks and deliverables involved with your specific project.

Also, from time to time, I mark sections of interesting technical information with the technical stuff icon. If you're like me, you'll zero in on this information first because software project managers tend to have a curious love of technical details but feel free to skip this information if you want. You may want to focus more on the tons of information that you're responsible for juggling as a software project manager.

How This Book Is Organized

With the exception of The Part of Tens, the parts of this book follow the sequence of the seven phases of the software project life cycle, as detailed in Chapter 1. However, you don't need to read the book from cover to cover in order to use this kit successfully.

Each chapter covers an aspect of software project management and provides an opportunity to create your project plan, schedule, and crucial project documents using the templates and toolkit contained on the CD-ROM.

Part I: Defining Your Software Project

In this part, you and your project team will start out with a high-level overview of the seven phases of the software development process in Chapter 1. In Chapter 2 you learn, hands-on, the steps of defining requirements involved for conceiving and justifying a new software project. By getting involved from the product's inception, you will be especially prepared to lead your development team through the remaining project phases for a successful software project. Chapter 3 walks your project team through a variety of analysis phase meetings, including the project kickoff, project brainstorming, and WBS meetings.

Part II: Building and Tracking in Microsoft Project

Your effort as a project manager of a new software project can be simplified by using project management software tools, such as Microsoft Project. In Chapter 4, you get off to a great start by effectively using Microsoft Project to begin building your software project plan. Here you learn about summary tasks, and Gantt charts, project schedules, and task durations. Chapter 5 shows you how to use proven software estimation methodologies and software tools. By the end of this chapter, you will accurately estimate your project parameters, enabling you to assign the optimal amount of resources, and even humans, to your project with a reasonable degree of certainty. In Chapter 6 you use Microsoft Project to assist you in optimizing your project plan through modifying scope, adjusting schedules, and reallocating resources.

Part III: Making Your Software Happen

It's not enough to gather and analyze the requirements for your software project. Your project team also needs to design and build the software and documentation in order to deliver a fully functional product to your customers. Chapter 7 covers the design phase, where your project team will participate in several meetings to design your software product's data model, functional architecture, information flow model, prototype sales demo, and documentation. Here is where you develop both functional specifications and detailed design specifications. Chapter 8 details the development phase, which involves the development or production of your software, involving a very similar process in the manufacturing of any other product.

Part IV: Testing 1, 2, 3. . .

After your software and documentation are designed and built, they still need to be fully tested. Your project team also needs a mechanism in place for handling project change and risks. Chapter 9 will show your team, step-by-step, how to develop a comprehensive Software Quality Assurance strategy. You find out about test plans, test cases, test automations, bug tracking, configuration management, metrics reporting, and change control. Chapter 10 helps you manage changes that creep into your project through the effective development and implementation of a Change/Risk Management plan.

Part V: Releases, Support, and Implementation

Another big challenge in bringing your newborn software product from mere vaporware to alpha, beta, and finally a generally available release, is successfully build configurations, implementations, and a 24x7 world-class support package. In Chapter 11, you learn what it takes to put together your final software product and to support that product. Chapter 12 covers the implementation phase — the final phase of the development cycle. Here you learn what happens after you create a product and need to adapt it for specific customers.

Part VI: The Part of Tens

This part summarizes key concepts, as well as providing an executive summary of the big issues project managers and project teams will encounter during your software project adventure. Chapter 13 provides ten tips for effective project management.

Part VII: Appendixes

There are two appendixes included in the *Software Project Management Kit For Dummies* for your reading enjoyment. Appendix A is a glossary of important software development and project management terms. Appendix B gives you the full scoop on how to install and use the wealth of templates and tools contained on CD-ROM.

Icons Used in This Book

This icon points out a valuable template or software tool to be used for managing your software project.

This icon points out an important issue that you want to be sure to remember.

This icon gives you helpful advice on subtle or complicated issues.

This icon gives you a heads-up on issues that can have a detrimental impact on your project.

This icon shows you technical information that you can skip if you like.

Where to Go from Here

You're the boss (in this book and in your project), so I won't tell you where to go (and hopefully, neither will your team!). But I can tell you that you can turn to Chapter 1 to overview the software development process and to tailor this book to your needs. If you work for a large software company that has a marketing department, then you can probably skip Chapter 2, which details the process of gathering requirements at your customer's site (your marketing department probably does this for you). Or, you can go straight to Appendix B, which tells you how to install the software and templates that put the *hands on* in, uh, hands on.

Part I
Defining Your Software Project

The 5th Wave   By Rich Tennant

©RICHTENNANT

HAPPY HOLIDAYS

"I hear some of the engineers from the mainframe dept. project managed the baking of this year's fruitcake."

In this part . . .

I just heard the outstanding news — you've been
selected as a new software project manager! Yesterday,
you may have been just another nerd cranking out Y2K
COBOL code or you may have been handling entirely different types of projects in another industry. But tomorrow
you get to start leading a team of developers on a hot new
e-Commerce project. Before you can move into management, cash in on your stock options, and start spending
quality time in your hot tub, however, you need to figure
out how to manage your software project to completion,
handling the schedule, resources, and costs. It's a tall
order!

Part I starts out by giving you an overview of the seven
phases of the software development cycle. In particular,
you focus your attention on gathering your customers'
software requirements and your team's ability to solve
your customers' problems within the available. You then
graduate to doing the up-front brainstorming work that's
so important to getting your project off on the right foot.
By the end of this part, you should see the outlines of
your project taking shape and have the various tasks and
details laid out and ready to assign to your team.

Chapter 1

Understanding the Software Development Process

● ●

In This Chapter

▶ Reviewing the phases of a software project

▶ Getting along with sales and marketing

▶ Relating to customer support

● ●

As far as I know, you can't get a degree in software project management — at least not yet. The mantle of *project manager* usually falls to an experienced code writer/software developer. So chances are good that before you begin to manage software projects, you already have a firm grasp on the technical issues involved in the development and coding of software (if not, I explain enough of the central concepts throughout this book to help you fake that you at least have a clue).

Software project management, however, requires more than an understanding of data models, user interface principles, and the difference between an elegant algorithm and a complete kludge. You also need major project management skills, and more to the point, software project management skills. You may be the best darned code writer in your company, but at the same time, you may be completely lost when it comes to estimating and managing the myriad details and parallel processes involved in a software project.

Don't worry! This book provides you with a first-aid kit of software project management tools that enable you to successfully manage a software project right from the get-go!

This chapter presents you with a high-level overview of the entire software-development process. You also get a glance at the activities that occur after the software project has been completed and the product goes out the door to the customers. So, grind some Java beans for a fresh mug and hop to it!

The Seven Phases of Software Projects

Join me in a trip to the dawn of cyber-time, to a time when the Y2K bug was first being coded into RAM-starved programs, when men still wore white lab coats in air-conditioned rooms and fed cards to dinosaur-like mainframe computers, and when Homebrew Club hackers burned the midnight ale in front of kit computers.

Even in those lyrical days of yore, code writers developed and followed a protocol called the *software development process.* (Primordial code warriors liked words such as *protocol* that sounded technical and impressive.) All the software development process refers to, however, is a process for developing a software product from concept to finished product.

The software development process is often divided into phases that roughly identify what is going on at the time in relation to the project as a whole. In the "real world," every major software project in computerdom has probably been developed in phases. The exact number of phases and their precise names vary depending on the software outfit you may be working for or which of the million or so books you happen to be reading on the subject. (Good choice on the book you're currently reading, by the way!)

For the purposes of this book, the software development process can be broken down into seven phases, as shown in Figure 1-1.

The purpose of dividing software development into phases, such as those shown in Figure 1-1, is so that you can see light at the end of the proverbial tunnel. Often — and particularly if you're in the middle of a huge project — you can easily get lost and feel that you're never going to make it to the end of the project. The phases of software development serve the same purpose as mile markers on the highway, enabling you to gauge your progress and ascertain what you still need to do.

The seven phases that I detail in Figure 1-1 are somewhat arbitrary. In fact, some texts divide the development process into fewer phases, while others use more. There is, however, a method to this seven-phase madness: I selected these seven particular phases because they represent a complete project development cycle for a generalized approach to development.

The needs of those who develop software (mainly your needs, as the responsible party) vary as much as the software itself. The necessary development phases for someone creating a monitoring program for a nuclear powered submarine are different than those of someone creating a checkbook balancing program. (Balancing a checkbook is, of course, a much more complex and difficult process.) The seven phases of software development that I use in this book are general in nature — they can work for anyone developing a program. The bottom line, however, is for you to feel free to adapt the phases as they appear in this book to your own needs and the specifics of your project.

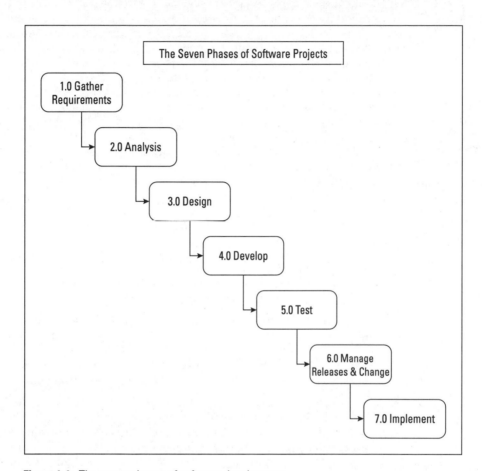

Figure 1-1: The seven phases of software development.

The following sections address each of the seven phases. Take a moment to read them, as they form the basis for the balance of the chapters in this book.

Phase 1: Gathering requirements

The first phase of your software project is to gather your requirements. This phase may sound as if it's a relatively easy one, but it's always the most crucial. Any miscalculations in this phase are always the most expensive to correct later.

Gathering software requirements begins as a creative brainstorming process in which the goal is to develop a cool idea (or vision) for a new product that no other software vendor has thought of. Exactly how this vision evolves and who develops it depends greatly on the size of your company. Often, in established software organizations, the marketing group plays the major role in dreaming up new software product ideas. If you work for a brand new startup, however, *you* may play a significant role in the genesis of the software's overall vision, as may the organization's founder. New software product ideas normally materialize as a result of analyzing market data and interviewing customers about their product needs.

The main function of the requirements gathering phase is to take an abstract idea that fills a particular need or that solves a particular problem and create a real-world project with a particular set of objectives, a budget, a timeline, and a team. (See, I told you that this phase was crucial.) This process includes the decision of whether each particular idea is worth pursuing at all. Some of the highlights of the requirements-gathering phase include:

- ✔ **Collecting project ideas:** Here is where you have fun and let your hair down (assuming you haven't pulled it out already). Coming up with project ideas can prove an expansive exercise that involves many people — including, I hope, your potential customers.

- ✔ **Gathering customer requirements and proposed solutions:** If you intend to customize solutions for customers, you need to focus on solving your customers' particular problems and fulfilling your customers' needs. Do the results of your project solve one of the top three problems of your customer? How universal are the problems that your software solves?

- ✔ **Justifying the project:** Deciding whether a particular project is more or less likely to make your company successful is an important part of the requirements-gathering phase. You (or your marketing department) must figure the return on investment for the project and conduct a cost/benefit analysis. But even if another department is crunching the numbers for whether a project makes sense, you need the ability to justify the project to your team members and to interested managers.

- ✔ **Submitting the Request for Proposal:** The *Request for Proposal* is an important document that senior management uses to decide which projects are likely to show a profit and, therefore, are worthy of allocating a budget for further testing and study. Although approval of an RFP doesn't guarantee that a project becomes a real piece of software, rejection guarantees that it never will.

- ✔ **Getting the team in place:** One of the requirements of any project is a team to work on the project. The team includes the project sponsor, a project manager, analysts, developers, database administrators, technical writers, quality-assurance testers, trainers, release managers, and possibly others.

✔ **Preparing the requirements document:** The *Requirements Document* (*RD*) is the deliverable that becomes the main input to Phase 2, the analysis phase. The RD is your main blueprint for the high-level description of the project that includes a summary of the problem to solve, the objectives of the project, the major features of the product, a documentation plan, a support plan, and licensing issues.

You can find detailed information on the requirements-gathering phase beginning in Chapter 2.

Phase 2: Analyzing

The main difficulty with feature lists that come from a marketing department is the everything-but-the-kitchen-sink syndrome. The main function of the analysis phase is for the project team to look carefully at the software's requested features with an eye toward what issues each may create in the actual coding.

Through hours of analysis, you can prioritize which features you can and can't reasonably include in the project, given your budgetary and scheduling constraints. You can think of the analysis phase as a time for thoughtful decision making with regard to must-have features, nice-to-have features, and if-we-had-another-five-years features. This phase is the time during which you decide what you think you can reasonably deliver.

Not all phases of a software project follow a linear progression. You can complete tasks of multiple phases in parallel, thereby shortening the overall duration of the project. The analysis phase, however, depends on your completing the deliverables that you provide during the requirements-gathering phase — particularly, the Requirements Document.

After your project team extensively analyzes the Requirements Document from Phase 1, the project's team members create several deliverables. These deliverables, as I describe in the following list, act as input to other parts of the process:

✔ **Project Scope Document:** The *Project Scope Document* document is the most critical deliverable in the analysis phase. The PSD document prioritizes and limits the high-level deliverables from the RD to a manageable list by project phase; it also includes time estimates for completing each requested feature. Your project team and the product marketing manager typically undergo extensive negotiations before all stakeholders approve the PSD.

✔ **Work Breakdown Structure:** Successful project management includes the ability to take complex tasks and break them down into manageable chunks that you can achieve relatively easily. The *Work Breakdown Structure* is your first-pass effort at defining the tasks necessary for completing your project and assigning resources to those tasks.

✔ **Baseline Project Schedule:** You can use a wide range of software tools to schedule and track your project. One such tool is Microsoft Project. By using the documents that you develop to this point, you can then develop a baseline schedule in Microsoft Project that serves as a measuring stick for the duration of your project.

Information on the analysis phase's deliverables starts in Chapter 3.

Phase 3: Designing

If you have experience as a software developer, the design phase is probably among your favorites. The design phase is where you really begin to solve (conceptually, at least) the technical problems that you face in making your project a reality. In this phase, the relationship of the code, database, user interface, and classes begin to take shape in the minds of the project team.

You can probably find as many approaches to software design as you can software designers. I espouse a generic approach to software design that's flexible enough to work with virtually any software project, but you need to remain aware that many other approaches exist.

During the design phase, your project team is responsible for seven primary deliverables: the data-model (or schema) design, the user-interface (UI) design, the prototype design, the functional specifications, the documentation plan, software quality assurance (SQA) test plan and test cases, and the detailed design specifications. You can break down the deliverables for this phase as follows:

✔ **Data model, or schema:** The primary objective in designing the data model, or schema, is to meet the high-level software specifications that the Requirements Document outlines. Usually, the database administrator (DBA) on your project team designs the data model for the software project.

✔ **User interface:** The *user interface* is the first part of the software application that's visible to the user. The UI provides the user with the capability of navigating through the software application — for example, by pointing and clicking through drop-down menus in Windows-based applications. The UI is often known in the software industry as the look-and-feel aspect of the software application. Ideally, you want to design your software application to provide an interfacce that's as user-friendly and cosmetically attractive as reasonably possible.

✔ **Prototype:** After the data model and UI designs are ready, your project team can design the prototype for the project. Your sales and marketing teams generally can't wait to get the prototype in their hands to show it off to sales prospects and at industry trade shows. You develop all later versions of your software from this initial prototype.

✔ **Functional specifications:** From a high-level standpoint, the functional specifications provide the definitive overview of what you're including in the project. This deliverable incorporates many of the documents that you prepare to this point, gathering them into one place for easy reference.

✔ **Documentation plan:** The technical publications manager or the technical writer on the project writes the documentation plan. The plan provides an overview of the software product you're documenting, the recommended documentation processes and procedures, and a list of document deliverables for the project.

✔ **Detailed design specifications:** Just as the functional specifications provide a high-level view of the project, the detailed design specifications lay out the detailed blueprint of how you intend to develop the project. The design specifications include every document that you create to this point (including the functional specifications) but provide detailed — and, in some cases, step-by-step — information on how you intend to implement the specifications.

✔ **Software quality assurance test plan and test cases:** Other very important deliverables that you create during the design phase are the Software Quality Assurance test plan, test cases, test data, entrance test plan (criteria), and in some cases any test automation requirements. Chapter 7 provides a closer look at the design phase and these deliverables.

Phase 4: Developing

After you design the data model, user interface, prototype, documentation plan, functional specifications, detailed design specifications, and software quality assurance test plan, the next logical step is to start coding the actual software, writing the documentation, and developing the SQA test cases, entrance criteria, and automations. Software coding includes building the data model and programming the user interface and application. If your analysis and design efforts are superb, actually developing the software shouldn't be too arduous a task.

As you develop your software, documentation, SQA test plan, and test cases, you go through several distinct versions, each of which you can consider a release of the product. These releases are as the following list describes:

✔ **Pre-alpha:** This condition describes any release that is, well, pre-alpha. *Pre-alpha* basically means that individual modules are ready, but you haven't yet combined them into a functional unit.

✔ **Alpha:** This release is the first functional version of the software. In the *alpha* version, the fundamental structure of the software is in place, as is about 60 percent of the functionality.

✔ **Pre-beta:** You typically have many, many pre-beta releases of software. This term describes any release that's functional but not ready for testing on the general public. You normally use pre-beta software for in-house testing.

✔ **Beta:** The *beta* version is the release that the public gets to see for the first time, although not every project may entail an actual beta release.

✔ **GA:** The *GA* (or *generally available*) release is the software that you're ready to install for use by your customers. This term refers to the finished version of the software for which everyone's waiting.

Seeing software progress from the conceptual stage to concrete modules to fully functional reality is exciting. You can find more information about developing your software in Chapter 8.

Phase 5: Testing

Testing isn't isolated to only one phase of the project but should be practiced throughout all phases of the project. Your entire project team will find themselves conducting many tests, usually in tandem with the actual development process, whether they're testing the design specifications, actual code, or documentation. Thus the fine line between Phase 4 (development) and Phase 5 (testing) often blurs. This blurring isn't a problem; you just need to understand that a line really is there.

In a perfect world, after developing each unit of the software product, the developers go through an extensive testing process on the software. Your project team ideally includes at least one representative from your company's Software Quality Assurance group who participates on the project from beginning to end.

After the module reaches an acceptable level of functionality, the developer(s) perform a thorough unit testing of each software component and module, as well as conduct integration testing of all combined modules, before even thinking of handing it off to the SQA engineer(s) for complete system testing. Unfortunately, in the real world, people often skip the unit-testing step because the company has no software SQA processes in place or because of poor project planning and scheduling (and sometimes for both reasons). As project manager, your job is to make sure that you *don't* skip this part of the process — testing throughout the entire development process is important to the quality of the product you want to produce.

After you develop the individual modules and combine them (or integrate them, if you want to use the lingo) into a functional software build, you perform what's known as *integration testing*. Instead of looking at how individual modules perform, this testing exercises the modules as a whole, as well as their interactions with other modules. Integration testing is often very rigorous and demanding on the software.

Finally, as you prepare later builds of the software, system testing takes place. This part of the process is when you conduct in-house testing in simulated live conditions. System testing is the most rigorous of all the testing you conduct and is when you really put the software through its paces.

Software products that don't undergo rigorous testing and SQA processes usually result in an onslaught of bad feedback and product defect reports from unhappy customers. These complaints can overload your technical-support staff and injure your company's reputation. Chapter 9 provides the full scoop on testing and SQA procedures.

Phase 6: Managing releases and change

As a software project manager, you work closely with the release manager (also referred to as the configuration manager) and SQA manager to determine whether each unit, module, and integration version of the software follows the specifications that the Requirements Document, the Statement of Scope document, and other documents spell out. Release management depends on the testing phase. (In other words, you can't manage releases until the releases are ready, and you can't release anything until it passes the unit, integration and SQA system tests.)

The following two important release management tools can assist your team in making the decision whether a release is ready for delivery or whether you need to hold it back:

- **Defect tracking system:** This tool helps you list, quantify, and manage defects (bugs) and enhancement requests in your software. It is, in effect, a database in which you catalog your bugs and then note the status of fixing those bugs. In large software projects, a tool such as this one is especially valuable because bugs can spring up everywhere during the different tests that you conduct on your software. Your customers are forever requesting new enhancements as well. Provided on the CD-ROM is a trial version of *TRACKdefect* software provided by Soffront, Inc.

- **Automated source control:** This category of tool essentially provides transaction control for your program source code. *Transaction control* refers to tracking each change to the source code as it occurs. Automated source control software maintains all previous versions and builds of the source code, which you can pull up at a moment's notice. The benefit here is that this process provides an audit trail to help you track down bugs that some change to the source code may introduce.

If you're the project manager for a software project, someone obviously believes that the project is large enough or important enough to warrant a full-time manager. I can guarantee that, if your project is that large or that important, it's certain to demonstrate a tendency to change over time. People come up with new ideas, marketing has strokes of genius, and customers often have second thoughts. Regardless of the reason, changes inevitably start to creep into the original scope of your project.

You need, therefore, to devise some way to manage the propensity for change. In software circles, this device is known as a *C/RM (change/risk management) plan*. The plan enables you to specify the acceptable process for making changes to the project and can also pull some semblance of order out of potential chaos (as well as prevent you from pulling out your hair).

You find out more about managing change in Chapter 10 and about software releases in Chapter 11.

Phase 7: Implementing

After your customers sign their lives away on the dotted line, they're ready to begin their software implementations. At that time, your consulting organization and partners are ready to rake in the big bucks! The implementing phase is what I call the dividing line because it delineates both the end of your public software-release project and the beginning of yet a new software project that encompasses many of the previous phases — only this time, they're not for the general product but to meet the specific needs of your customer.

The implementation phase involves adapting and applying many of the strategies that the development team uses in your project (including gather requirements, analysis, design, develop the customizations, testing, and so on). The difference between the application of these strategies in the implementation phase and in earlier project phases is that the focus is now on meeting the specific requirements and desired feature set of a particular customer. Thus, you can also think of the implementation phase as the creation of a new, customized version of your software.

If you're the manager of the original development team, the implementation team's manager is most definitely going to stay in contact from the customer's site with you and your staff. The implementation team needs to understand whether particular adaptations are possible and schedule the deliverables with input from the customer. Be responsive to the needs of this team and find answers to their questions as quickly as is practical. Your aid is invaluable in making sure that the new customer becomes a happy long-term customer.

If, on the other hand, you're on the implementation team yourself, the implementation phase is your lifeblood! The consulting arm of your software company generally takes the lead on customer installations, implementations, and adaptations. If you're the project manager of the implementation team, you play a similar role to that of the project manager of the development team, but instead of defining and coding the software requirements from ground zero, you define and code the specific software-adaptation requirements of your customers. You want to stay in close contact with the development project manager because that person knows the project from the inside out and can get you the answers that you need.

Your analysis at the customer site defines the gap between the plain-vanilla software and your customers' wish lists of software features. (Sometimes, in fact, this analysis is known as *gap analysis* for this very reason.) In Chapter 12, I go into considerable detail concerning an on-site project's design, development, and test efforts on the newly defined gap requirements for a customer. Figures 1-2 and 1-3 show a checklist that overviews the project management process.

Looking at the Relations

You belong to a company that's much like a large family. (Well, isn't that what your Human Resources manager told you? Hopefully, your company family isn't too dysfunctional.) You have brothers and sisters in other departments who're hard at work trying to figure out how to further the goals of the family.

You don't do your job in a vacuum, nor are you the only person responsible for your project. Other people at your company also are likely to have a large stake in your project. In most companies, you need to concern yourself with two other primary departments: the sales and marketing department and the customer support department. The following sections take a look at your relationships to these sibling departments.

Your relationship to sales and marketing

After the software quality assurance team fully tests the final software product and it becomes available to the public, your sales team starts to pound the pavement. Sure, you may have customers with so much money that they purchase all the vaporware your marketing group feeds them, but sales efforts don't begin in earnest until *after* the software becomes available.

Working on software projects without first having a customer base is like building mansions in the low-rent district. You need to identify a market for your product *before* you begin creating the product. So the sales effort of the software project really begins during the project's requirements gathering phase.

Software Project Management Checklist

Phase	Milestones/Deliverables
1.0	**Gather Requirements**
1.1	Collect Marketing Data
1.2	Survey Customer Requirements & Proposed Solutions
1.3	Justify the Project
1.4	Prioritize Project Ideas
1.5	Submit Request for Proposal (RFP)
1.6	Approve RFP
1.7	Write Requirements Document (RD)
1.8	Write Beta Test Plan
1.9	Identify Project Sponsor & Project Manager
1.10	Get Project Team in Place
1.11	Build Work Breakdown Structure (WBS)
1.12	Build Preliminary Project Plan (Schedule: Critical Path, PERT Chart, & Gantt Chart)
1.13	Estimate, Optimize, & Finalize Project Plan
1.14	Create Baseline Plan in Microsoft Project
2.0	**Analysis**
2.1	Write Project Scope Document (PSD)
2.2	Create Entity Relationship Diagram (ERD)
2.3	Create Data Flow Diagram (DFD)
2.4	Define Data Dictionary
2.5	Perform Object-Oriented Analysis
3.0	**Design**
3.1	Design Data model
3.2	Write Functional Specifications
3.3	Design Storyboards (Prototypes)
3.4	Write Detailed Design Specifications
3.5	Write Documentation Plan
3.6	Write Beta Test Plan
3.7	Write SQA Test Plan
3.8	Write SQA Test Cases
3.9	Write Customer Support Plan
3.10	Write Training Plan
3.11	Write Risk Management Plan

Figure 1-2: Software Project Management Checklist. Page 1 of 2.

Phase	Milestones/Deliverables
4.0	**Develop**
4.1	Develop Application
4.2	Develop Data Model
4.3	Unit Test
4.4	Integration Test
4.5	Develop SQA System Test Plan
4.6	Develop SQA System Test Cases
4.7	Write Documentation
4.8	Write Training Courseware
5.0	**Test**
5.1	System Test
5.2	Track Defects
5.3	Regression Test
6.0	**Manage Release and Change**
6.1	Configuration management
6.2	New full releases
6.3	Maintenance releases
6.4	Defect and enhancement tracking
7.0	**Implement (At Customer Site)**
7.1	Install Beta Test System
7.2	Beta Test Software
7.3	Track Defects & Report to Customer Support
7.4	Gather Requirements for Customizations
7.5	Analysis (Gap Between Customizations & "Vanilla")
7.6	Design
7.7	Install "Vanilla" Development System (GA Release)
7.8	Implement/Adapt Software
7.9	Unit Test Adaptations
7.10	Integration Test Adaptations
7.11	Acceptance Test
7.12	Cut-over Development to Production (Pilot)

Figure 1-3: Software Project Management Checklist. Page 2 of 2.

You don't normally carry any responsibility for the sales or marketing aspects of your product other than to deliver something that these departments can promote and sell. Most organizations receive lots of advice from their sales and marketing department well before you come into the picture. The sales and marketing department is usually full of highly paid experts who tread a parallel course to the personnel in your department, anticipating the point when a prototype and later a finished product is ready.

By now, your company is holding itself out to the business world as a fierce competitor in a target market niche. Your marketing group has promised delivery of your product by a certain target release date. The common error is to overcommit and underdeliver.

You and/or your marketing and sales teams, as well as members of the software project team, often work in collaboration with prospective customers from the presale product demos and negotiations clear through to the final approval of the contract.

If you happen to be the project manager for an implementation team (working for the consulting arm of your company), you play a very important role in the sales cycle. The goal of the sales and marketing department (as well as that of the implementation project manager) is to sell the customer the most lucrative combination of products and services possible, which is likely to include software applications, implementation consulting, and training.

After the sales contract is a done deal, a handoff from sales to your consulting organization's implementation project team marks the beginning of the final phase of the development of the project: installing, implementing, and customizing the software at the customer's site.

Your relationship to customer support

Another important postrelease activity that often goes without recognition is that of customer support. Planning, analyzing, designing, developing, testing, documenting, training, releasing, installing, implementing, and adapting software are terrific, but do these tasks really mark the end of the line for a project? What happens *after* the customer's implementation — after the consulting team signs off the project and takes the red-eye flight home? Who takes the telephone calls and reads the flutter of e-mail reporting product defects and enhancement requests?

The answer is the customer support department. These folks perform the thankless job of answering questions and reporting problems 24 hours a day, seven days a week. They lie in bed sweating through the sleepless nights with cellular phones and pagers under their pillows, dreadfully awaiting the support nightmare call in the wee hours of the morning. Meanwhile, the project manager and developers are fast asleep, with visions of stock options dancing in their heads.

A hallmark of a first-rate software company is not only to crank out high quality software, but also to offer world-class customer support all the time. Believe it or not, you, as project manager, have a stake in making sure that the customer support department fulfills its mission. And you're likely to find that some of your development staff needs to work with customer support to make sure that you completely satisfy the customer.

As project manager, you don't control customer support. The customer support department has broad responsibility — typically for the entire range of your company's products. You, on the other hand, are limited in responsibility to a single product or product line. You need to work with the customer service department to keep them up to speed on your project so that they can anticipate any support needs or potential problems. Good communication with the customer support department throughout the final phases of the project also eases your handing off the project to them at the appropriate time.

I cover the topic of supporting your software in more detail in Chapter 11.

Chapter 2

Defining Your Software Project's Requirements

*O*f all the good ideas for software products, only a handful actually meet the needs of your company and your customers. In the fiercely competitive software industry, the reality is that successful projects begin with winning product ideas. Before your company invests substantial time and resources into a project, management needs to know that the product has a reasonable chance of providing a solid return.

Typically, a product marketing manager is responsible for researching and generating new product concepts and for setting requirements for any upcoming projects. In a medium- or large-sized company, this manager may be someone in another department (or may even be the entire department); in a small company, it may even be *you*. (Which hat are you wearing today, Ms. or Mr. Entrepreneur?)

Even if you're not directly responsible for the marketing efforts of your company, you can benefit by understanding what goes on at product inception. By involving yourself in the project at such an early stage, you better prepare yourself with an understanding of the product's vision. This preparation is often necessary for you to successfully lead your project team through the remaining project phases.

In this chapter, you discover how to define the requirements of a new software project. You can follow these nine general steps:

1. **Collect project concepts.**

   Before you can select which software project to pursue, you must identify a wide range of potential project concepts.

2. **Prioritize the project concepts.**

   You need to pick the three to five software project ideas that represent the highest probability of success from all possible candidates.

3. **Gather customer requirements and proposed solutions.**

   You now need to obtain a clear definition of the problem that the customer needs you to resolve, along with proposed solutions for that problem.

4. **Select and justify a project.**

   After you gather your marketing data, customer requirements, and proposed solutions, you need to determine which projects are justified.

5. **Submit and approve the Request for Proposal.**

   In order to launch your software project, you must present your project to the powers-that-be and await their blessing. You will submit a Request for Proposal for your project's approval to your executive management team or company's board of directors.

6. **Identify the project sponsor and project manager.**

   After executive management blesses your software project idea from on high, the next step is to identify a project sponsor and assign a project manager.

7. **Get the project team in place.**

   Finding the right people for your software project as well as keeping your project team members up to speed on cutting-edge technologies and project management methodologies are constant challenges for a software project manager.

8. **Prepare the Requirements Document (RD).**

   The Requirements Document, commonly referred to as the Product Requirement Document or the Statement of Work, is the single most important document in a software project. In the RD, you thoroughly define the customers' requirements (problem) before your project team can begin designing and developing the software solution to the problem.

9. **Conduct the project kickoff meeting.**

   As project manager, you will coordinate the scheduling and agenda for the project kickoff meeting with the product marketing manager and your core project team.

Collecting Project Ideas

Your software's target market consists of customers with a number of business needs that they are looking to solve with the deployment of your software. It's crucial to address as many of the customers' needs by using optimal software solutions, which differentiate your software from the competition. Before you select which software project to pursue, however, you must identify a wide range of potential product ideas.

You can identify potential project ideas in a number of ways. Some of these methods you can use internally, within your department or company, while others involve dealing with outsiders — you know, those people you hope may someday purchase your software. The following list presents some of the most effective ways in which you can identify project ideas:

- ✔ **Conducting internal company-wide brainstorming sessions for new product ideas:** If your company's large enough, a brainstorming session among colleagues can bring fresh and potentially profitable ideas to the foreground.

- ✔ **Researching market trends and literature:** This method is particularly important if you're entering a target market in which you face already entrenched competition. You can often gather an impressive amount of material directly from the Internet.

- ✔ **Analyzing the competition:** Gathering literature about your competition's products is only the starting point. A full analysis discloses competitive products, the current and future trends of your software market segment, and neglected market needs. Another good tactic is to obtain copies of your competitors' software, and then install and run it in your test lab to identify the strengths and weaknesses. Then, you can capitalize on the design of your software to incorporate those features your competition failed to address.

- ✔ **Interviewing your customers onsite:** Using carefully prepared questions can help you determine the direction in which to proceed with a project, as well as what software features you need to implement in the project.

- ✔ **Surveying your customers:** Surveys are often used at trade shows and conventions. They provide you with a way to target a large cross section of your prospective customers. Often, you can get a great deal of information at a trade show for the price of a trinket or T-shirt bearing your company name.

- ✔ **Soliciting feedback from user groups:** User groups typically exist in larger cities and, of course, online. If you can identify a group in your target market, you can often garner significant insights that illuminate what actual product users deem important.

✔ **Looking back at features planned in previous releases:** Another great source of features to consider for future releases (assuming this isn't your first release) derives from looking back at your previous requirements document(s) to see which features weren't included. You can carry these features forward to future releases.

If possible, use more than one method of gathering project ideas. You may get ideas from one source that you wouldn't get from another. For example, you may be surprised by the different ideas that are generated from a survey at a trade show versus through customer interviews.

As you identify potential project ideas, don't throw anything out — toss every idea into the pool for now. Don't spend a lot of time discussing the merits of each idea or its feasibility at this point; that part of the process comes later. The purpose here is to gather ideas in a creative burst of energy. You're likely to be amazed, too, at how one idea leads to others that you may not have considered before.

The length of time that you spend on the identification process depends on your resources and the approach you're taking. If you're conducting customer surveys, the process takes longer than if you're simply brainstorming within your department. In no case do you want this process to last any longer than three or four months. If you've spent any time in the software industry, you know that the market can change quite significantly within six months to a year. The faster that you can identify ideas, the faster you can bring them to market and meet the needs of today's customer.

To cut down time at the front end of the project cycle, consider keeping a perpetual idea list to which anyone can add items whenever they want. This list keeps growing over time, and you can refer to it whenever the company or group is ready to consider a new project.

Provided below are some sample customer interview and survey questions. Typically, representatives from your marketing, sales, and customer service organizations will conduct interviews at customer sites. You could also use these questions if you happen to be an implementation project manager collecting the requirements for a customer site implementation. Written surveys are a good tool to use to gather the requirements from your potential customer base at trade shows for example.

Prioritizing Project Ideas

Imagine for a moment that you work for one of the ten million Internet start-up companies. In the Internet arena, about 100 zillion projects may have merit and make money. Okay, that's an exaggeration; maybe only ten billion ideas have merit and only five of them have any real chance to make you money. Most of the project ideas sound cool, and you and your marketing crew feel as though you can tackle any of them. The harsh reality, however, is that you must draw a line somewhere. You need to pick the three to five ideas that represent the highest probability of success.

Remember, however, that today's great idea may soon become yesterday's BetaMax machine in the fiercely competitive software marketplace. Think carefully through alternative software solutions and technologies that may supersede the need for your product.

As you attempt to pare down your idea list, some ideas prove easy to dismiss while others may seem very attractive. Ending up with an original idea list containing hundreds of candidates isn't all that unusual. After your first pass through the list, you may pare it down to a dozen (or two) solid candidates. But this amount is still too large. Your resources are limited, after all, so you need to cut your list down to no more than five potential projects.

Often software companies employ the strategy of planning for a few versions (two or three) ahead of time. Dividing features among the different versions allows the product to reach the market and generate some income.

Use the following questions — which I present in no particular order — as a starting point to help you prioritize and select projects:

- ✔ **Which project holds the largest sales potential?** Face it — sales help make the world go 'round. You can make the greatest software in history, but if it possesses no sales potential, then why bother? You can create a product that reminds users when to wipe off their monitor, for example, but you can probably also identify many other projects with far greater sales potential.

- ✔ **Which project addresses the largest unmet need in the proposed market?** If you can identify an unmet need of your customers, you're well on the way to a winner. Of course, you must meet that need according to customer expectations, which I discuss in the "Gathering Customer Requirements and Proposed Solutions" section, later in this chapter.

- ✔ **Which project can my team complete in the shortest time?** As you already know, the software market changes quickly. The faster that you can get a quality product to market, the faster you can earn a return on your development investment and the better chance you face of shutting out any potential competition.

- ✔ **Which project offers the least competition?** You're likely to face at least some competition in the marketplace. If your target market offers few competitors or (better still) few competent competitors, your chances of success increase dramatically.

✔ **Which project provides the most compelling reason for customers to buy your software instead of the competition's?** As you're ruminating over how to implement your project, you can identify features that set your proposed product apart from any competing products. You may also discover intangible reasons that add to your product's potential success, such as great customer service, company reputation, and complementary products that you already market.

✔ **Which project has the lowest probability of introducing new risks to your customers?** Even if your product is absolutely great, if it doesn't work politely with other software or increases the potential for computer down time, you run the risk of bad press and bad word-of-mouth advertising from your customers. Products that don't increase the customer's risk are eminently more saleable and more profitable in the long run.

✔ **Which project offers the lowest liability potential?** Today's society is extremely litigious, and some projects carry a greater risk of liability than do others. If, for example, you create a program that instructs people how to perform home appendectomies for fun and profit, such a program is inherently riskier than one that merely calculates the position of astronomical bodies.

After you finish analyzing your potential projects, you should have your final list of three to five projects in hand, along with written reasons as to why these projects are the best for your company to pursue. These reasons can come in handy during later stages of the project. At some point, for example, your company's executive management team may call you to stand before it and answer tough questions about why they should choose your project over your colleagues' proposals.

The experience of justifying your project to management can prove either exhilarating or humiliating, depending on how thoroughly you do your homework. The work that you perform at this stage can make all the difference in the world as to whether your project gets the green light from management or winds up in the software shredder.

Gathering Customer Requirements and Proposed Solutions

With your top whiz-bang product ideas in hand, you're ready to gather more information. Wait! Didn't you just do that a while back? Well, yes, you did. But that information didn't focus on any particular projects. Now you need to zero in on your top ideas and gather the information that can help you make them successful.

Each product idea must represent a potential solution to a customer problem. The problem may be well known, or it may be one that the customer doesn't even recognize yet. You need a clear definition of the problem that the customer needs you to resolve, along with proposed solutions for that problem. This stage is where you begin to flesh out your project idea so that you can make sure that its features address the needs of the customer.

The following list includes some common questions that can help you to initiate a requirements gathering dialog with your customers:

- **What problems are your customers trying to solve?** The customer may, for example, need a way to retrieve up-to-date information about sales of a particular product.

- **How do your customers currently deal with these problems?** The customer may be dealing with the problem by referring to printed summary reports of weekend sales.

- **What are the limitations of the current alternative solutions?** Determine what software solutions your customers currently has available, including what the competition has to offer, to solve their problems. Then, determine what limitations are inherent with those alternative solutions. Finally, think big, have vision, dream up software solutions that overcome the limitations of the existing alternative solutions and better meet the needs of your customers.

- **What high-level software features do your customers require?** When gathering the customers' requirements take a top-down approach, seeing the big picture rather than getting mired in the details. Pick six to ten high-level features that the majority of your customers are asking for. The detailed features can be fleshed out later in the process.

Notice that you need to provide answers to each of these questions that are as specific as possible. Avoiding ambiguity and subjective answers is very important. Saying, for example, that the possible solution is to "deliver a good sales report on demand" simply isn't acceptable. Such an answer leaves open to interpretation the meaning of *good*. Differing interpretations can lead to problems down the road in the development process. In this example, a specific framing of the possible solution may be to "deliver a sales report that includes sales data broken down by quarter, territory, and salespersons, in real time upon demand by the user."

This requirement implies (and rightly so) that you may need to ask many follow-up questions of your customers. *Exactly what do you mean by good?* is a logical follow-up to the proposed solution that I describe in the previous paragraph. The answers that you receive may lead to other questions as well. For example, you may get general responses, such as a complete sales report. You then have to follow up again, asking, "What do you mean by *complete?*"

Just as important as finding the right solutions is identifying the right problems that require the solutions. Finding the right solution to the wrong problem doesn't pay the bills. Asking the correct target questions can help reduce the chance of error in making your plans.

The *Software Project Management Kit For Dummies* CD contains a Customer Requirements Survey template (Customer Requirements Survey.dot), which is an excellent requirements-gathering tool. An example of a filled-out survey is shown in Figure 2-1.

You can complete a new customer-requirements survey form for each new project idea by following these steps:

1. **Enter the customer profile information, including the primary contact's name, title, customer name, and location.**

   This contact name is that of the person you talk to when completing the survey form. In Figure 2-1, for example, the customer profile contact information is that of Rich Requirements of Problematics, Inc. He's the CEO and project sponsor in the Calamity City location.

2. **Enter the Problem Summary in ten words or less.**

   The limitation on words means that you (and the customer) need to carefully think through the problem and make sure that you state it succinctly and unambiguously.

3. **Enter the Current Problem Description in detail.**

   Here is where you can go into more detail about the problem. Make sure that you elicit as much information as possible from the customer and enter all the salient details in this section.

4. **Enter a Proposed Solution in detail.**

   You don't describe your solution here but the solution your customer proposes. Ask the customer to suggest a solution to the problem.

5. **Enter the Risks/Costs of implementing the proposed solution.**

   Often, customers can see problems with a solution before you can. Ask your customer about any drawbacks to the proposed solution and what costs may accrue from the proposed solution. This figure is not the final cost of the project, of course, but a ballpark figure that allows you to judge your cost estimates for the implementation prior to preparing final estimates. You may also want to provide information regarding how the customer arrived at the estimate.

6. **Enter the potential Benefits/ROI (return on investment) of implementing the proposed solution.**

   Here is where you can discuss with the customer the benefits of the customer's proposed solution. This is seldom the final ROI that you submit with your proposal, but it provides a useful barometer of the customer's interest (and investment) in the project.

Template 2-1 Customer Requirements Survey

Customer Self-Service Web Customer Requirements Survey	
Primary Contact's Name: Rich Requirements	**Company:** Problematics, Inc.
Title: CEO, Project Sponsor	**Location:** Calamity City

Problem Summary: Customer Service client-server system is inadequate.

Current Problem Description: Problematics' current customer service client-server software requires a proprietary software client on every customer service representative's machine. This makes the software very costly and difficult to scale to a large customer service staff of 2,500 representatives, worldwide, and growing exponentially.
Problematics' customer service representatives always seem to be understaffed and overworked. Despite several staff increases customers' calls and backlog increases. Customers are unable to access their account information online. The only access they have is by telephoning Problematics' Customer Service staff. Due to poor customer service, Problematic has lost several big accounts estimated at least a $3,000,000 loss.

Proposed Solution: The Customer Self-Service Web software does not require any proprietary software client to be installed on workstations. Only Internet browser software is required to access the Customer Self-Service Web interface and database. Customers will have direct access to all their data online via the Web. Customers will be able to resolve most of their inquiries and issues online, without having to make telephone calls to Problematics' customer service representatives.

Risks/Costs: To roll out Customer Self-Service Web software for 2,500 employees with unlimited external customer access, licensing, extensive software customization, on-site consulting, and training services, is estimated at $1,500,000.
Many of Problematics' customers are pretty set in their ways of doing business, who may be reluctant to use the Web self-service, still insisting on telephoning in their issues to Problematics' to hear a live voice. There are number of security defects plaguing the Customer Self-Service Web software which still need to be worked out by the vendor. Until these issues are resolved, customers will not have a high confidence in the security of their company's private data.

Benefits/(ROI): The benefits of implementing the Customer Self-Service Web software at Problematics far outweigh the risks and costs, as follows:
- Lower backlog and faster resolution of customer issues by 150%.
- Increase customer satisfaction by 300%.
- Optimize customer service staff and reduce overhead costs by 90%.
- Increase quality of customer information by 75%.

Figure 2-1: A sample Customer Requirements Survey.

Don't rush through the process of gathering customer requirements, but do the job expeditiously. The actual number of people you interview — and from whom you solicit responses — depends on the scale of the project. Make sure, however, that you get enough feedback to ensure a wide variety of input to your project.

You're gathering customer requirements and solutions for each of your three to five possible project ideas. Make sure that you treat each project idea independently, giving each your full attention as necessary. Make sure that you don't talk with a customer about more than a single project idea at a time. Doing so may compromise the quality of the answers you receive.

Justifying a Project

After you gather your marketing data, customer requirements, and proposed solutions, you're ready to evaluate your top potential projects. You now need a method of determining which projects you can justify. You need to use two sets of criteria to evaluate each project: internal criteria and external criteria. The primary tool for determining internal criteria is your ROI analysis from a software vendor's perspective. The chief tool for external criteria is a cost/benefit analysis for your customers.

Before executive management makes its go/no go decision for a software project, the managers take a close look at your justification analyses. Thus, you want to spend significant time with these justifications to make sure that they're accurate and that your assumptions are correct.

You need to perform an ROI analysis for each of your three to five top prospective projects. That way, you can examine the bottom-line figures to determine where to best spend your time and resources. After you finish the analysis, you should have a single project on which to proceed. The other projects return to the idea list for future consideration.

As you return projects to the idea list, make sure that you keep all the paperwork you generate with the ideas themselves. That way, you needn't redo most of your work if you consider the project again in the near future.

Figuring a return on your investment

Internally, your organization needs a product strategy designed to return the highest possible return on investment. Management, financial, and high-level marketing folks all understand the meaning of an ROI form. The form enables them to know at a glance whether a product is likely to be profitable and how soon your software company can realize that profit.

Exactly how you figure an ROI depends on your company. If you work for a well-established company or for a company that's part of a larger company, you may have very specific internal forms that you need to use in conducting an ROI analysis.

Even if you're not required to do so, you should still perform at least a rudimentary ROI. Doing so allows you to know when you can expect to see a return on the money you must shell out while developing your software.

On the *Software Project Management Kit For Dummies* CD is a Microsoft Word template *(Project Candidate ROI Analysis.dot)* that you can use for figuring return on investment. Figure 2-2 shows an example of what the template looks like.

Your main challenge in using this template to evaluate the return on investment of a software project is to quantify each factor into a specific dollar amount or percentage. To fill out the ROI template, follow these steps:

1. **Identify project's developmental expenses and enter them into the Expenses column of the ROI spreadsheet.**

   Development expenses include costs incurred during the entire software development cycle. A great source for your estimates is to look at any historical data that your software organization may have tracked on similar projects.

   If you're short on historical information upon which to base your estimates, consider using a third-party tool, such as Marotz Cost XPert, a trial version of which appears on the *Software Project Management Kit For Dummies* CD. Cost XPert provides cost information and estimating from a huge database of real-world software development projects.

   Examples of development expenses can include:

   - **Fixed labor expenses, such as marketing, analysts, and developers**
   - **Variable labor expenses, such as third-party consultants, and clerical work**
   - **Office space rental/depreciation**
   - **Marketing and advertising costs**
   - **Hardware and third-party software expenses**
   - **Development tool expenses**
   - **Training expenses**

Template 2-2 Project Candidate ROI Analysis

	Candidate 1	Candidate 2	Candidate 3	Candidate 4	Candidate 5
Project name					
Forecasted Project Expenses					
Fixed labor expenses (marketing, analysts, developers, etc.) Variable labor expenses (third-party consultants, clerical, etc.) Office space rental/depreciation Marketing and advertising costs Hardware and third-party software expenses Development tool expenses Training					
Total Forecasted Expenses	$0	$0	$0	$0	$0
Forcasted Project Revenues					
Software sales Consulting implementation and training engagements Maintenance and technical-support packages					
Total Forcasted Revenues	$0	$0	$0	$0	$0
Forecasted Revenue - Forecasted Expenses	$0 = $0	$0 = $0	$0 = $0	$0 = $0	$0 = $0
Forecasted Expenses					
ROI (%) = (Revenue - Expenses) / Expenses	0.00%	0.00%	0.00%	0.00%	0.00%

Figure 2-2: A blank ROI template.

2. **Forecast the project's revenue potential and enter the total in the Revenue Estimates column of the ROI template.**

   Again, a great source for your estimates is historical data tracked on similar projects. Three common revenue sources in the software industry are:

   - **Software sales**

   - **Consulting implementation and training engagements**

   - **Maintenance and technical support packages**

3. **Calculate the project's ROI.**

   Now, you're ready to plug the aggregate expense and revenue figures you estimated in Steps 1 and 2 into the below ROI formula, as illustrated below (remember that these figures are all estimates at this point).

   ```
   ROI (%) = (Revenues - Expenses) ÷ Expenses
   ```

   Figure 2-3 shows a sample of completed ROI form for a mythical software project.

Examining costs and benefits

Your customers need to perform a cost-benefit (payback) analysis on the proposed software, even if your customer is just another department in your own organization. Your customers want to know why they need to invest in your software as a replacement for their existing systems rather than something that a competitor offers.

The cost-benefit analysis that your customer conducts is probably fairly detailed because most customers have their own internal financial procedures to which they must adhere. Requesting to see a summary of the cost-benefit analysis is a good idea, however, because doing so enables you to perform the following tasks:

✔ **Gauge how financially committed the customer is to your project.**
  After you know how much the customer thinks is riding on the project, you have a good idea of how much emphasis the customer is likely to place on your work.

Template 2-2 Project Candidate ROI Analysis

Project name	Candidate 1 Customer Self Service Web	Candidate 2 Calendar Self Service Web	Candidate 3 Project Management Self Service Web	Candidate 4	Candidate 5
Forecasted Project Expenses					
Fixed labor expenses (marketing, analysts, developers, etc.)	$1,130,000	$1,150,000	$1,250,000	$0	$0
Variable labor expenses (third-party consultants, clerical, etc.)	$245,000	$275,000	$225,000	$0	$0
Office space rental/depreciation	$35,000	$45,000	$55,000	$0	$0
Marketing and advertising costs	$35,000	$45,000	$30,000	$0	$0
Hardware and third-party software-expenses	$70,000	$80,000	$75,000	$0	$0
Development tool expenses	$100,000	$125,000	$350,000	$0	$0
Training	$50,000	$55,000	$250,000	$0	$0
Total Forecasted Expenses	$1,565,000	$1,650,000	$1,885,000	$0	$0
Forcasted Project Revenues					
Software sales	$1,500,000	$1,300,000	$1,200,000	$0	$0
Consulting implementation and training engagements	$50,000	$40,000	$37,500	$0	$0
Maintenance and technical support-packages	$150,000	$130,000	$120,000	$0	$0
Total Forcasted Revenues	$1,700,000	$1,470,000	$1,357,500	$0	$0
Forecasted Revenue - Forecasted Expenses	$135,000	-$180,000	-$527,500	$0	$0
Forecasted Expenses	$1,565,000	$1,650,000	$1,885,000	$0	$0
ROI (%) = (Revenue - Expenses) / Expenses	8.63%	-10.91%	-27.98%	0.00%	0.00%

Figure 2-3: Example of a completed ROI form.

Customer Self-Service Web Cost-Benefit Summary

Benefits	Costs/Risks
Quality ✓ ✓ ✓ ✓	Existing System ✓ ✓ ✓ ✓
Operational Effectiveness ✓ ✓ ✓ ✓	Operational Ineffectiveness ✓ ✓ ✓ ✓
Cost Savings ✓ ✓	Staffing Costs ✓ ✓
Software Savings ✓	Software Cost ✓

Figure 2-4: A blank cost-benefit summary.

✔ **Identify any false assumptions that the customer may have about the software.** If, for example, the customer expects your software to save them more than a million dollars each year, even though your best estimates put the savings at closer to $300,000, you may need to talk with the customer to resolve the discrepancy. The customer may be basing these assumptions on a higher transaction level than you were planning for the software, or the customer may be looking at using the software in many locations while you were planning on only a couple.

You want to head off any misunderstandings early in the process rather than at the time that you actually deliver the software.

On the *Software Project Management Kit For Dummies* CD is a Microsoft Word template (*Template 2-3 Cost-Benefit Summary.dot*) that you can use as a pattern for the cost-benefit summary. As you can see in Figure 2-4, the document isn't very extensive.

In filling out the document, your customer will list the benefits on the left side of the form and the costs and/or risks on the right side. Some examples of items that may appear on the benefit side include the following:

- ✔ **What benefits are inherent in adopting the new software?** These benefits may include a better user interface, greater ease of use, more powerful functions, and more useful reports.

- ✔ **What are the benefits to operations in using the software?** Such benefits may include lower overhead, improved workflow, increased productivity, fewer defects, and easier integration with existing systems.

- ✔ **How much money does the customer save by using the software?** You can develop estimated figures to show savings over the course of a year or 18 months for *hard* and *soft* dollar savings as a sales strategy. *Hard dollar savings* are those reduced operation costs such as labor costs. These costs are easily identifiable and go directly to the bottom line. *Soft costs,* on the other hand, are often more difficult to define in terms of dollars, such as customer satisfaction. Monthly breakdowns aren't necessary, but quarterly projections enable you to determine the expectations of the customer. Based on these average estimates, the customers can calculate their own hard and soft dollar savings in using your software.

These examples represent only a few of the items that you can include in such a benefits summary. The exact information that you list here depends on the nature of the project and your relationship with the customer.

The cost/risk side of the summary often reflects the antithesis of the benefits side. Here you want to enter the anticipated downside to adopting the new software. Some ideas for this side include the following:

- ✔ **What cost must you associate with purchasing or leasing the software?** This figure may include not only the easily identifiable dollar figure, but also hidden costs, such as temporary staffing increases. This figure needs to be an actual bottom-line cost that you can balance against the cost of keeping the existing system in place. (This figure ends up on the cost side because purchasing new software is often more expensive than keeping legacy systems. If that's not the case here, you can move this item to the benefits column.)

- ✔ **What is the effect on personnel?** If the customer is using this software in a new department or for a new function, they need to determine the costs of hiring, training, and outfitting new employees. This figure is often the largest on the summary.

- ✔ **What is the cost to operations in keeping the existing system in place?** Some examples may include higher overhead, lower productivity, and more defects.

In filling out the cost-benefit summary, you need to make sure that the customer provides as accurate information as possible without going into too much detail. I don't make that statement to sound funny. I simply mean that you want to provide aggregate totals for financial and personnel figures (for example, $1.2 million instead of "money") but not to get into a breakdown of the aggregates. A good general rule is that, in most cases, you keep the cost-benefit summary to no longer than a page or two. Figure 2-5 shows an example of a completed cost-benefit summary for a mythical software package.

In some cases (for example, in developing commercial software for the retail market), you may actually need to develop the cost-benefit summary yourself. If so, you can base your cost-benefit estimates on information from focus groups or customer surveys.

Submitting the RFP and Getting Approval

After you finish gathering customer requirements and analyzing the cost and benefits of your software project, you may think that you've done quite a bit of work. However, before you can get to the joyful time of coding, you must present your project idea to the powers-that-be and await their blessing. The vehicle for this sacred event is known as a Request for Proposal. This request may sound very formal and it can be.

The actual requirements and expectations for this benchmark document vary, depending on the company. In some small companies, you may accomplish this entire stage over a cup of coffee or around the water cooler. In larger companies, you may need to request presentation time on the corporate agenda a month in advance. Executive managers and boards of directors can be very busy. Regardless of the formality (or lack thereof) in your organization, you need to carry out the RFP stage in writing. You must provide a record as to the nature and scope of the project, what you envision the result of the project to be, and what the financial expectations are.

In some companies, the RFP actually serves as a preliminary test document for whether the project is even feasible. The RFP may include a budget request for a feasibility study as well as a target date for completing the study. If your situation requires a feasibility study, someone in your marketing group usually spearheads it. This study starts with your original marketing analysis, your ROI figures, and the customer interviews and surveys; then it goes into an in-depth, focused analysis of this information. The feasibility study results in a coherent plan of attack for you to use in carrying out the project.

Customer Self-Service Web Cost-Benefit Summary

Benefits	Costs/Risks
Quality ✓ State-of-the-art ✓ Friendly user interface ✓ Rich functionality ✓ Meets current business needs	Existing System ✓ Obsolete ✓ Unfriendly user interface ✓ Limited functionality ✓ Doesn't exactly match current business model
Operational Effectiveness ✓ Lower overhead: requires 10 less employees to operate ✓ Higher throughput: 12,000 more transactions per month ✓ Fewer defects by 40% ✓ Easily integrated with other software	Operational Ineffectiveness ✓ Higher overhead: requires 10 additional employees to operate ✓ Lower throughput: 12,000 less transactions per month ✓ More defects by 75% ✓ Proprietary—difficult to integrate
Cost Savings ✓ Revenue increases by 3% ($250,000) per year ✓ Costs decrease by $575,000 per year	Staffing Costs ✓ Increase staff by 10 people for transition period ✓ Training costs estimated at $22,500 for first year
Software Savings ✓ $200,000 per year after first year	Software Cost ✓ $700,000 increase for first year

Figure 2-5: An example of a completed cost-benefit summary.

After the completion of a feasibility study, the corporate executives examine the results and make a decision. If they approve the project, work can proceed apace. If they don't approve it, you can always go back to the idea list you worked up at the beginning of the process.

In reality, the RFP contains many of the same items as the Requirements Document that I describe in the section, "Entering the Big Time: Doing the RD," later in this chapter. Additionally, it contains budgetary information that relates to project costs and time frames. In fact, most RDs are simply a subset of a full RFP, with additional information that you glean at subsequent steps (such as during a feasibility study).

Identifying the Project Sponsor and Project Manager

After executive management blesses a project from on high, the next step is to identify a project sponsor and assign a project manager to the project.

Project sponsor: The grand pooh-bah

The *project sponsor* is the boss, the person who acts on behalf of the customer. This person (or sometimes a group) is responsible for making sure that the project is up to snuff as customers are likely to view it from their perspectives. The project sponsor approves every step of the project and makes sure that the product meets each benchmark.

As you can tell, the role of the project sponsor is multifaceted. The primary responsibilities of the project sponsor generally include some or all of the following:

- Providing executive management-level approval and support for the project
- Assisting in the project strategic planning process
- Assuming the role of primary contact for executive decision making
- Approving the project's final scope, goals, objectives, schedule, and budget, as well as any changes to those items

Project manager: Chief cook and bottle washer

The project sponsor often is responsible for picking the project manager. The project manager carries the hands-on responsibility for the project's big picture, overseeing the project's day-to-day progress. The project manager acts as the liaison between the project sponsor and the development team.

Effective project managers coordinate the activities of a team of employees representing every area of their organization. Everyone also perceives you, the new project manager, as the primary expert resource for the project. So, suddenly, you're the expert! (Perhaps for the first time in your life.) If anyone has any questions concerning the project, they come to you because you're the person in charge.

As the project manager, you have several responsibilities, including the following:

- ✔ Selecting the project development team
- ✔ Identifying and implementing software project management practices
- ✔ Providing effective project planning, scheduling, budgeting, and risk and change control (for further details on the risk and change control process, check out Chapter 10)
- ✔ Communicating effectively with the project sponsor and your team members

In many ways, a good project manager is a generalist. You're the one with a good overall view of the project and the methods necessary to accomplish that project. You must be able to explain the needs of the organization (which the project sponsor embodies) to the manufacturers of the project code (which your development team embodies) and vice versa.

A critical duty of the project sponsor is to formalize the project manager's appointment by communicating this fact effectively to everyone with an interest in the project. After the project begins, you want no question to remain in anyone's mind as to who's the manager of the project. If you're filling the role of project manager informally, make a special request to your project sponsor to make your appointment known.

Getting Your Project Team in Place

Although you shoulder a great deal of the responsibility for the project, you can't do all the work yourself. The success of your project depends, in good measure, on the people working with you and how you manage and motivate them.

Finding the right people for a particular software project isn't always an easy task. Getting and keeping your project team members up to speed on cutting-edge technologies and project management methodologies is a constant challenge for a software project manager. On a given project, a number of sources — including your own software company, third-party business partners, and perhaps a customer's IT staff — may pull your team members in any number of directions. Your team members may have different backgrounds and skill sets from one another. Some team members may require training on project management processes and tools, while others may need a primer on different project skills, such as using HTML or JavaScript.

In your previous life — before you managed projects — you were probably an experienced software developer. Now, in your new role as project manager, your staff members will look up to you as the high-tech guru and as their new mentor for answering any questions. For example, your team may ask how to use Microsoft Project scheduling and tracking functions. Or, they may ask you a difficult programming question.

Keep in mind that some of your team members may come from your old staff, while others know nothing about your background and management skills. Just because you're the new project manager doesn't necessarily mean that you suddenly know everything there is about your software project. Remember you're the "high-level" person — the generalist. Give yourself and your team permission to delegate and refer the hard questions to the subject matter experts.

You want your software development team to include whomever you deem necessary to enable you to accomplish your goal of finishing the project. This ideal lineup may include some of the following positions:

- **Business Analyst:** This person typically examines the RFP and other existing documents for the project and translates them into the requirements document (see the following section). A business analyst is also helpful in understanding the specific business processes that a customer follows and not just in how the software is implemented to meet the customer's requirements.

  For example, your customer may be looking to automate their workplace business processes, such as purchasing supplies, mail, and manual paper transactions. Your customer looks to your analyst to determine what e-Commerce, e-mail, procurement, and automated workplace solutions will best meet their business process needs.

- **Developer/software engineer:** Normally, you have several developers and software engineers on your team. They create and debug the software's code and make sure that the program works as everyone expects. They're key team members in helping you successfully complete the project on time. Typically, a software organization's development organization can be split into two groups: application development and engineering.

- **Database administrator:** If the project relies on storing, processing, archiving, and transmitting data, you need a database administrator on the team. Because virtually every program of any scope involves at least one of these aspects of data manipulation, you may just as well face the fact that you need this person.

- **Technical writer:** One of the team members you most often overlook is the technical writer because they don't do Windows (or Mac code either, for that matter). But the technical writer performs the important function of producing the documentation that explains how the software operates and, sometimes, how it works behind the scenes, too. You need this person on the team from the very beginning because a tech writer can often spot problems that affect your implementation of the program while translating your product concepts to the written page.

✔ **SQA test engineer:** At some point, you need to test your software. Testing is where an SQA (software quality assurance) test engineer comes in. SQA engineers develop effective test suites that exercise your software and help expunge errors before the customer discovers them. (You don't want the customer to discover errors; that's *really* bad.)

✔ **Trainer:** You use a trainer primarily during the implementation phase to help customers integrate the software into their routines. Trainers work closely with technical writers and software engineers to uncover the intricacies of the software and stay one step ahead of the customer.

✔ **Configuration/release manager:** A configuration/release manager uses configuration management software to create the daily software builds for development, up to and including the final general release build that is provided to the customers. The configuration/release manager also coordinates the development team in adhering to sound development practices, such as ensuring that the correct fixes for all urgent defects are present in the build. When you're ready to invite your customer (or the public) to sample and use your software, the release manager is right there to handle the first feedback and resolve concerns.

I provide a Project Team Skill Matrix template (Project Team Skill Matrix.dot) on the *Software Project Management For Dummies* CD. You can use it to help make sure that you cover all your bases in relation to your development team. Figure 2-6 shows a completed matrix.

Customer Self-Serve Web Development Team Skill Matrix

Team Member	Project Sponsor	Project Manger	Analyst	Developer / Engineer	Database Admin	Technical Writer	SQA Test Engineer	Trainer	Release Manager
Dilbert	X								
Monica		X		X					
Hillary					X				
Kenneth			X	X			X		
Bill			X	X					
Austin									X
Felicity						X		X	
Dr. Evil							X		
Mini-me							X		
Forrest			X						

Figure 2-6: A sample Project Team Skill Matrix.

To use the matrix, just enter the names of everyone on your project team down the left side of the form and then put check marks in each column for each skill a person possesses.

The matrix does nothing more than help you identify the skills that each person on your team possesses. Notice in the example that some team members possess more than one skill. This overlap means that you can draw from the talents of more than one person for each skill area necessary to your project team.

Entering the Big Time: Doing the RD

Your fundamental goal during the requirements phase of every software project is to understand exactly what problem your customers are trying to solve. Granted, you spend a good deal of time identifying which problems are most beneficial for your company to solve, but you're identifying problems nonetheless. The problem equates to the specific software needs or requirements of your customers and target market.

The Requirements Document (sometimes known as the Product Requirements Document or Statement of Work) is the single most important document in a software project. Before you and your project team can even begin thinking about a solution to the customer's problem, you must thoroughly define the customers' requirements and clearly write them down in the RD.

The RD provides a detailed description of the proposed software's requirements or feature set. The RD doesn't, however, contain every little nit-picky detail down to how you implement items in code — it's not that detailed. But the RD does cover every feature the user can access and discusses the effects of that feature. You can, therefore, view the RD as a "laundry list" of features that are essential for the project.

Creating a requirements document

In larger organizations you, as project manager, don't typically have a hand in developing the RD; rather, your job is implementation. Smaller organizations, of course, offer a different story. There, the hat of project manager may be only one of several that you wear. You need to understand how to put together an RD so that you don't wind up out in left field without a glove if you do find yourself responsible for creating one.

I provide a requirements document template (Requirements Document.dot) on the *Software Project Management Kit For Dummies* CD. You can use it to create your own RD (if someone else doesn't create it for you). Complete each section of the template specifically for your project by using the information in the template itself. Following are the major sections of a typical RD and what sort of information each section contains:

✔ **Overview:** This section contains the top-level summary of what the RD covers. It reflects the intention of the document and the project that it describes.

✔ **Problem Summary:** This section summarizes the basic problem that your customer faces. It provide specifics if you're orienting the focus of this project toward a specific customer's business scenario. You can use the information that the Customer Requirements Surveys gather as a starting point for completing this section and the sections to follow.

✔ **Project Objectives:** This section contains a clear and simple statement concerning the primary goals and objectives of the project.

✔ **Major Required Features:** This section is often the longest in the RD. It starts out with a high-level, prioritized statement of features that the project requires. It then contains detailed information concerning how to implement the features to meet the needs of your customers.

✔ **Environments/Platforms:** This section consists of nothing more than a quick statement about the hardware, operating system, and software combinations on which you're basing the project. It provides guidance for the SQA test engineer in putting together test suites for the project.

✔ **Ease of Operability:** This section details how the project approaches the concept of "user friendliness." It focuses primarily on the user interface that the software uses.

✔ **Compatibility/Integration/Migration:** If the project is to develop a new version of existing software or software that you're designing to work with other software, you describe these relationships in this section. The focus is on how to achieve compatibility, integration, and migration during the course of the project.

✔ **Documentation/Training:** This section lists the key publications that the project requires. The technical writers and trainers on the development team use the information here to determine what they're creating.

✔ **Support/Maintenance:** Provide detailed customer support and ongoing software maintenance (sustained engineering) requirements in this section. The information in this section helps project team members understand how your company intends to support the product after they finish work on it.

✔ **Pricing/Licensing:** The legal department (in- or out-of-house) uses this section to develop the pricing and/or licensing documents that you use with the product. You want to list only exceptions to your company's established practices — things out of the ordinary. If you can use standard pricing and licensing practices, you can state that here, too.

Examples of exceptions to a company's established practices may include skipping a beta release or waiving maintenance and customer support fees in order to realize revenue for an initial public offering valuation.

The RD template on the CD that comes with this book contains a short instruction statement for each of these areas. You can also refer to Appendix A, which contains a sample RD that I developed by using the template. The RD reflects the needs of a mythical software project to which I refer at various places throughout this book.

You need to understand that the RD is a benchmark working document. It's the major document on which you and your development team base your work. Thus, you must keep it very flexible. Usually the product marketing manager or the project manager creates the RD. You can adapt the RD to meet your needs throughout the course of the project. The major point on which you need to focus is to be precise and complete in creating the RD. You can't expect your subsequent work to be complete or of quality if the basis for that work (the RD) is shoddy or faulty.

Putting the RD to work

The product marketing manager or the business analyst usually prepares the Requirements Document specifically for you and your project team, depending upon the size of your software organization. Your team uses the RD as its roadmap for developing all the other project deliverables during the remaining software development phases. The RD acts as the authoritative blueprint to which everyone refers in developing the project plan, the data model design, the detailed design specifications, the product's user publications, and even the actual coding of the software.

Marketing typically presents the RD to your project team during the project kickoff meeting, which I discuss in Chapter 3.

Your project team must not write a single line of code, create a single publication, or develop a single test plan until you have a written an RD that gathers, finalizes, and obtains approval from all stakeholders for all the project's requirements. To proceed without such a document is the riskiest course you can take as a project manager. If you do, you may end up wasting time, money, and other resources — all of which looks very bad on your employee review.

Because the RD is your guide to how to proceed with the development project, you and your development team — but especially you as project manager — must intimately acquaint yourselves with it. After you receive the RD, therefore, you need to ask questions, look for initial problems, and generally tear apart the document so that you're sure that you have a handle on it.

Much of the actual work that your team does in relation to the RD begins with the project plan brainstorming meeting, which I discuss fully in Chapter 3.

Chapter 3

Coordinating Team Meetings

· ·

In This Chapter

▶ Conducting the project kickoff meeting

▶ Brainstorming software project ideas

▶ Developing the Statement of Scope and Project Scope Document

▶ Creating the work-breakdown structure of milestones and tasks

▶ Estimating task durations

· ·

*A*fter a software project gets the go-ahead, the product-marketing manager typically drafts a Requirements Document. As I discuss in Chapter 2, the RD describes the proposed requirements — or feature set — for the high-level software you're going to design. A series of project meetings that involve you, as project manager, puts the RD to work. This chapter covers the three meetings that help you get the project off the ground smoothly — specifically, the project-kickoff meeting, the project-brainstorming meeting, and the work-breakdown structure meeting.

Each of these meetings is vital to the success of the project, as the following sections describe.

Project-Kickoff Meeting

As project manager, you coordinate the scheduling and agenda for the project kickoff meeting. You should invite the product marketing manager, project sponsor, and your project team. I strongly recommend reserving a conference room with a whiteboard and an easel with a notepad. Also, provide several packets of large Post-its for all attendees to jot down notes during the course of the meetings.

If you have many details to cover, consider requesting a video camera to record the meeting.

The main agenda items to discuss at this meeting include the following:

- Introducing the project team members and project vision.
- Presenting the Requirements Document — see Chapter 2 for complete details on creating an RD.
- Conducting a question-and-answer session regarding the RD.
- Identifying the project name.
- Presenting the Project Team Skill Matrix, which describes the project team's roles and assignments.
- Creating the Project Scope Document, which is your project team's response to the marketing department or the customer.
- Agreeing on a future meeting schedule and agenda.

Marketing (possibly assisted by the customer if this is a site-specific product) presents the RD to your development team during the project kickoff meeting. For the purposes of the sample project that I develop in this book, the following list provides an example of a high-level feature set that you can identify for the *Customer Self-Service Web* project. This feature set is the major item that you pull from the RD and focus on at the project kickoff meeting. The following list describes the feature set for this particular project:

- **A Web-based case tracking form:** This feature should be designed so that customers can enter software issue reports and customer profile information via a Web browser.
- **Key customer profile information:** This feature should be updated automatically as data is entered via a Web-based input form. The data is stored in a back-end relational database, such as Oracle, MS-SQL Server, or Sybase.
- **E-mail notification system:** You can add a system that fires off an e-mail to customer service for new cases that customers open.
- **Auto-escalation of case priority and approval of workflow functions:** You can customize your application to use an auto-escalation feature. To do so, create program modules to enable the system to automatically escalate the case priority, which in turn sets off a workflow to management. For example, if a case sits for several days with no customer response, you can set an auto-escalation that increases the case's priority and sets off a workflow that fires off an e-mail to the customer-service manager.
- **Internal case management reports:** These reports can include critical metrics for management use, such as the total number of cases opened or closed on a given workday by customer support representatives.

✔ **External case-tracking summary reports for customers:** The reports are viewable via Web browser and can include a summary of all the open and closed cases by customer, along with the current status by case number.

The nature of the project kickoff meeting is purely informational. During the meeting, the product marketing manager or your customer presents the RD and the feature set while you and your project team primarily sit and take notes. During this time, however, you want to encourage team members to ask questions that help clarify any of the points that you cover during the meeting.

Remind your team members to concentrate on understanding the project vision instead of worrying over the technical difficulties at this point. You actually decide which features are feasible during the project brainstorming meeting (which I discuss in the following section).

If you're a project manager for a software implementation at an off-site customer location, the same project meeting, RD, and PSD processes apply — only the players and roles vary somewhat. Instead of the product marketing manager gathering the requirements and writing and presenting the RD, for example, the implementation manager and the customer assume these responsibilities.

Project Brainstorming Meeting

Your second project team meeting during the analysis phase is known as the project brainstorming meeting. The purpose of this meeting is to give your development team the opportunity to analyze the RD that the product marketing manager presents during the project kickoff meeting (as I discuss in the preceding section).

Depending on the complexity of the project your team is undertaking, the project kickoff meeting may prove relatively short. If so, you may want to immediately convene the project brainstorming meeting. If not, and if you have a reasonable amount of time built into the project schedule, you may want to schedule the project brainstorming meeting for a few days or even a week after the kickoff meeting. This interval provides team members with time to review and individually analyze the RD. Such forethought and analysis can lead to a much more fruitful project brainstorming meeting.

Brainstorming the project scope

Here's where you go to the whiteboard and do the following team brainstorming activity:

1. **Draw a line down the middle of white board.**

2. **Add the following column titles, one on each side of the line:**

   In Scope   Out of Scope

3. **Pass out a hard-copy of the Requirements Document (RD) and pad of Post-its to each team member.**

4. **Instruct the team to write down all the software product features in the project to as fine a degree of detail as possible. These ideas are later placed on the whiteboard in either the In Scope or the Out of Scope area.**

Emphasize to the team that all ideas are fully accepted and unfiltered during the brainstorming session and that criticism of ideas is unacceptable. Also, clarify that only a single feature is to be written on each Post-it.

5. **Paste Post-its under the appropriate column, discussing with your team the reasons why each feature may or may not be within the project scope.**

This exercise is useful in not only determining which features your team believes can feasibly make it into the product, but also in finding possible solutions that may make a feature that your team may have thought impossible become suddenly feasible.

During the project brainstorming meeting, you want to focus on several different areas. The following list describes the primary items that you want to nail down:

✔ **Make sure that everyone understands the scope of the project.** The scope of a software project defines exactly which modules, components, and features are within the project scope and outside of scope. Often, the details of the RD can obscure the true scope of a project (the old can't-see-the-forest-for-the-trees syndrome). As project manager, you need to understand the project's scope better than anyone. Discuss your vision with your project team and make sure that you all have a firm understanding of the project's scope.

✔ **Define the primary project goals.** You can often restate your project goals directly from the major feature set for the project. Don't rely solely on the marketing types, however, to define these goals for you; you need to elicit the expertise of your project team to develop a firm set of goals that everyone on the project believes to be doable. Here's another opportunity for a team brainstorm activity by listing the goals on Post-its and adding them to the whiteboard.

✔ **Identify basic project assumptions.** Almost as important as goals are the assumptions on which you base those goals. Every project carries some underlying assumptions, and you must identify them. This is yet another opportunity for a team brainstorm activity where you can list the project assumptions on Post-its and add them to the white board.

Pose some questions to your project team; for example, what do you assume to be the transaction load on the software at an actual customer site in production? How many maintenance people are available to support it? And what additional software does the customer require to use the product you're making? Questions such as these are critical to the success of the project. Failure to accurately identify the assumptions behind a project can sink that project just as quickly as pursuing the wrong goals.

✔ **Identify the resources that you require.** Every project consumes resources, and yours is no exception. The personnel sitting around the table at your project brainstorming meeting are but a portion of the resources on which you need to draw. You may also need to identify how much computer time (or equipment) you need, what software tools are necessary, how many beta testers you're going to have, and whether you may need the help of any other departments.

✔ **Estimate a preliminary project schedule.** After you identify the scope and resources, you need take a crack at estimating the time necessary to complete the project. One of the important deliverables of the project kickoff meeting is an estimated project completion date. You can handle the detailed task durations in a subsequent project team meeting that determines the Work Breakdown Structure task network. For more details on the WBS, please refer to the "Work Breakdown Structure Meeting" section later in this chapter.

✔ **Estimate a preliminary project budget.** After you identify the resources and schedule that you need, setting up a preliminary budget is a relatively easy task. You may even want to create more than one budget, basing each one on different development scenarios (for example, best-case, most-likely, and worst-case possibilities).This is also a good place for a whiteboard treatment conducive to a lively team discussion.

Two major tools can help you accomplish the goals that your team sets during the project-brainstorming meeting: the Project Optimization Matrix and the Project Scope Document. You develop these tools during the course of the project brainstorming meeting, and you use these documents for the balance of the project. I discuss each of these tools in depth in the following sections.

The Project Optimization Matrix

The three primary ingredients of every project are scope, resources, and schedule. You, as project manager, must balance the scope of the project against your budgetary and schedule constraints — and that means donning your mediator's hat. Scope, resources, or schedules are not unlimited, and changing one of the three requires changes to one or both of the remaining ingredients. For example, you can't increase the scope of your project without either increasing the available time or adding to the project's resource pool (possibly by hiring temps). Likewise, you can't push the project out the door ahead of schedule without cutting features or increasing your budget so that you can add resources to the project (or both). You have to reach compromises with your project sponsor about where the priorities for your project lie.

Your team uses the Project Optimization Matrix to identify the priorities for your project's scope, resources, and schedule, and for making project plan adjustments in response to project changes. The POM is a useful tool because it helps you see what possible wiggle room you may have in your project's scope, resources, or schedule. Depending on the project goals and mood of your project sponsor, this amount of wiggle room can vary significantly, as illustrated in the examples provided in Figure 3-1.

The *Software Project Management Kit For Dummies* CD contains a Project Optimization Matrix template (Project Optimization Matrix.dot), which is a great starting point for developing your POM. Figure 3-1 shows you a filled-out sample of a POM.

Figure 3-1:
A sample
Project
Optimization
Matrix
(POM).

Project Optimization Matrix

	Fixed (High)	Variable (Medium)	Variable (Low)
Scope (Deliverables)			
Resources (Budget)			
Schedule (Time)			

In the POM example that I provide in Figure 3-1, Monica (the project sponsor) has definitively said to Bill, the project manager, "You have no slack time in this project schedule." However, the resource variable is the most flexible. Thus, Bill, can possibly add additional resources to his project (maybe even a legal counsel or two) to make his schedule less inflexible.

Alternatively, if the project sponsor doesn't want to provide you with all the resources that you need, you can try to see whether you can further limit the project's scope by modifying and deleting certain project tasks. For example, you can reduce the project's scope by reducing certain noncritical software features. By reducing the number of features, you reduce the design, development, and testing critical task durations, which in turn shortens the overall project schedule.

The Project Scope Document (PSD)

The Project Scope Document is also commonly known as the Statement of Work. The PSD gives your project team the opportunity to provide a formal response to features proposed in the RD. Typically, your product marketing manager lists every possible software feature in the RD that the marketing team presents to your team at the project kickoff meeting.

Speak now or forever hold your peace. In your PSD, your team indicates, in their professional opinion, which software features listed in the RD are in the project's scope, as well as those deemed to be out-of-scope. In addition to formally responding to the RD, you will also get valuable input by asking pointed questions during the project brainstorming meeting.

Your PSD begins with a Statement of Scope, followed by a list of the project's primary goals. Do you remember your high-school English teacher harping on the importance of a thesis statement, or your statement of the overall goal of your composition? You may remember writing silly stuff such as: *In this paper, I prove that ketchup is the undisputed king of hotdog condiments* — making this statement, without fail, the last sentence in your introductory paragraph. (Can you spell *obsessive-compulsive,* teach?) Well, the SOS acts as a sort of thesis statement for your project, outlining the project's primary goals as well as defining its boundaries.

You can think of the PSD as your we-can-do-these-things-but-we-can't-go-there manifesto. The PSD serves as the development team's reality check to the sometimes rose-colored feature set that the marketing team delivers. The PSD also provides a means for the project sponsor and project team to manage customer expectations.

Before trying to craft a PSD, you first need to try answering the following important set of questions during the project kickoff meeting:

✔ **What is the scope of project?** You should already have determined the answer to this question earlier in your project kickoff meeting. Remember — determining the scope of the project is one of the major tasks that you must accomplish during the project brainstorming meeting. If you can't definitively answer the question by this point, you can't develop the PSD.

Keep in mind that your team needs to put on their critical thinking caps to balance marketing's vision of the project scope with the realistic costs of each feature. At the end of the day, your team, project sponsor, and the marketing group need to work on a preliminary agreement or compromise on the project scope — the software feature set. Often, the compromise means that a lengthy feature list of an RD is broken out into several phases or subprojects, as opposed to having finish everything for the initial rollout.

After reaching a preliminary consensus for a targeted project scope, you can begin writing the PSD, beginning with the high-level SOS as your thesis.

✔ **What software business requirements appear in the RD?** Your marketing team's surveys of your target customer base define the business requirements that appear in the RD. Also, your project sponsor can go a long way toward helping you clarify your customers' business needs. The project sponsor should have a firm grasp on market demands and your leadership's vision of the software product that they expect to result from your project.

Some examples of customer business requirements for the Customer Self-Service Web project may include gathering requirements on the customers' business rules, how many external customers they expect to service with the software, and the nature of their lines of goods and services that such a system will support.

✔ **What software functional requirements appear in the RD?** Part of your effort in defining your project's scope involves gathering and analyzing the software's functional specifications. Defining the software's functional requirements involves translating your customers' business requirements into technical software features. The functional requirements for the Customer Self-Service Web project include the Web-based input and output form design, automatic escalation of cases, storage and retrieval of particular cases, and so on.

✔ **How do you intend to design the look and feel of the user interface?** Another important issue that needs to be addressed in the PSD is the scope and features of your software's user interface. Because your customers don't deal with the behind-the-scenes algorithms and other code that underlie your project, they rely solely on how easy the software is to use and whether the appearance of the software seems intuitive to them — a consideration that lies squarely within the domain of the user interface.

In the Customer Self-Service Web project, some UI considerations may include whether you intend to support frames, whether the main entry screen looks like a particular form, and whether right-clicking will be supported. Marketing and the project sponsor should express which UI features they believe customers are interested in. However, you and your project team also need to develop a good idea of how you're going to put that interface together to understand the overall scope of the project in this area by clearly expressing your opinions and reservations in the PSD.

✔ **What are the high-, medium-, and low-priority features of the project?** The focus of the project brainstorming meeting that I discuss earlier in this chapter in the section titled "Project Brainstorming Meeting" is determining which features are within and which features are outside the scope of your project. Having come to an understanding with your project sponsor about the features that you can reasonably include in your project, your next challenge is to determine the relative priority of each in-scope feature compared with all the other in-scope features.

You should meet first with your project team to discuss the technical difficulties that underlie each feature and which features your team feels are central to the development of the project. Using this information and the Project Optimization Matrix that I explain in the previous section, you should draft a priority list of product features that you place within the PSD for approval by management.

Before you submit the final PSD, you should run your priority list by the project sponsor. You're better off letting the project sponsor do some behind-the-scenes checking, negotiating, and explaining before you go live with your PSD.

✔ **Which high and medium features can you reasonably deliver by the target date?** You can obviously skip this step if every feature is high priority. If you're lucky enough to have a project in which different features have different priorities, you can figure out which ones you can finish first, how long each takes, and which features' completion dates fall beyond the estimated project completion date.

✔ **Which features need to be deferred to a subsequent release?** If you firmly feel that some of the project features that made the cut still fall outside the scope of the project, you need to identify those features and defer them until later. Of course, you must do so in consultation with your project sponsor so that everyone understands this decision on an organizational level. Now's your chance to ask whether a feature that everyone agrees adds to the utility of the project must be included in this project or whether it can be deferred until a future release or upgrade.

✔ **Do you need more information from the marketing team or from the customer?** By this point, you need to know what the project entails and what the customer expects. Now, therefore, is the time to request additional information if any points do remain unclear.

✔ **How is your design going to affect the data model?** You find out more about the data model in Chapter 7. For now, just know that the term refers to how the program uses and manages data. The answer to this question becomes critical to the scope of work if the program requires the retention of tons of data (which may require additional hardware) or if it modifies the data that your customers' organizations currently collect and retain.

As you answer these questions, try to think back to the time that you last went shopping for a new car. You had a certain budget and a feature set for the automobile in mind. The feature set probably included a brand, a model, a specific color, and so on. You had these items in mind *before* the salesperson accosted you as you wandered into the showroom. As you discovered how high the cost was for each feature, you may have quickly crossed items off your original wish list. You faced a real wake-up call as to which features really fell in the must-have category, the important-but-you-can-live-without category, and the add-on-nicety category.

Keep in mind that an SOS is a detailed but succinct statement outlining the project's goals and deliverables that serves as the thesis statement of the PSD. The *Software Project Management Kit For Dummies* CD contains an SOS template (Statement of Scope.dot). Figure 3-2 shows you a sample SOS and PSD that I've already filled out.

The PSD may not seem such a big deal if you go only by what you see in Figure 3-2, but it can take you and your team quite a while to hammer out. It presupposes a lot of work on your part (and that of your development team) to decide what you're putting into the project and what, by necessity, you're leaving out. The following sections may shed additional light on how you can accomplish some of the tasks necessary in successfully completing the SOS. Figure 3-3 shows a blank Statement of Scope Document.

Defining project goals

In defining the goals and objectives of each phase of your project, you go through the same prioritization process as the marketing team uses in creating the RD. Keep in mind that, typically, you can't possibly complete all the features that your marketing department and your customers request within the time allotted for the project.

Suppose, for example, that you're sitting in your project brainstorming meeting in early February and that your company's Chief Technology Officer mandates a drop-dead date of June 19 for the first phase of the project. (He does so very kindly, of course, and passes this information on to you through your project sponsor.) This schedule, unfortunately, gives you only four months to get the job done. Yikes!

Customer Self-Service Web
Statement of Scope

Ojectives

Instructions: *Provide a clearly stated statement of three to five high-level project objectives which must be accomplished.*

The scope objectives of Phase I of the *Customer Self-Service Web* project include: (1) Internet self-service transaction processing for external customer support case tracking and reporting; (2) internal customer service metrics reporting; and (3) customer-profile data access.

Development and Implementation Phases

Instructions: *If the project will be developed and/or implemented in phases, provide an overview of each phase.*

The *Customer Self-Service Web* product will be released in phases, with additional functionality added in each release. The first release will focus on basic call-tracking transactions and basic reporting features. Phase I of the project will have a considerably smaller scope than what is described in the functional specifications of the Requirements Document (RD).

Features

Instructions: *Provide a list of product features which are the specific software components of the product within the project's scope.*

Phase I of the *Customer Self-Service Web* will include the following features:

- Web customer self-service transaction processing
- Case record entry
- Update and correction capability
- Customer profiles
- Search and retrieval
- Tracking and reporting

Out of Scope Items

Instructions: *Indicate any features which may be desirable but are considered outside the scope of the project.*

Only the *Customer Self-Service Web* management features listed above are included in Phase I of this project. With the exception of the update and correctional capability, the rest of the enhanced features listed in the Requirements Document will not be included in Phase I of this project.

These additional functions include Computer Telephony and Internet (CTI) technology, knowledge database, online Customer Forum, and auto-generated ("push") software releases and service packs, which will be added in later releases.

Figure 3-2:
A sample
Statement
of Scope
and Project
Scope
Document.

[Project Name]
Statement of Scope

Ojectives

Instructions: *Provide a clearly stated statement of three to five high-level project objectives which must be accomplished.*

Development and Implementation Phases

Instructions: *If the project will be developed and/or implemented in phases, provide an overview of each phase.*

Features

Instructions: *Provide a list of product features which are the specific software components of the product within the project's scope.*

Out of Scope Items

Instructions: *Indicate any features which may be desirable but are considered outside the scope of the project.*

Figure 3-3:
A blank
Statement
of Scope
Document.

The following steps offer a recommended approach to help you maintain your sanity:

1. **Assign priorities to all the features that the Requirements Document lists.**

    This prioritization process requires some negotiation with your marketing group, project sponsor, and customers, but you can't avoid it. You must determine which features are "must haves" (high priority), which are important but are really features that they can live without (medium priority), and which features are merely "add-ons" or enhancements (low priority).

    An important criterion for lowering the priority of a particular feature and determining whether to include or defer a particular feature is to weigh its proportionate level of difficulty to develop against its proportionate level of functionality. One measurement of level of difficulty is the effect of a proposed feature on the design of the data model and on your existing application design. The level of functionality is a measurement of the degree of necessity as dictated by market demand.

The following are some sample questions you can ask to help your team determine whether to include or defer features in the PSD. Does the feature require only the addition of a couple new columns to an existing data table and a simple new input form? Or does the feature mandate, for example, additional dependencies between tables that require a complete redesign of the data model or the addition of a multipart input form into the application interface? Is this feature an absolute necessity to the functioning of the software, or can its development be deferred to a subsequent release?

2. **Categorize all the requirements by priority into the following three lists:**

   • **Phase I:** High-priority features.

   • **Phase II:** Medium-priority features.

   • **Phase III:** Low-priority features.

In the Phase I listing for our Customer Self-Service Web project (refer to the Statement of Scope and Project Scope Document shown in Figure 3-2), you notice that I list only the top five high-priority features for completion. Several other medium- and low-priority requirements I determined to be out of scope for Phase I, and so I deferred them to later phases of the project.

Developing budgets

One of your principal responsibilities as project manager at the beginning of any project is to estimate the project budget. In putting together your budgetary estimates, make sure that you include the following areas:

✔ **Salaries:** Although your project team members are full-time employees getting paid salaries based upon a forty-hour week. However, most of your team members will probably work on your project on a part-time basis. Therefore, you generally budget salaries for a given project as a percentage of each resource's total available time.

✔ **Third-party consultants:** In addition to utilizing full-time salaried team members, software project teams often consist of third-party consultants on the payroll. Consultants typically charge by the hour, often at a high rate, in exchange for their specialized experience and skills they bring to the table. You need to set aside a small fortune in your budget to cover these costs.

✔ **Development tools:** Depending upon the project, you almost always need development tools, including hardware and third-party software programming tools. Most of the time, these items can be reused for multiple projects. Depending on the requirements of your company, you may need to budget these items by amortizing the total cost and life of the assets as a function of the total duration of the project. Keep in mind tools, hardware, and software are fixed assets that are used on a full-time basis, potentially used for multiple projects, and costs should be spread across all projects that benefit from their use.

✔ **Facilities:** Similar to the use of development tools, hardware, and software, facilities such as office space, cubicles, chairs, and desks can be reused for multiple projects. Depending on the requirements of your company, you may need to budget for these facilities by amortizing the total cost and life of the assets as a function of the total duration of the project. You should spread the costs of fixed assets — which are used on a full-time basis potentially for multiple projects — across all projects that benefit from their use.

✔ **Documentation:** Every software product needs to be documented for the customers, including release notes, installation instructions, administration and user guides, and online documentation tools. Documentation costs need to be factored into your project's budget, including sufficient staffing writers in your technical publications group, as well as the required tools.

✔ **Testing:** In order to ensure that your software product reaches the desired level of quality for your customers' ultimate use, there needs to be testing throughout the development cycle including unit, integration, Software Quality Assurance system, and beta testing at designated customer sites. In addition to budgeting for enough SQA testing engineers and automation test scripting tools, beta-testing may involve members from your consulting team to travel to beta tester client sites. Therefore, testing costs need to be included in your project's budget.

✔ **Training/courseware:** Often a software project involves special training needs for your project team. For example, you may want to purchase a copy of this *Software Project Management for Dummies Kit* for your entire team and hire a third-party company to provide project-management training to your team. In the age of the Internet and multimedia, offering Web-based training and computer based training is very important. The success of the product (and future releases) depends on the fraction of users who become power users. Thus, training and courseware costs need to be factored into your project's budget.

In addition, you may have other budgetary items that your team requires to accomplish the project (pizza, Jolt Cola, and so on). In some companies, there may be a requirement to follow the accounting procedures and processes of your finance department.

Whenever you're planning to allocate resources and budgeting for a new project, look at any historical data available from previous projects. The more that you base your project-resource estimates on empirical data — what came in on time and on budget and what didn't — the higher is the probability of your project's success in this area. Do your homework!

One big area to look at for budgeting is whether your project needs to include the initial development and packaging cost estimates for the product in the figures that you submit. Some companies may require such information. If so, you need to work with outside vendors or your manufacturing department to pull together reasonable figures for manufacturing, packaging, and distribution.

For an example of how to put the budget together, consider the information in Table 3-1. This proposed budget is for the *Customer Self-Service Web* project example that I cover on the CD and elsewhere in the book. Each preliminary budget starts with a single figure that represents the total estimated expenditure for each budget category.

Table 3-1	Preliminary Budget for the *Customer Self-Service Web* Project
Budget Item	*Estimate*
Salaries	$450,000
Consultants	$10,000
Development Tools	$150,000
Facilities	$45,000
Training/Courseware	$10,000
Total	$660,000

As you work on the project, you necessarily must keep track of your expenditures. In some companies, you may receive periodic budget printouts from your finance department. Make sure that you manage these figures closely; they may make or break your reputation with the company.

After you finish the project, you often need to prepare a budget summary that shows your original estimates, your actual expenditures, and the variance between the two. Table 3-2 shows an example of such a summary, basing its data on the information in Table 3-1.

Table 3-2	Budget Summary for the *Customer Self-Service Web* Project		
Budget Item	*Estimate*	*Actual*	*Variance*
Salaries	$450,000	$478,568	$28,568
Consultants	10,000	7,500	−2,500
Development Tools	150,000	147,300	−2,700
Facilities	45,000	50,000	5,000
Documentation	10,000	12,789	2,789
Total	$660,000	$696,157	$36,157

The wonderful world of project management provides an entire toolkit of project estimators to assist you in allocating resources and developing budgets throughout the life of the project. In Chapter 5, I give you an opportunity to develop time, cost, and resource estimates for your project by using a variety of tools for estimating the cost and schedule of a software project. (You can also find many of these tools on the *Software Project Management Kit For Dummies* CD that comes with this book.)

Work Breakdown Structure Meeting

Think of a software project as a multitasking effort. In this section, you find out how to break your project down into tasks and how to start tracking those tasks. In preceding sections, you formulate and enter your high-level project's scope, goals, and assumptions. In this section, you begin to look at your project in greater detail, focusing on who is going to do what and how long they have to do it.

The place to start creating your development plan is in the work breakdown structure meeting (sometimes known simply as the WBS meeting). Here you start to break the project down into constituent parts and define the phase-structure of the project's tasks. This process involves the following three key steps:

1. **Identify software project phases and milestones.**
2. **Assign numbers to phases and tasks.**
3. **Estimate task durations.**

The following sections delve into each of these steps in more detail. You can either create the WBS on paper (boo, hiss!), or you can use a software program to help you out. I suggest that you use Excel; it's on many people's computers and is very easy to use for the type of data that you compile in a WBS.

Step 1: Identify software project phases

A high-level Project Scope Document that defines the project goals isn't enough to build an effective software-project schedule. You need to further break down the work into more manageable and meaningful chunks, identifying project phases, and their associated tasks through a project management tool known as a *Work Breakdown Structure* (*WBS*).

You want to start identifying the WBS by first identifying the major phases that mark each major project-development stage in the software development cycle (such as gather requirements, analysis, and so on). Remember that you have seven phases in the software development cycle, which I explain in Chapter 1.

The phase list for the *Customer Self-Service Web* project example is summarized as follows:

- Gather requirements
- Analysis
- Design
- Development
- Test (Software Quality Assurance — SQA)
- Manage release and change
- Implementation

Figure 3-4 shows an example of how your Excel worksheet probably looks after you enter these seven major steps. You don't have much to see here yet; you're just at the beginning of developing your task list.

You can further break down each of the tasks shown in Figure 3-4 into subtasks, which you can then break down even further. If you have a programming background, you may notice that this iterative process of breaking down tasks is similar to modularizing a software program — you define the major task and then break it down into component parts that, after you complete them, represent the entire task.

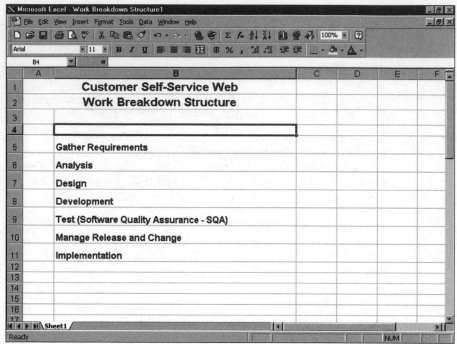

Figure 3-4:
Starting
your task
list at a
high level.

You're still dealing with concepts at this point and not with the implementation of these concepts. Don't worry yet about how you can accomplish something; just identify the project's phases and tasks as something that you need to accomplish. Keep in mind the analogy of the writing process that you employ in creating a good report or story: You first define the thesis statement, which is your project's Statement of Scope and high-level features in the Project Scope Document and then you outline the major themes along a discrete timeline — your project's critical tasks along the critical path. The project's *critical path* is the sequence of tasks that must be finished on or ahead of the project completion date in order for the project to be completed on schedule.

Finally, you successively break down the software project phases into tasks and then into subtasks until you have a complete outline of how your project is to proceed. Figure 3-5 shows an example of what such an outline may look like.

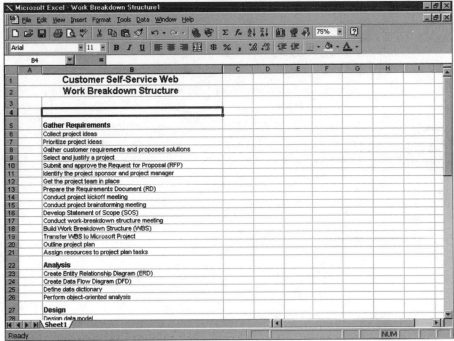

Figure 3-5:
Filling in the
details of
the Work
Breakdown
Structure.

Step 2: Assign numbers to the tasks and subtasks

I strongly suggest that you number every software project phase and task in your WBS task network. This step may sound trivial, and in some respects it is. But this numbering comes in handy at a later date, when you want to track the relationships of milestones and tasks throughout the project.

Projects change over time. As you get into the groove of creating your software, you may discover new milestones and/or tasks that you need to do — ones that you fail to envision early on. As you add new milestones and/or tasks to the task network list of WBS, you push older tasks down a line. Assigning task numbers early in the process enables you to easily track how a specific task carries through the project, all the way from start to finish.

You can assign phases and tasks to a software project as follows:

1. **Assign phases whole numbers such as 1.0, 2.0, 3.0, and so on.**

2. **Assign tasks numbers beginning with the first digit of an associated phase, such as 1.01, 1.02, 1.03, and so on.**

3. **Assign subtasks by adding another period and set of numbers, such as 1.01.01, 1.01.02, and so on.**

You can also alternate between digits and letters in tasks to make it easier to read and remember. For example, you can have a subtask as 1.A, 1.B, and so on, and nested subtasks as 1.A.01, 1.A.02, and so on.

Figure 3-6 shows an example of how your updated WBS may now look, with numbering applied to each task.

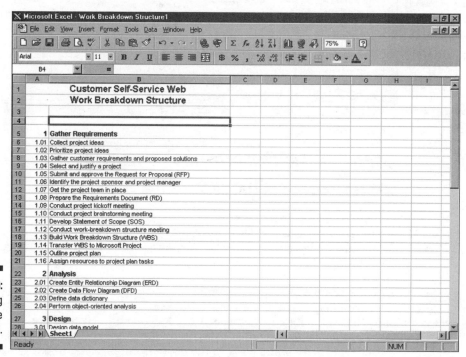

Figure 3-6: Numbering tasks in the WBS.

Step 3: Estimate task durations

By definition, milestones are project benchmarks that are assigned 0 day durations (time). It's the tasks associated below each milestone with assigned durations that your project team need only focus on during your WBS project team meeting. Your estimate of how long each task is to take is only your best guess, but nailing these estimates makes you look like a genius at the end of the project.

Estimating is critical so that you have at least an idea of how long your project may take to finish. The best approach to take is to update the project schedule as frequently as you can. As time goes by, your estimates will become more accurate. As you estimate the project's task durations while filling in the WBS (task network), you don't need to get any more precise than the number of days each task may take — so what if you're a few minutes or hours late for the software release party!

Adding durations to your Excel worksheet is easy — just add a column to indicate the number of days each task requires. The *Software Project Management Kit For Dummies* CD contains an Excel template (Work Breakdown Structure.xlt) that represents a starting point for a WBS just before you enter any durations.

For some tasks, you don't need to use estimates — instead, you can use actual figures. Many of the tasks that you list in the 1.0 gather requirements phase, such as 1.01 Collect Marketing Data, 1.02 Survey Customer Requirements & Proposed Solutions, and so on may already be complete. If so, just make sure that the durations you give for these tasks represent reality.

You're a perceptive and well-informed project manager (but don't let it go to your head). You already know that you can accomplish many tasks at the same time that other tasks are being accomplished. But don't worry about that quite yet. Just enter a duration for each task as if it's the sole task you're performing at the time that you do it. So if you figure that you can accomplish three of your tasks in a single day, you don't enter a duration of .33 days for each of them; instead, you enter a duration of one day for each of them.

As you enter durations, make sure that you include the word *day* or *days* along with the duration itself. Thus you enter a duration as **4 days** rather than simply as 4. Don't enter a duration for a particular phase (or for a task that contains subtasks). Microsoft Project interprets these as summary tasks and sets their duration to be the sum of the durations of the tasks that comprise them. Figure 3-7 shows an example of how a filled-in WBS may look.

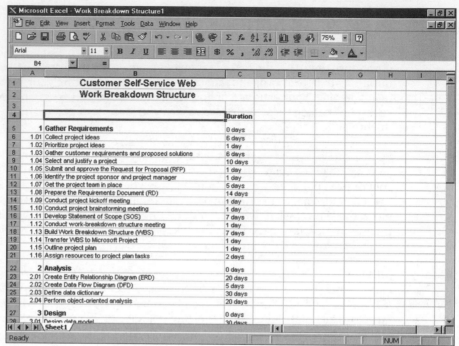

Figure 3-7:
Adding
durations to
your WBS.

After you enter the durations, you're still not through with your WBS. Indeed, what you have so far acts simply as the starting point for working in more powerful project management tools. Make sure that you save your Excel WBS; you use it right off the bat in Chapter 4.

The Statement of Scope, your project's "thesis statement," taken together with the WBS of supporting details, is often known as the Project Scope Document. (Don't you *love* all these abbreviations?) I refer to the PSD often in the following chapters of this book.

Part II
Building and Tracking in Microsoft Project

The 5th Wave

By Rich Tennant

"This isn't a quantitative or a qualitative estimate of the job. This is a wish-upon-a-star estimate of the project."

In this part . . .

Ever seen a project manager perform black magic with Microsoft Project? With a click of the button, these prestidigitators can make half the time in your schedule disappear. Well, now's you're chance to pull a few rabbits out of your own hat. And here you thought that this project management stuff was all work!

In Part II, you discover how to start building your software's Gantt Chart schedule using Microsoft Project. You enter milestones, tasks, durations, and build task relationships. You can also use Project to help you optimize your project plan by adjusting project scope by modifying tasks on the critical path, changing your schedule by playing with time, reallocating resources, and reducing costs.

Finally, entering your project information into Project, you have a good way of tracking whether your project is still on schedule and under budget (or if it's time to ask your rich uncle to buy you some extra time and resources).

Chapter 4

Scheduling and Outlining Your Project

· ·

· ·

Suppose that you're both the primary architect and the contractor of a construction project for a new high-rise building. As such, you're responsible both for the design of the building and for knowing when to have the crane on the lot and when you need the windows delivered.

Before your construction crew even thinks about setting that first girder, you (as architect) must spend several months drawing up elaborate blueprints of the skyscraper, trying to ensure that every detailed specification appears in the plans. As the contractor, you're responsible for scheduling every conceivable task, subtask, and milestone (phase) of the construction project, as well as ensuring that optimal resources are available to complete each of the tasks necessary to finish the building's construction.

The roles of architect and contractor in the skyscraper project parallel the dual roles of designer and scheduler that a software project manager fulfills. As designer, you create your software project plan as the blueprint for the project. As the scheduler, you need to sweat the details of the timing of the various phases of the project. The better that you think through and the more that you detail your project schedule, the higher is your probability for overall success on the project. In this chapter, you find out how to build and refine a software project schedule by entering tasks, editing existing tasks, inserting new tasks, adding milestones, and outlining your project into an organized structure of summary tasks and related subtasks.

Analyzing the Work Breakdown Structure

Your project team starts creating your software project plan during the *work breakdown structure meeting,* which I cover in Chapter 3. The WBS is a listing of the milestones (the seven software project phases) and tasks associated with the project.

During the WBS meeting, your project team starts to break the project down into logical units of work and to define the phase-structure of the project's milestones and tasks. This process involves the following three key steps:

- ✔ Identify software project milestones and tasks.
- ✔ Assign numbers to milestones and tasks.
- ✔ Estimate task durations.

Enter WBS tasks into Microsoft Excel

This WBS Excel spreadsheet provides three important benefits for your project-planning process as it goes forward from this point:

- ✔ **Work-in-progress document:** A WBS in spreadsheet form provides a work-in-progress document that you can print out for subsequent team meetings. Your team members are free to pencil in any notes and any recommended changes to the preliminary WBS that they want to make. After each subsequent meeting, you can add any newly agreed-upon changes to the spreadsheet.

- ✔ **Historical reference:** The WBS spreadsheet is a good historical point of reference for your current project, as well as for planning estimates for similar, future projects with greater accuracy.

- ✔ **Data repository:** The WBS provides an excellent source of project data when you're ready to enter your tasks, durations, and assignments into Microsoft Project. Although you can import your WBS data into Microsoft Project, doing so is probably more difficult than just finding an assistant to type the tasks into Microsoft Project. After your WBS Excel spreadsheet is complete, I recommend that you print it out for use when you begin entering your project data into Microsoft Project.

After you establish a team consensus on the WBS and you're ready to finalize entry of your project's tasks into Microsoft Project, I recommend that you first perform the following important tasks:

- ✔ Conduct a work breakdown structure team meeting.
- ✔ Enter the WBS tasks into Microsoft Excel, as shown in Figure 4-1.

For the complete skinny on the WBS team meeting and how to create your WBS in Microsoft Excel, please check out Chapter 3.

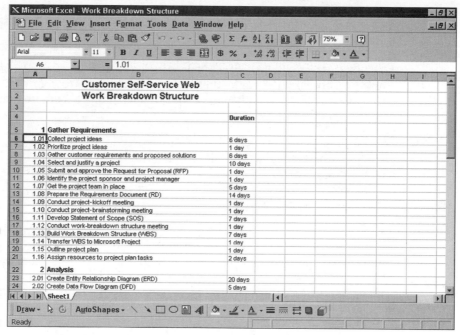

Figure 4-1:
Reviewing
your WBS in
Microsoft
Excel.

Building a task network and critical path

The task network provides a graphic representation of the Work Breakdown Schedule task list that you create in Microsoft Excel, including start and finish times for only the critical tasks, which are those that you must complete to successfully finish the overall project.

The Critical Path Method and Program Evaluation and Review Technique are the two primary project-management tools that project managers traditionally use to create a task network. CPM and PERT provide a graphical representation of the series of critical project tasks that you define in the WBS, which network along the project's critical path.

Based on your research and estimates, you determine the project's critical path. The critical path is the total duration of the tasks that are necessary to accomplish your project's goals (as the Project Scope Document defines them).

The question that you need to keep asking yourself is "Is this task *critical* to the completion of the project?" Try to avoid the tendency of adding *non*critical tasks to your task network by first carefully prioritizing tasks.

You're always best off starting with the high-level tasks that follow the project stages, which are the major milestones of the software development cycle, as shown in the Excel spreadsheet in Figure 4-1. In that example, you see seven critical tasks (project phases), which include gathering requirements, analysis, design, development, testing, managing releases and change, and implementation.

The process parallels the writing process you follow in creating a good report or story: You first define the thesis statement (similar to your Project Scope Document) and then outline the major themes along a discrete timeline — your project's critical tasks.

The detailed subtasks come later. Of course, you find many variations of the implementation phase of the development process across various software-development firms. The basic software project phases have remained relatively constant since the 1950s however, when the U.S. military initiated the first megalithic application projects for its mainframes.

You find out as a software project manager that, after you establish your WBS, Critical Path, and Gantt Chart, you're well on your way to effectively identifying and managing your project's critical tasks. You can also add some "float" to the tasks along the critical path, which provides some flexibility to the schedule for unforeseen project change. You can now schedule the project by using Microsoft Project. So get your PC and mouse ready to byte into this chunk of cheese!

Using Microsoft Project

The world is full of all sorts of tools that you can use to manage your project. One such tool is known as, appropriately enough, Microsoft Project. Microsoft Project enables you to enter and track the individual tasks that make up a project. You can then print all sorts of graphs, charts, and reports, basing them on the information that you enter into the program.

The beauty of a tool such as Microsoft Project is that it enables you to quickly and easily see where your bottlenecks are and to allocate resources accordingly.

The *Software Project Management Kit For Dummies* CD contains an evaluation version of Microsoft Project 2000. It's a full-blown version of the software that you can use for 90 days (after which time it insolently refuses to work). If you don't already have Microsoft Project on your system, take a moment to install the software. If you already have some Microsoft Office products on your system, you're likely to find Project very easy to use. If you're not that familiar with the interfaces that Microsoft uses, getting up and running generally takes only marginally longer than it does for those familiar with its software.

You may wonder how exactly Microsoft Project relates to this chapter — good question! Quite a bit, actually. In this chapter, you're discovering how to schedule and outline your project. If you read through Chapter 3, you get a pretty good idea of how to create a good outline for your project. In this chapter, you find out how to use project management software (in this case, Microsoft Project) to start working with that outline.

The purpose of this chapter (or even this book) isn't to try to teach you how to use Microsoft Project. If you need to know how to use the software, I suggest that you refer to a seminal work on the subject — such as *Microsoft Project 2000 For Dummies* by Marty Doucette (published by IDG Books Worldwide, Inc.). If you want to find out how to use this tool to accomplish your larger task — managing a software project — read on; that's why you and I are here.

Setting the Start Date of the Project

Every project must have a start — having a starting point makes reaching the end much easier. Microsoft Project enables you to easily change the starting date for your project. After you first import your WBS from Excel, Project assumes that you want to start the project today, right now, immediately. Because this assumption is probably not a good one, you may need to change the starting date of your project. To do so, simply follow these steps:

1. **Choose Project⇨Project Information from the menu bar.**

   Project displays the Project Information dialog box, as shown in Figure 4-2.

2. **Click the down arrow next to the Start Date drop-down list box.**

   Project displays a handy-dandy calendar with a circle around today's date.

3. **Click the arrow buttons to locate the month you want to begin.**

4. **Click the date that you want the project to begin.**

   If you want a starting date of 2/1/2000, for example, you first need to ensure that the calendar for February 2000 appears by using the arrow buttons to locate February 2000 calendar; then you click the first day. Check to make sure that Project updates the Start Date text box with your choice (for example, to `Start Date: Tue 2/1/00`).

   I base the Project files on the CD-ROM on the assumption that the Customer Self-Service Web project begins with `Gather Requirements` as its first phase. If you're also using `Gather Requirements` as the beginning phase of your project, make sure that you pick as your Start Date the date when the Gather Requirements phase begins.

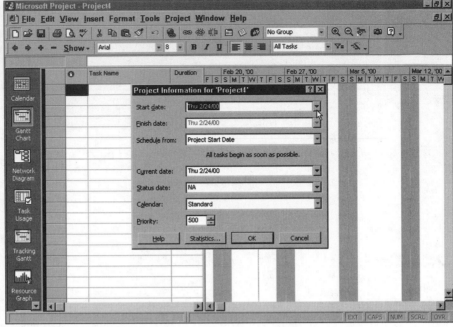

Figure 4-2:
You can
change
information
for your pro-
ject in this
dialog box.

4. **Click OK.**

Project updates all the calendars and schedules that appear in the
Project window.

Transferring Tasks to Microsoft Project

Although you can import your WBS from Microsoft Excel into Project, the
process is really more trouble than it's worth. Instead, you're better off entering (or even *better* off having an assistant enter) the tasks from Excel into
Project. The easiest way is to type them, one-by-one, into the default Project
view, called the Gantt Chart view. The Gantt Chart view consists of two elements, as shown in Figure 4-3:

- **The Gantt Table:** This is on the left side of the Project screen. You enter
  the information about your project's tasks here.

- **The Gantt Chart:** This is on the right side of the Project screen. This
  chart provides a graphical representation of your project's task durations and how the tasks relate to one another.

Gantt table   Gantt chart

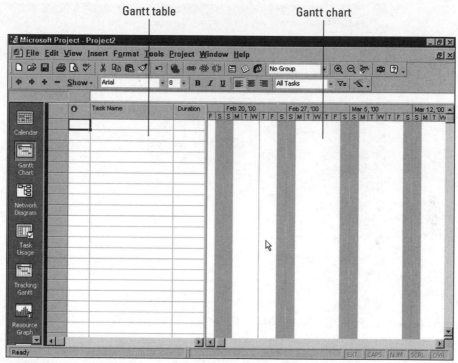

TECHNICAL STUFF

Figure 4-3:
Microsoft
Project in
Gantt Chart
view.

A *Gantt Chart* is a way of graphically representing the duration of tasks against the progression of time. You use the Gantt Chart view of your project right from the point that you start using Project, whether you know its formal name or not. (Now you do!)

To enter tasks into Microsoft Project, make sure that you're in Gantt Chart view and then follow these steps:

1. **Click in the topmost cell in the Task Name column.**

   For example, you can type **Gather Requirements** in the Task Name field, which is the first task that appears in your WBS Excel spreadsheet.

2. **Type the task description.**

3. **Press Enter.**

   You see a screen similar to Figure 4-4.

In the Duration column, Project prompts you to enter a duration estimate, but you can skip entering the duration for now. Just zip down the Task Name column, entering the critical tasks that appear on your WBS document one-by-one until all tasks are input, as shown in Figure 4-5.

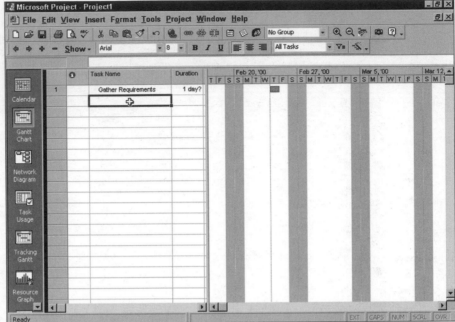

Figure 4-4:
Entering your project's tasks in Microsoft Project.

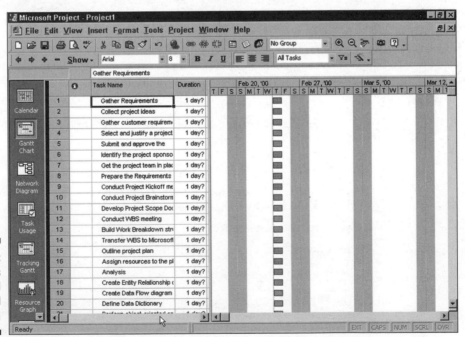

Figure 4-5:
All tasks present and accounted for, sir!

Good work! Entering the tasks is a bit time-consuming, but it isn't difficult.

Do you find clicking and dragging a drag? Luckily for you, the *Software Project Management Kit For Dummies* CD contains a Project file that you can use to save those precious mouse clicks. Just load up CSSW1.mpp from the samples folder for Chapter 4 on the CD.

Entering Task Durations

After you have your tasks all listed from your WBS document, you can go ahead and enter all the durations from your Excel WBS document into Microsoft Project.

The easiest way to enter task durations is to simply follow these steps:

1. **Click in the appropriate Duration cell.**

   For example, click in the Duration cell for the second task, Collect project ideas.

2. **Type the duration.**

   Sure, you can click the spinner buttons to go up or down a day at a time, but who needs that aggravation? For example, type **6d** for 6 days.

3. **Press Enter.**

Project moves you down to the next task and you can quickly repeat the process.

If you know how to use the ten-key numeric pad, you can really cook through this process. Here are some timesaving keyboard shortcuts to use as you enter your task durations:

- **m:** Type m for minute (5m).
- **h:** Type h for hour (3h).
- **d:** Type d for day (7d).
- **w:** Type w for week (2w).
- **mo:** Type mo for month (2 mo).

You're going to become a pro at this project-management stuff real soon!

Understanding Milestones and Phases

You may already know what milestones are, but making sure that you do before proceeding is a good idea. Every project has its milestones, and these particular tasks closely relate to the phases of a project. In Microsoft Project, you can define phases and milestones as follows:

- ✔ **Project phase:** A *phase* is a grouping of related tasks in which each task has a discrete start and finish time that add up to the complete project's duration. This structure represents the project in seven phases: gathering requirements, analysis, design, development, testing, release/change management, and implementation.

- ✔ **Project milestone:** A *milestone* is a task that you don't actually perform — and thus it has no start/finish times. (Don't confuse it with a grindstone, however. That's the thing you keep your nose to during the life of the project.) Milestones provide a symbolic representation, a "time to celebrate," either at the start or end of a phase. Think of milestones as intermediary goals or big steps, which provide checkpoints along the path of the overall progress of your software project.

To illustrate how milestones work, think of your job as a software project manager as analogous to that of a race car driver racing in the Indy 500. Each checkpoint through which the racer passes represents both the celebration of the completion of a phase of the race and the celebration of the beginning of the next phase. (Either way, celebrate good times, come on!)

In Microsoft Project, you make a task into a milestone by entering its duration as **0 days**. Project displays a black diamond in the Gantt Chart. Entering 0 days for the duration makes sense if you think about it. A milestone really doesn't take any time to happen, you just say *we're here.* An example of a milestone of most software projects would be, for example, the project sponsor's sign-off on an important document, such as the Project Scope Document.

A phase is a longer period of time, which encompasses several tasks. I describe how you enter phases in the following section.

Behold — The Summary Task

In your software project, the *summary tasks* are the main phases of the software-development process. Why two phrases to describe the same thing (phase and summary task)? Well, humans tend to think about phases, and Microsoft Project thinks of summary tasks.

You don't really enter a task as a summary task. Rather, you simply indent the tasks below it. How's that? Just follow these steps to transform a run-of-the-mill task into an all-powerful summary task (also known as a phase, *sheesh*):

1. **Click the number of a task that you want to subordinate in the gray column on the left-hand side of the of Gantt table.**

   For example, the Collect Project Ideas task is part of the Gather Requirements phase, so click the number 2.

2. **Drag your mouse down the gray column until you reach the last task that you want to subordinate.**

   Doing so highlights all the tasks in between, as shown in Figure 4-6. (Note, these tasks must be contiguous.) For example, select through number 16, the last task in the Gather Requirements phase.

3. **Click the Indent button.**

   You've created a summary task. For example, Gather Requirements is now a summary of the tasks within its phase in Figure 4-7.

   Repeat Steps 1 through 3 for each of the other six major milestone tasks (that is, the software-project phases of analysis, design, and so on) in your project. As you do so, you notice that your project looks quite a bit more organized in the Project window, differentiating as it is between its summary and subtasks. (It's certainly easier to understand at a glance.)

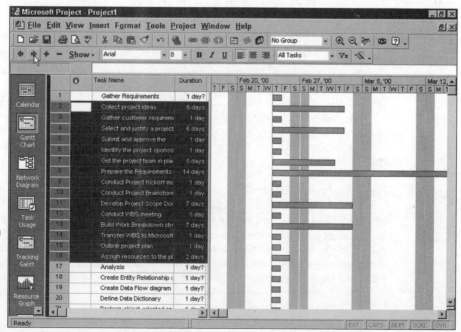

Figure 4-6: Highlight the tasks that belong in a phase.

Subordinate tasks

Summary task

Duration of this phase

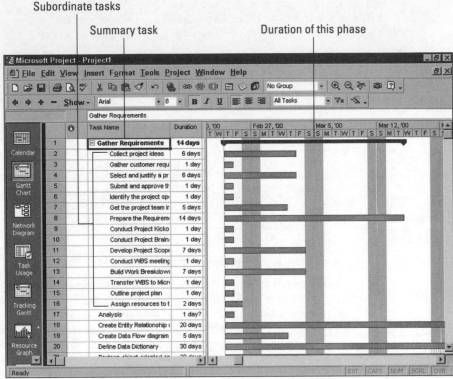

Figure 4-7:
Voila!
Gather
Require-
ments is a
summary
task.

By definition, the summary task's duration is the sum of the durations of its related tasks. Notice that the duration of Gather Requirements is 14 days, which is the same as the subordinate task with the longest duration (Task 8, Prepare the Requirements document). What this tells you is that right now, Project assumes that all the tasks within the Gather Requirements phase all start at the same time and progress in parallel. Wouldn't it be wonderful if that were the case? Unfortunately, some tasks can't take place until other tasks are complete. Skip to the section titled "Linking Tasks" for a solution to this little dilemma.

Be careful not to confuse a summary task with the term milestone. In the preceding section, I define a *milestone* as having duration of 0 days. A *milestone* is a task that you don't actually perform, having no start/finish times. Milestones thus provide a symbolic representation, a time to celebrate, either at the start or end of a project phase. A *summary task,* on the other hand, is not merely symbolic but is a summation of the durations of all related, dependent tasks for a given project phase.

Outlining Project Tasks

Whenever I hear the word *outlining*, I cringe at memories of all the bone-headed English professors who hashed up my terrific essays with red marks and insisted that I outline my topic before writing a word. In fact, before I began writing this *For Dummies* book, I suffered from flashbacks to college days after the first thing that came out of the editor's mouth was the need for me to grind out a detailed, proposed table of contents — another form of outline. I suspect that they're all in cahoots, actually.

Despite the degree of pain and suffering that you may have to endure from outlining a project, however, the outline provides you with a logical structure and a roadmap to follow throughout the development of any project, whether literary or for software.

The good news is that outlining is merely a matter of subordinating tasks to other tasks. In the section titled "Creating a Summary Task," earlier in this chapter, I take you through the process of subordinating a set of tasks to another task, thus defining a phase of your project. Well, defining phases isn't all that you can do — you can also add further levels of hierarchical detail by promoting and demoting tasks to your heart's content.

Linking Tasks

You're probably asking yourself, "Self, shouldn't I be scheduling some of these tasks to happen only after other tasks are complete?" *Good question!* You compliment yourself — while making a mental note to schedule that overdue psychiatric appointment. Your instinct is good. Many tasks on a software project are dependent upon each other, which means that you can't start one task until the task on which it depends is complete.

Every project has a group of tasks that make up the longest period that that your project requires. These tasks are known as *critical tasks,* which collectively create a network of dependent tasks, which together make up the *critical path*. You must finish all critical tasks on time to complete the entire project on schedule. In other words, critical tasks, by definition, have no float or slack time. Other, shorter duration tasks may be taking place in parallel with the critical path tasks, but they probably don't have other tasks waiting on them.

 In creating the critical-path task network in Project, you're sure to find the Link feature invaluable. The seven phases of the software project (gather requirements, analysis, design, and so on) serve as the important markers along the critical path, under which the rest of the critical tasks fall.

Beginning Task 36 (Code Application Components), for example, doesn't make much sense until Task 27 (Write Detailed Design Specification) is complete. Your innate knowledge of the software-development process tells you that actually writing code depends on your first completing the design specifications for that code. (And people wonder how you got your job as project manager! Amazing.)

In the following sections, I tell you all that you ever wanted to know about creating links between tasks.

Establishing links

At the time that you first enter your WBS from your Excel worksheet, Project assumes that every single task can run concurrently. Fat chance! Typically, a software project encompasses many different tasks that start and finish in linear succession, often along a critical path. To create dependencies between tasks in Microsoft Project so that one task starts after the other in a linear succession, you need to use Project's Link feature.

So that you can understand how to link tasks, follow these steps to link task 36 (Code Application Components) to Task 27 (Write Detailed Design Specification):

1. **Select the task that you want to link to another task by clicking its number at the left side of the task description.**

   Select, for example, Task 27 (Write Detailed Design Specification). Just click the number 27 at the left side of the description. That action selects the single task.

2. **Press and hold the Ctrl key as you select the other task you want to link to the task that you select in Step 1.**

   Press and hold the Ctrl key as you click the number 36 (Code Application Components). You now have two tasks selected.

 3. **Click the Link Task button.**

That's it! Project links the tasks, making the assumption that Task 36 starts at the completion of Task 27. (Project makes this assumption because Task 36 physically falls after Task 27 in the task list.)

After you link two tasks, a couple things happen to your project. First, if you scroll the Gantt Chart to the right, you see a blue arrow at the end of Task 27 that connects to Task 36 (see Figure 4-8). This connecting arrow is a graphic indicator that Task 36 starts right after Task 27 is complete.

Blue arrow indicates linkage between tasks

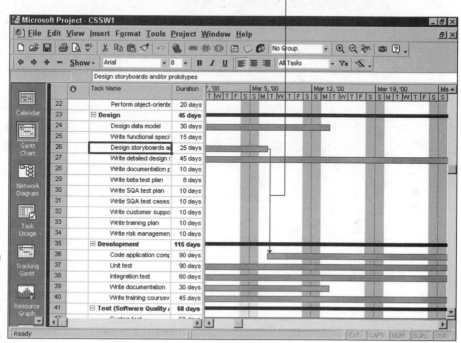

Figure 4-8:
Linking two
tasks in
Project.

A *Gantt Chart* is a way of graphically representing the duration of tasks against the progression of time. You use the Gantt Chart view of your project right from the point that you start using Project.

You can also take a look at your task list and notice that the duration of the Development task jumps from 90 days to 135 days. Why? Because, as shown in Figure 4-10, the time span between the start of the earliest Development subtask and the end of the last (which is now task 36) is 135 days. Linking tasks can affect your project this way by pushing out the end of your project — sometimes considerably.

You need to spend some considerable time specifying linkages between tasks. How you establish those linkages depends on the tasks you set up in your project. You must, for example, link all the tasks along the critical path. (I provide a definition of a critical path at the beginning of the preceding section.) Don't rush yourself as you think through the process. In fact, you may want to call on other members of your development team to help fine-tune the linearity of your project.

Changing link types

Project includes different types of linkages that you can establish between tasks. You have the following four types of links that you can use:

- **Finish-to-Start (FS):** If you use this type of link, the current task can't start until the predecessor task is complete.

- **Start-to-Start (SS):** If you establish this type of link, the current task starts at the same time as the predecessor task.

- **Finish-to-Finish (FF):** With this type of link, the current task finishes at the same time as the predecessor task.

- **Start-to-Finish (SF):** If you use this type of link, the current task can't finish until the predecessor task starts.

By default, Project assumes that you want to use the FS (Finish-to-Start) linkage. To change the linkage between tasks, follow these steps:

1. **Select the second task in the linked pair.**

   Just click the task number at the left side of the task line. This action selects the single task.

2. **Click the Task Information button.**

   Project displays the Task Information dialog box.

3. **Select the Predecessors tab at the top of the dialog box.**

   The Predecessors tab is the second tab in the Task Information dialog box, as shown in Figure 4-9. This tab lists the links between the selected task and any predecessor tasks.

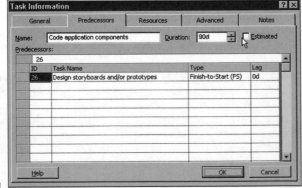

Figure 4-9:
Project keeps track of links between tasks.

4. **Click in the cell in the Type column of the Predecessors table for the predecessor task containing the link that you want to change.**

   A small down arrow appears at the right side of the field.

5. **Click the down arrow.**

   Project displays a drop-down list of five link types. These links include the four types that I list at the beginning of this section, along with a None selection (which blows away any link).

6. **Select the new link type that you want to use to link the two tasks and click OK.**

Project makes the changes to your project and updates all dependent tasks to reflect the change in this link.

Setting up links between tasks can prove quite time consuming. If you're just starting project management and following along with the sample project that I develop in this book, you may be happy to find that the *Software Project Management Kit For Dummies* CD contains a Project file with links that are already established. To find out where to locate this file, check out Appendix B. The file is called CSSW2.mpp, and it gets you going with the correct links in place.

Modifying the Task List

After you organize a nifty project outline, your work is done, right? Wrong! As you work through your project, you're undoubtedly going to face numerous times when you need to modify your task list. After all, even the most well-organized project managers (such as yourself) may periodically forget to include critical summary tasks or subtasks.

Microsoft Project supports three ways to modify your original task list. The most common scenario for modifying your task list arises if you forget to include certain tasks. No worries! Microsoft Project is as flexible as Gumby doing the splits, giving you the capability to insert an unlimited number of new tasks between existing tasks. On the other hand, you may want to just rearrange the original order of the tasks. Or you may simply want to delete any tasks that you no longer want to include or that become unnecessary. Project covers you for all three possibilities, as the following sections describe.

Inserting new tasks

Suppose that you suddenly realize that you left out an important task from your project. Not to worry! Modifying your task list in Project is a cinch! Just follow these steps to insert a new task:

1. **Make sure that your project file is open.**

   Open a file by clicking the Open button. Project displays the File Open dialog box. Select your project file from the list of files in this dialog box and click the Open button to open your project, as shown in Figure 4-10. If your project doesn't open in Gantt Chart view, click the Gantt Chart View button on the view bar.

2. **Select the task in the list where you to want to insert a new task.**

   Project inserts the new task above the task that you select. Select Task 17 (Assign resources to project plan tasks), for example. Figure 4-10 shows you an example of such a project file. You always select the task before which you intend to insert a new task. (Just click the task number at the left side of the task line to select it.)

3. **Press the Insert key.**

   Project adds a new, blank task to the list just before the task that you select in Step 2.

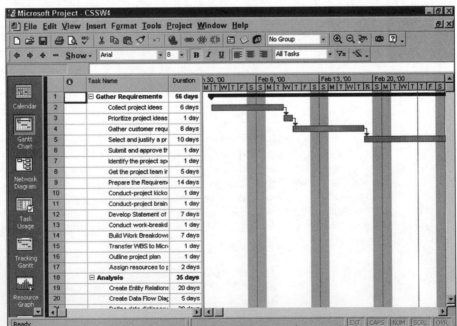

Figure 4-10:
An open
project file.

4. **Type a task name to replace the blank task that you insert in Step 3 and press Enter.**

   For example, I type **Establish Project Task Links** and then press the Enter key. Project assigns the task a number and increments all the task numbers below the inserted task by one.

   After you finish adding the new tasks for your software project, you also need to enter the appropriate durations you're assigning to each task, as well as to establish any links for the task. I give you information on linking chores in the section "Linking Tasks," earlier in this chapter.

5. **Enter a duration for the newly inserted task (in Step 3) in the blank Duration column and press Enter.**

   For example, I type a new duration of **10 days** and press the Enter key.

Moving tasks

Moving tasks and their durations in the task list is as easy as dragging and dropping at the click of your mouse. You can either move a single task or an entire group of tasks, depending on your mood that particular day. To move tasks, ensure that your project is open and follow these steps:

1. **Select from the task list the first task (or tasks) that you want to move.**

   Just click the number to the left of the task. This action selects the single task. To move more than one task, select the first task and then press and hold the Shift key as you select the ending task in the series. You now have a task or a series of tasks selected.

2. **Click the task number (or a task number in the series) and drag the task (or tasks) to a new location in the task list.**

   As you move the mouse, a light gray square line magically appears around the selected tasks, showing you where the tasks are moving.

4. **Release the mouse button after you reach the place in the list where you want to move the task.**

   Voila! The tasks play musical chairs!

 If you move tasks that already have links to other tasks, you may need to double-check and reset your links after the move is complete.

Deleting tasks

Even the perfect software project manager makes mistakes. For those rare occasions, Project enables you to easily and completely erase tasks. Of course, that doesn't necessarily mean that you don't need to complete the task later — unless you can also delete the task in your boss's copy of Project!

To delete a project, simply select in the task list the task that you want to delete and press the Delete key. (You can also choose Edit⇨Delete Task from the menu bar, but why make life hard?) Poof! The task is gone.

Aggghhhh! That soul-felt cry of anguish comes after you realize that you deleted the wrong task. But before you take a long walk off a short balcony, Bucko, you do have hope. If you realize your mistake right away, you can use Project's Undo feature. All you need to do is take either of the following actions:

✔ **Click the Undo button.** Immediately, your dearly departed task returns from the great beyond.

✔ **Choose Edit⇨Undo Delete from the menu bar.** This process takes just a bit longer, but the critter still returns to the land of living tasks.

Chapter 5

Assigning Resources and Estimating Costs

In Chapter 3, I tell you how to build your preliminary software project plan. Your plan essentially includes three basic parameters: scope (work to do), schedule (time to do it in), and resources (budget for the project). Too often, software project managers make haphazard estimations of their project's parameters. Even worse, they often base their final project plan and resource assignments on "gut feelings" rather than on empirical data and methodologies. An alarming number of software projects fail because managers assign resources to the project prematurely, basing these assignments on inaccurate estimations of the total work load of the project, the time such work requires, and the resources necessary to complete the project.

After you build your preliminary software project plan, you and your project team need to take charge of your project's destiny by following these few, simple project estimation guidelines that enable you to optimize your project's scope, schedule, and resources with a high level of accuracy:

1. **Study your history.**

2. **Pick a scheduling estimation method.**

3. **Associate project team members with the right tasks.**

4. **Use metrics software tools to estimate staff time, task durations, and project costs.**

Taking a Lesson from History

Philosopher and poet George Santayana said, "Those who cannot remember the past are condemned to repeat it." Stay mindful of the poetic and philosophical importance (and the importance to the posterior of the project manager) of conducting a bit of historical research of your own. Whenever you're planning to allocate resources and are budgeting for a new project, examine any historical data that you can find from previous, similar projects. (Assuming, of course, that you work for a company that tracks such information on a project-by-project basis.)

The more you base your project resource estimates on empirical data — lessons that derive from what did and didn't work before — the higher the probability of your own project's success.

Start by checking to see whether your company keeps project files. Perhaps a similar project is even currently in process. If such project files exist, locate where your company keeps them and determine which, if any, apply to your current situation. You want to ensure that the project (or projects) that you select to examine are similar in scope and purpose to yours.

After you get your hands on these project files, make a beeline for their final budget summaries. You need to check out what resources were originally allocated to your respective projects and determine whether those estimates were on target. Because similar projects tend to share many of the same tasks and phases, you can check to see what were the actual durations of the tasks for those projects and then compare them against those you formulate for your project, as I describe in Chapter 4. (*Note:* In dealing with allocating staff resources, task duration often directly relates to monetary expense.)

Make sure, too, that you look for any problems the teams encountered in any previous projects similar to yours. Such research can help you avoid such problems in your project.

Finally, in researching historical costs, make sure that you take history itself into account. Costs change over time because of inflation, labor rate changes, and other factors. Make sure that you try to look at historical elements in terms of today's costs. If you're basing your data on figures from three years ago, research the rate of inflation over that time period as well as the state of labor availability and any other factors germane to your project. Careful attention to detail can help you avoid nasty cost-overrun surprises at the end of the process.

Following these guidelines can make your life much simpler and even help you sleep at night. (You face a smaller chance of experiencing night sweats over budget overruns and staffing shortfalls.) I discuss each guideline in the remaining sections of this chapter. By the end of the chapter, you can expect to accurately estimate your project parameters, enabling you to cover the optimal number of software features (scope), optimize your project schedule, and budgeting and assigning the ideal amount of resources to your project with a reasonable degree of certainty.

Using Cost Xpert to Estimate Costs

What if you don't have convenient historical information to use in your estimations? You aren't sunk because the *Software Project Management Kit For Dummies* CD-ROM contains trial versions of two excellent software project-cost and schedule-estimating tools: Cost Xpert and Strategy Xpert from Marotz, Inc. These tools provide the following benefits:

- **Cost Xpert** helps you estimate your projects by using a large database of real-world software cost information. You can export your Cost Xpert data directly into Microsoft Project.

- **Strategy Xpert** guides you through the process of prioritizing your management decisions to optimize your project's strategic objectives. By prioritizing your management decisions and nailing down your project's strategic objectives, you can optimize the use of limited project resources (time, money, and humans).

In this section, I describe how to use Cost Xpert to gather some pretty accurate estimates for your project. For complete online documentation, double-click the Cost Xpert Help icon from the program menu for complete online documentation or point your Web browser to www.costxpert.com for help using the Cost Xpert tool for estimating your project's costs.

For information on installing Cost Xpert and Strategy Xpert from the CD, check out Appendix B.

After Cost Xpert is installed on your hard drive, you can start the program by choosing Start⇨Programs⇨Cost Xpert 2.1⇨Cost Xpert 2.1. The main Cost Xpert window appears, as shown in Figure 5-1.

The Cost Xpert main window contains five tabs:

- **Project**: This tab is selected by default when you start Cost Xpert. This tab is divided into four subtabs:

  - **Company**: Enter customer project information on this subtab, including company name, address, phone, fax, and e-mail.

  - **Estimator:** Enter estimations of the project start and end dates as well as overall duration in months on this subtab.

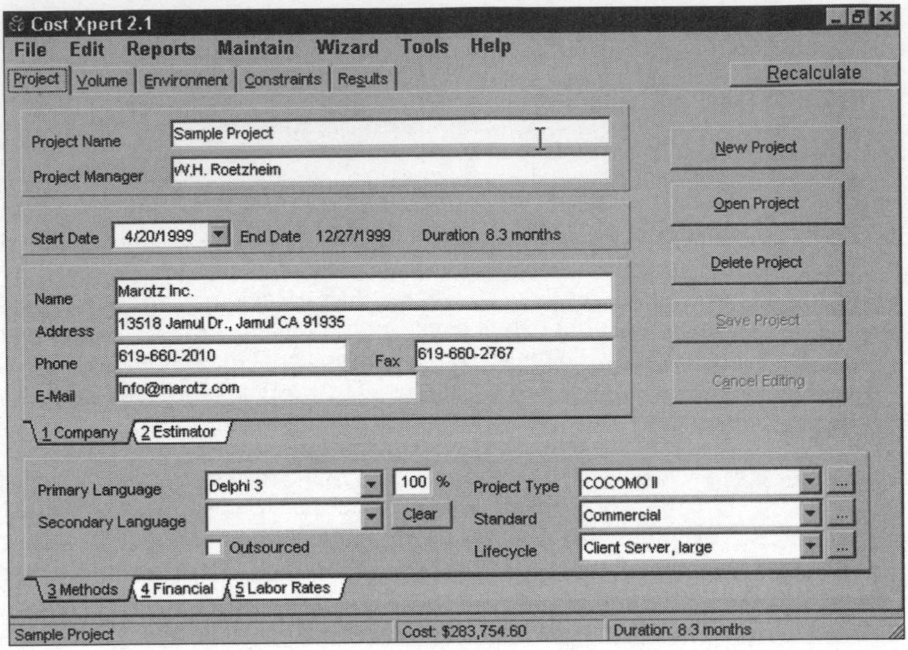

Figure 5-1:
The main
Cost Xpert
window.

- **Methods:** Enter important software development information on this tab. For example, if your project uses two programming languages, you enter that information in the Primary Language (% used) and Secondary Language (% used) areas. Enter coefficients of estimated development effort, Standard (such as Commercial, IEEE, and so on), Project Type (for example, Commercial, MIS, End user computing, and so on) and Lifecycle (such as client/server, large, standard, small, and so on).

- **Financial:** Enter important financial estimation information for your project on this tab, including: average trip cost, inflation factor percentage, number of users for the project, annual change traffic percentage, average cost per hour, total projected person months, and total projected project cost.

✔ **Volume:** The Volume tab is where you enter your project estimates for the total programming volume. This tab is divided into six subtabs: SLOC, Function Points, GUI Metrics, Object Metrics, Bottom Up, and Top Down. For definitions and applications of each of these volume estimators, refer to the "Approaching Estimation" section later in this chapter.

✔ **Environment:** Enter the estimates of your project's development environment on this tab. This screen is divided into four subtabs: Experience, Volatility, Project, and Policy.

- **Experience:** Enter estimates of the level of experience of each team member on your project team on a scale of 0 to 100 percent (ranging from Very Low to Very High).

- **Volatility:** On this tab, you enter an estimate of the amount of project design and development rework that is likely to occur due to changes in project scope in the customer's software requirements. This is a critical estimate that can significantly affect the overall estimates of your development effort.

- **Project:** Enter technical environment capacity planning estimates on this tab, such as computer turn-around time, database size, execution time constraint, main storage constraint, product complexity, and required product reliability.

- **Policy:** Enter estimates in the development environment's policies on this subtab. For example, how modern your programming practices are, how much you should reuse of your software components, and the degree of Use of S/W (software) Tools.

✔ **Constraints:** Enter your project's estimated constraints on this subtab, as shown in Figure 5-2. The Constraints screen is divided into eight sections: Time-Cost Trade off, Review Time, Plans and Requirements, Minimum Review Time, Testing and Integration, Cushion, Overlap, and Risk Tolerance.

✔ **Results:** This is the task that provides the results of how your project's actual results compared against the planned estimates. This screen (tab) is divided into six subtabs including: Correlation, Tasks, Risk, Labor, Maintenance, and Deliverables.

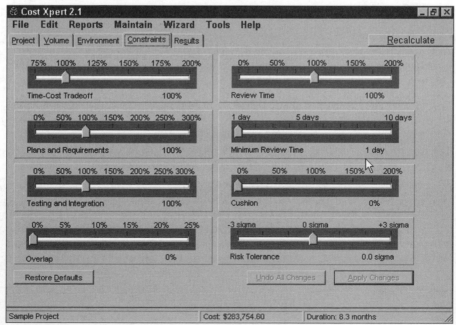

Figure 5-2:
The Cost
Xpert
Constraints
tab.

Approaching Estimation

Over the years, managers have developed many different approaches to estimating the cost and necessary resources for various projects. Depending on the size of your project, you can consider several different approaches to estimating what you need. The following examples represent the more common approaches available for making such estimations:

- **Top-down Approach:** In making a top-down estimation, you first estimate the total work involved in completing the project tasks and then work backward to determine how much work to allocate to smaller subtasks. This approach is useful when the schedule is inflexible, but where resources can be added to the project. This approach is generally applicable only to smaller, less-complex projects.

- **Bottom-up Approach:** The bottom-up estimation method approach is the opposite of the top-down approach. The first step in making an estimate is to decompose each project phase into tasks (as you do with your WBS in Chapter 3). Then assign a measurement of duration (time) to each task (for example, workdays, hours, months, and so on). Finally, you total all the task durations to arrive at a total duration estimate for the project. The bottom-up approach isn't to be confused with the *bottoms-up approach,* which often leads to headaches and regrets the next morning. This approach is generally applicable only to smaller, less-complex projects.

- **Lines of Code (LOC) Approach:** The lines of code estimation method is sometimes also known as the Constructive Cost Model. This approach has been around since COBOL programmers began typing their code on cards via now-fossilized keypunch devices that communicated with mainframe dinosaurs. This method estimates the effort of a programming task by its total lines of code, which is measured in thousands of lines of code (KLOC). After estimating the total lines of code that you need to complete a given task, you can then estimate the duration and cost estimates based upon historical metrics data tracked on any prior projects in your organization, such as KLOC's coded by a certain number of developers over a given period of time.

  For example, my team estimates the *Customer Self-Service Web* project at 10.5 KLOC for a project team of ten developers. If your historical metrics say that the total cost of each line of code is $10, then you could estimate $105,000 for the total cost for the project. You often use this approach for medium and large projects. Some significant metrics that can be calculated through the LOC approach include:

  - **KLOC:** Total lines of code (in thousands)

  - **Development productivity factor:** KLOC/developer-time period

  - **$ Cost per LOC:** $/LOC

- **Documentation:** `Pages of documentation/KLOC`
- **Cost of training and user support**
- **Software Quality:** `# of Defects/KLOC`

✔ **Function-Points Analysis Approach:** To use the function-points analysis estimation technique, you must first count all the inputs (for example, input screens/forms, tables, and so on), outputs (such as reports), user interfaces, files, and so on that you need to develop for your project. You then multiply these numbers by the resources necessary to arrive at an "average" input, output, and user interface. You determine the averages, of course, by your analysis of historical projects. You typically use a function-points analysis for medium and large projects.

✔ **User Interface (UI) Metrics Approach:** The user interface metrics estimation method measures the degree to which your system's "front end" interacts with the user. Your user interface includes all the icons, dialog boxes, menus, and so on that the project requires. This approach is appropriate for medium and large projects that heavily depend on the UI. After you determine the resources that you need to create the UI, you have the majority of your resource requirements for the entire project.

✔ **Object Metrics Approach:** You use the object metrics estimation method only if your development process involves the use of Object-Oriented Programming analysis and design. In estimating the work that you must do, you count all the objects that you need to develop your software. You can then base your estimates on which objects you can reuse from other projects and which ones you need to create from scratch. You often use this approach for medium and large development projects.

Notice that you traditionally apply each approach to projects of different sizes. Such application implies (and rightly so) that, before you can even decide on an estimation approach, you must have a feel for the size of your project. As a general guideline in the software industry, small projects involve an anticipated total cost of less than $50,000; medium ones range in cost from $50,000 to $1,000,000; and large ones cost at least $1,000,000.

As you manage your development project, remember to retain your flexibility. You don't, for example, want to feel constrained to using just one estimation approach. One approach may take into consideration factors that another approach may overlook or ignore. Using different methodologies enables you to synthesize and cross-check your final project estimates from a variety of methods and viewpoints and make the best use of available information.

After you have a good estimate in hand, you may want to apply what's known as the *DeMarco ±15% Rule*. This rule helps remove the inherent "human-factor" bias in making duration estimates. The rule derives from the assumption that, even if you make a reasonable estimate of a task's or total project's duration, you're equally likely to either over- or underestimate it by 15 percent. You can apply this rule to a project of any size that you want.

Allocating Human Resources

One of the most critical tasks to the success of a project is your allocation of human resources. I describe how to put together your development team in Chapter 2 and give you quite a bit of information on how to work with the team in Chapters 3 and 4. In this section, I cover how to assign tasks to each member of the team.

This task is where your Development Team Skill Matrix comes into play. (You first create that document at the time that you put together your team, as I describe in Chapter 2; see Figure 5-3.) The matrix enables you to see, at a glance, who possesses the requisite skills to best take on a given task.

You need to sit down and, using the matrix, make a first-pass decision on who to make responsible for which tasks. Don't get ahead of yourself, though — you don't want to make your final decisions until you actually sit down with your development team and let them to go over what you put together, too. Your best course is to hammer out any problems at this point and then make the hard decisions together. For example, too many programming tasks may be assigned to one programmer. So, you and your team may have to identify some volunteers to take some of the tasks off of the plate of the overworked programmer.

Leveling resources

As project manager, you want to make sure that you assign resources evenly among your team members — and that you assign them to the best team members possible for each specific task. In project management terms, this process is commonly known as *resource leveling*. You aren't using resources optimally — or levelly — if you assign tasks, for example, to team members who lack the ideal skill sets for handling those tasks. Similarly, assigning a truckload of tasks to just one highly skilled team member while others sit around twiddling their thumbs isn't the model of efficiency, either.

Customer Self-Serve Web
Development Team Skill Matrix

Team Member	Project Sponsor	Project Manger	Analyst	Developer / Engineer	Database Admin	Technical Writer	SQA Test Engineer	Trainer	Release Manager
Dilbert	X								
Monica		X		X					
Hillary					X				
Kenneth			X	X			X		
Bill			X	X					
Austin									X
Felicity						X		X	
Dr. Evil							X		
Mini-me							X		
Forrest			X						

Figure 5-3: A sample Development Team Skill Matrix.

You can consider a number of varying factors while figuring out to whom to assign which task. As you make your first pass on who gets what task and, later, as you thrash out the details with your team members, you want to keep the following ideas in mind:

- ✔ **Assign tasks to project team members according to their technical expertise.** Use your Development Team Skill Matrix to help you match expertise to task requirements. Make sure that you keep abreast of any changing areas of expertise among team members.

- ✔ **Assign critical tasks to the most skilled and reliable staff.** Some tasks form the foundation for other tasks, and others must be "done right and on time" to successfully complete the entire project. You want to assign these tasks to those team members on whom you can rely most. (You're likely to know who those people are because their reputations often precede them.) For example, the lead programmer often assumes responsibility for defining new classes in the project while delegating the coding of the class's member functions to other programmers.

- ✔ **Assign related tasks to the same team member.** As you look over the tasks that you need to complete for your project, you often see patterns start to emerge. These patterns generally appear because many tasks closely relate to one another. Wherever possible, assign these related tasks to the same person. Doing so often speeds up completion of the tasks, because the subject matter expert doesn't have to stop and cross-train someone else.

- ✔ **Keep geographic considerations in mind.** Some of your team members may sit just a door or two away from other team members, while others may be miles away from everyone else. In assigning tasks that require close coordination (such as documentation and training-program responsibilities), keep members' geographic locations in mind. If you assign tasks requiring close coordination to members who're geographically close to one another, you increase your likelihood of finishing these tasks on time simply because you're improving communication among those working on such task.

- ✔ **Be mindful of personality issues.** In choosing your team, you pick a set of pros; that goes without saying. But personality issues can crop up even among pros. Make sure that you're aware of any such clashes between certain team members before you make your assignments. Doing so can save you grief and blown schedules later.

Some companies use the Meyers-Briggs Personality Index to identify the personality types (including leaders) of potential project team members. The MB index is a good way to check whether you have optimally placed your project managers and team members on projects possessing compatible personality chemistries.

Reviewing task durations

After you assign and level your tasks, you need to review the durations you assign to these tasks. In this area especially, you really need to rely on the expertise of your people. Show them the schedule that you first cast in Chapter 3. Then ask them to help you determine whether these durations are viable.

Obviously, the individual members of your development team are going to pay the most attention to the specific tasks to which you've assigned them. Make sure, as you discuss the situation with them, that they agree with the durations you've set or that they can give you a valid reason for changing one. Your negotiation skills may come into play here, particularly if you know of reasons why a particular task can't take as long as a team member insists it must.

One tool that you can use in working with team members on reviewing durations is known as a Human Resources Estimation Worksheet. Happily, the *Software Project Management Kit For Dummies* CD includes a template for this worksheet (Human Resources Estimation Worksheet.dot). You can use it to create your own worksheet for your project.

The worksheet enables you to indicate all the various tasks for the project, to note to whom you assign each task, and to specify how long each task is to take. Figures 5-4, 5-5, and 5-6 show an example of a filled-out Human Resources Estimation Worksheet.

Compared to all the work you perform on other phases of your project, filling out the worksheet is easy. The first column correlates to the WBS and the task list that you create in Chapter 3. The second and third columns you create in this section. Your team members now need to focus on the fourth column of the worksheet, making sure that the durations you enter here are appropriate, reasonable, and achievable.

After the durations are firmly in place, ask your people to provide you with a list of constraints on their time. Certain team members may, for example, have such other demands on their time that they're not available to you on Fridays, or they may have a vacation coming up. You need this information when you later to finalize the project schedule.

Customer Self-Service Web
Human Resources Estimation Worksheet

Project Tasks	Resource	Team Member	Estimated Total Effort (days)	Daily Rate	Estimated Cost (days _ rate)	Actual Cost
1.01 Collect project ideas	Product Marketing Manager	Roseanne	6	$400	$2,400	?
1.02 Prioritize project ideas			1		400	
1.03 Gather customer requirements and proposed solutions			6		2,400	
1.04 Select and justify a project			10		4,000	
1.05 Submit Request for Proposal (RFP)			1		400	
1.06 Identify project sponsor			1		400	
1.08 Prepare the Requirements Document (RD)			14		5,600	
1.05 Approve RFP	Project Sponsor	Dilbert	1	$800	$800	
1.06 Identify project manager			1		800	

Figure 5-4: An example of a completed Human Resources Estimation Worksheet. Page 1 of 3.

Project Tasks	Resource	Team Member	Estimated Total Effort (days)	Daily Rate	Estimated Cost (days _ rate)	Actual Cost
1.07 Get the project team in place	Project Manager	Monica	5	$600	$3,000	
1.09 Conduct project kickoff meeting			1		600	
1.10 Conduct project brainstorming meeting			1		600	
1.11 Develop Statement of Scope (SOS)			7		4,200	
1.12 Conduct work-breakdown structure meeting			1		600	
1.13 Build Work Breakdown Structure (WBS)			7		4,200	
1.14 Transfer WBS to Microsoft Project			1		600	
1.15 Outline project plan			1		600	
1.16 Assign resources to project plan tasks			2		1,200	
3.11 Write risk management plan			3		1,800	
2.02 Create Data Flow Diagram (DFD)	Analyst/ Functional Architect	Kenneth Bill Forrest	3	$480	$1,440	
2.03 Define data dictionary			10		4,800	
2.04 Perform object-oriented analysis			7		3,360	
3.02 Write functional specifications			15		7,200	
3.03 Design storyboards and/or prototypes			25		12,000	
3.04 Write detailed design specifications	Developers /Engineers	Monica Bill Kenneth	25	S400	$10,000	
4.01 Code application components			75		30,000	
4.02 Unit test			15		6,000	
2.01 Create Entity Relationship Diagram (ERD)	Dbase Admin (DBA)	Hillary	20	$520	$10,400	
3.01 Design data model			30		15,600	

Figure 5-5: An example of a completed Human Resources Estimation Worksheet. Page 2 of 3.

Project Tasks	Resource	Team Member	Estimated Total Effort (days)	Daily Rate	Estimated Cost (days _ rate)	Actual Cost
3.05 Write documentation plan	Technical Writer	Felicity	10	$320	$3,200	
4.04 Write documentation			10		3,200	
3.06 Write beta test plan	SQA test Engineer	Kenneth	4	$320	$1,280	
3.07 Write SQA test plan		Dr. Evil	5		1,600	
3.08 Write SQA test cases		Mini-me	5		1,600	
5.01 System test			20		6,400	
5.02 Track defects			20		6,400	
5.03 Regression test			20		6,400	
3.10 Write training plan	Trainer	Felicity	6	$320	$1,920	
4.05 Write training courseware			30		9,600	
6.01 Configuration management	Release Manager	Austin	7	$440	$3,080	
6.02 New full releases			4		1,760	
6.03 Maintenance releases			4		1,760	
6.04 Defect and enhancement tracking			7		3,080	
3.09 Write customer support plan	Support Engineer	Howard	10	$320	$3,200	

Figure 5-6: An example of a completed Human Resources Estimation Worksheet. Page 3 of 3.

Estimating Project Costs

In this step, you and your development team use the software estimation tools that you decide are most appropriate for your particular project. (You choose an estimation method in the section "Approaching Estimation," earlier in this chapter.) You use your estimation method, along with the Human Resources Estimation Worksheet that I describe in the preceding section, to determine the cost of the resources you're applying to your project.

Take another look at the Human Resources Estimation Worksheet (refer to Figure 5-4). In this step, you're focusing on the fifth and sixth columns of the worksheet. (You can't complete the seventh column until you finally complete each task.) You already know how long each task in the project takes; now, you just need to apply dollar figures to these durations.

What figures do you use for your daily rate? They obviously vary by person because some positions naturally cost more to fill than others. You want to include in the daily internal-cost rate figures whatever costs your accounting department needs to track. Some companies, for example, require that you include allowances for fringe benefits; others may want only a billing rate to appear here and not an actual daily internal-cost rate.

In some companies, you may need to estimate project costs on your own; if so, your completed Human Resources Estimation Worksheet becomes a confidential document. After you start attaching labor costs to a project, company policy may prohibit personnel with positions below a particular level in the organization from being privy to the dollar figures. Make sure that you check with your human resources department to determine whether that's the case in your company.

Assigning Resources to Tasks in Microsoft Project

In Chapter 4, you find out how to set up your project tasks in Microsoft Project. In the preceding sections of this chapter, you do quite a bit of work, but none of it involves Microsoft Project. In this section, you fire up the old computer (or new computer, as the case may be) and enter the resource and estimation information that you determine in the preceding sections.

This section assumes that you've gone through a rigorous and sometimes harrowing estimation process, as I describe in the preceding sections of this chapter and that you're prepared to use Microsoft Project as a tool in assigning resources.

If you're starting this section without first doing any of the cost and resource estimation work that I describe in the preceding sections of this chapter, all I can say is — *don't!* Microsoft Project's output is only as good as the input that you provide, and if you fail to develop realistic estimates for your tasks . . . well, most coders are all too familiar with the term GIGO (garbage in, garbage out). Microsoft Project makes it easy to cut a day here and there out of your plan by changing a number in the project file. But changing numbers in Microsoft Project doesn't make the work take any less time to accomplish. Find out how long it takes (historically) to accomplish each task and plan for that amount of time.

If you want a "clean slate" with which to work (or on which to practice), the *Software Project Management Kit For Dummies* CD contains a Project file that you can use. The samples folder for Chapter 5 includes CSSW3.mpp, which represents the state of the Customer Self-Service Web project with the updated durations. You can use the file as a starting point for working with resources, as I discuss in the following sections.

Setting up resources

Before you can begin to assign resources in Microsoft Project, you must establish a resource list. This task involves nothing more than making sure that Microsoft Project knows the identity of your resources. To set up your list, you can access the Resource Sheet view icon from the view bar on the left-hand side of the Project window. Alternatively, you can choose View➪Resource Sheet from the Project menu bar. The initial Resource Sheet view appears, as shown in Figure 5-7.

The Resource Sheet view looks very much like a spreadsheet — in fact, you can use the view in much the same way as you would a spreadsheet. Each row of the view represents an individual resource that you have available to your project. All you need to do is grab your Development Team Skill Matrix (refer back to Figure 5-3) and start entering that information in the Resource Sheet. Start with the names of each team member, typing each in the Resource Name box. (You may take all of 30 seconds to type 10 names on the sheet.)

If you compare your Development Team Skill Matrix with the Human Resources Estimation Worksheet that you develop in the section "Allocating Human Resources," earlier in this chapter, you may notice that the latter document contains the names of people who don't appear on the former. This situation isn't unusual; perhaps the Johnny-Come-Latelys are new people added to the project after its start or represent short-term consultants pulled in for a specific task. Make sure that you enter on the Resource Sheet the names of all the people currently associated with your project. If you filled out a Human Resources Estimation Worksheet, you can enter those names into Microsoft Project.

With the initial names entered into the Resource Sheet, you can add details about each team member if you want. Simply double-click a name, and Project displays the Resource Information dialog box, as shown in Figure 5-8.

Notice that the dialog box enables you to add more details about each resource (meaning each project team member) than what appears in the Resource Sheet view of Project. You can add any details that you want to store for each resource. You may, for example, want to enter the position information from the Development Team Skill Matrix (project sponsor, project manager, analyst, and so on) in the Group text box.

If you're working with team members who split their time between your project and others in the company, you need to pay attention to some very important items in the Resource Information dialog box. The first is the Resource Availability area on the General tab (refer to Figure 5-8). Here you can specify whether the individual is available for the entire project or for only a certain date range.

You can also designate that an individual can only work on your project a certain percentage of the time by using the Assign Resources dialog box in Microsoft Project. The Assign Resources dialog box contains a Units box for each resource. By default, Microsoft Project assigns a unit of 1, meaning the resource is dedicated 100 percent of each working day to that project. If an individual's time is to be spread across multiple projects, you can adjust the units into percentages between 0 and 1 (for example, .5 would mean that the resource is available 50 percent of the time). For more information on assigning resources as units, you can refer to *Microsoft Project 2000 For Dummies* by Marty Doucette (published by IDG Books Worldwide, Inc.).

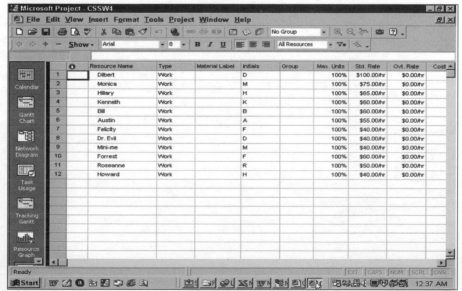

Figure 5-7:
The
Resource
Sheet view
of your
project.

Another important area of information appears after you click the Working Time tab. This tab contains a calendar so that you can specify on a day-by-day basis exactly when a person is available to work on your project, as shown in Figure 5-9.

You can change information in the calendar by selecting a date and then using the radio buttons and time ranges to indicate the hours that a person can work on that date. If you need to specify a company holiday, for example, simply click that date on the calendar and then click the Nonworking time radio button.

You can also click the Costs tab to enter information about how much using this particular individual costs the project (see Figure 5-10). You can pull this information directly from the Human Resources Estimation Worksheet that you develop in the section "Reviewing Task Durations," earlier in the chapter. The various project costs will be allocated from your project's budget.

The controls on the Costs tab enable you to enter up to five rate tables (A through E). Each table can contain differing rates for the same person. A team member may get different rates, for example, depending on the particular task that person's performing. On the sample Human Resources Estimation Worksheet that I provide on the CD, for example, the daily rate for Kenneth varies from $320 to $480, depending on the task he's performing (refer to Figure 5-2).

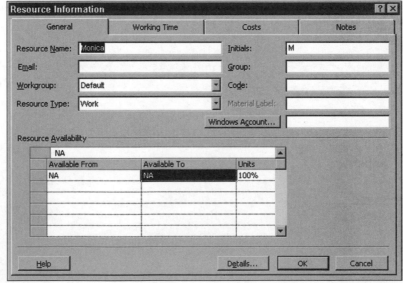

Figure 5-8:
The
Resource
Information
dialog box.

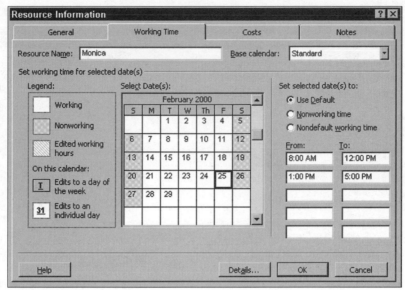

Figure 5-9:
The
Working
Time tab
of the
Resource
Information
dialog box is
where you
specify
individual
schedules.

As you enter rate information, make sure that you enter it by using per-hour rates and not daily rates so that individuals working only a percentage of the total workday on your project can be properly allocated and tracked in Microsoft Project.

After you finish using the Resource Information dialog box to change (or add) details to the resource information for an individual, click the OK button. The dialog box closes, and Project updates the information in the Resource Sheet view. You then want to update the same information for other team members. After you finish making these updates, you're ready to actually assign individuals to tasks.

If you don't want to tire out your poor little fingers by entering resource information, you can just load a completed sample file from the *Software Project Management Kit For Dummies* CD. The file CSSW4.mpp provides a sample project team, along with all the related costs for each member. Load it up and use it as you see fit. (Whoa! This CD thing is pretty cool!)

Of course, you need to change the names in the template to match your particular project. Hopefully, the majority of the sample data will apply to your project, to save you tedious data entry.

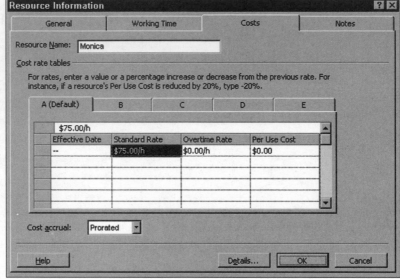

Figure 5-10:
You can use
the Costs
tab of the
Resource
Information
dialog box
to indicate
resource
costs.

Assigning a single resource to tasks

In this section, you start putting your Human Resources Estimation Worksheet to work, assigning tasks to people or people to tasks (as the case may be).

To assign a resource to a task for your project, follow these steps:

1. **Open Project to the Gantt Chart view for your project by clicking the Gantt Chart icon or by choosing View⇨Gantt Chart. Or, click on the Gantt Chart icon located on the right-hand-side vertical menu bar.**

   The Gantt Chart provides a graphical bar chart display of a project schedule. Where each Gantt bar represents a task's duration, and the lines connecting tasks show the task relationships.

2. **Select the desired task from the Gantt Chart you want to assign a resource. To assign multiple tasks to a single resource, hold down the Ctrl key and select the other tasks, and then release the Ctrl key.**

   Just click the number at the left side of the desired task. You can also select a range of tasks if you want to assign the same resources to all the tasks.

3. **Click the Assign Resources button on the toolbar, which has two over-lapping faces, or, by choosing <u>T</u>ools⇨ <u>R</u>esources⇨<u>A</u>ssign Resources from the top menu bar.**

   Project opens the Assign Resources dialog box, as shown in Figure 5-11. The dialog box lists all the resources that you define in the preceding section.

4. **Scroll through the list of resources in the dialog box and select the name of the person you want to assign to the task.**

   Just click the person's name in the resource list.

5. **Click the Assign button.**

   A check mark appears to the left of the person's name and the name appears next to the task duration indicator in the Gantt Chart.

6. **Repeat Steps 4 and 5 for each additional person that you want to assign to the task.**

7. **Click Close.**

   The Assign Resources dialog box closes. Voila! You've assigned the resources to your project.

You can still select from among your project tasks in Gantt Chart view while the Assign Resources dialog box is open. You don't, therefore, need to close the Assign Resources dialog box whenever you want to switch tasks in the Gantt Chart. This feature makes assigning resources to different tasks a breeze.

After you finish assigning resources to tasks, your Gantt Chart shows not only tasks and their durations, but also the names of the people you're assigning to each task.

Figure 5-11:
The Assign
Resources
dialog box
lists all your
resources.

Assign Resources

Resources from: 'CSSW4'

Dilbert		
Name	**Units**	
Dilbert		
Monica		
Hillary		
Kenneth		
Bill		
Austin		
Felicity		
Dr. Evil		
Mini-me		

Assign
Remove
Replace...
Address...
Cancel
Help

Deleting resources as necessary

After you complete the original assignments of resources to tasks, you're sure to face situations in which you need to delete resources completely from the project plan as changes arise in the project. For example, you can't always count on your project team members' availability 100 percent of the time. More than likely, their time will be shared across multiple projects. On occasion, project priorities may shift so that a team member may even be pulled off your project completely, in which case you will need to delete a given resource (team member). To delete a resource from an assigned task, follow these steps:

1. **Open Project to the Gantt Chart view for your project by clicking the Gantt Chart icon or by choosing View⇨Gantt Chart.**

2. **Select the task for the resources that you want to change.**

   Just click the number at the left side of the task line.

3. **Click the Assign Resources tool on the toolbar.**

   Project opens the Assign Resources dialog box. The dialog box lists all the resources you have available for the project (even though you may have already assigned certain resources to given tasks) to allow you the flexibility to add, reassign, or delete any resource from a given task any time during the duration of the project.

4. **In the Assign Resources dialog box, select the name of the resource that you want to remove from the project schedule.**

   Make sure that you select only a resource that displays a check mark to the left of the resource name on the list. These resources are the ones that you previously assigned to the task.

5. **Click the Remove button.**

   Project removes the check mark from the resource and, therefore, the resource from the task.

6. **Repeat Steps 2, 4, and 5 for other resources that you want to remove from the project schedule.**

   You don't need to perform Step 3 for each subsequent change unless you close the dialog box before you finish removing resources.

7. **Click Close.**

   The Assign Resources dialog box closes. You have now successfully deleted resources from your project.

Before you finish this phase of the project, you want to make sure that every task has a resource and every resource has a task. Save your work because you're almost to the point where you can create a baseline for your project prior to commencing actual development work.

To find out how to optimize your project and create a baseline, you can flip to Chapter 6. A *baseline* is a snapshot of your project plan at a given moment in time, which serves as a benchmark for measuring your project's actual progress versus your planned estimates. Usually, a baseline is established in Microsoft Project just prior to the project start date.

For example, your baseline on February 2, 2000 estimated it would take 61.5 days to complete the gather requirements project phase (milestone). However, your actual project status on April 25, 2000 is that you are 7 days (68.5 days have elapsed) behind scheduled baseline estimate. The baseline helps project managers get a reality check on the project status at a given point in time, so any necessary adjustments can be made before it's too late and out of hand.

Chapter 6

Optimizing Your Plan

● ●

In This Chapter

▶ Understanding the project baseline

▶ Examining the relationships in your project

▶ Using the Project Optimization Matrix

▶ Adjusting project scope, schedule, and resources

▶ Setting your project baseline

▶ Tracking your project's progress against the baseline estimates

● ●

Chapter 3 shows you how to build your preliminary baseline project plan in Microsoft Project. Chapter 5 provides an approach for accurately estimating and optimizing your preliminary project plan (to which your project sponsor puts her Monica on the dotted line and gives you a spiffy tie for a job well done).

In this chapter, you use Microsoft Project to assist you in optimizing your project plan by adjusting the project's scope, changing your schedule, reallocating resources, and reducing costs. Optimizing your plan entails changing your baseline estimates.

During your project planning process, you create a baseline plan with tasks and task duration estimates before the project start date. After the project begins, you use the baseline estimates as a point of reference to track the progress of the project. Chapter 6 shows you step-by-step how to create your baseline plan in Project.

A World of Related Elements

Every project (including yours) consists of three primary components: scope, schedule, and resources. (In fact, you can find several references in the preceding four chapters dealing with these three components.) The following list recaps each of the three elements:

- ✔ **Scope:** The scope of the project covers the work or tasks that you need to perform to complete the project in accordance with the goals and objectives you set out (or that management dictates to you, as the case may be).

- ✔ **Schedule:** Your schedule reflects the estimated duration or actual time that you require to finish each task in your project.

- ✔ **Resources:** Your resources are those people and things that you need to complete the project. Basically, if anything involving the project isn't part of the work itself or the schedule, it's a resource.

Notice that these three components are interdependent. If you change one of the elements, you typically affect one or both of the others. Among the more arcane of the arts of project management is the ability to change one element in order to positively affect another. Knowing just what to change and when to change it — and then doing so — is a large part of the optimization process. And much of this chapter focuses on just that topic.

Using the Project Optimization Matrix

So you reach the end of another day, and you're ready to submit the final proposal for your project schedule and budget to your project sponsor for approval. At last, you finish calculating your estimates. You've definitely proven that you can exploit every slick software tool under the sun!

You suddenly realize, however, that after the smoke and mirrors clear, your best cost estimate exceeds your project sponsor's budget allotment by more than $50,000! If that realization isn't aggravating enough, you also discover that your total project effort estimates exceed your project sponsor's original schedule by more than 125 business days.

No need to panic just yet. You can take a closer look at your handy Project Optimization Matrix (which you develop in Chapter 3) to determine what possible wiggle room you may have. Don't let the apparent simplicity of the POM fool you: This matrix can serve as a very powerful tool — as long as you base it on a sound understanding and agreement with your project sponsor as to your proposed project's scope, schedule, and resources. Figure 6-1 shows a sample Project Optimization Matrix.

Project Optimization Matrix

	Fixed (High)	Variable (Medium)	Variable (Low)
Scope (Deliverables)			
Resources (Budget)			
Schedule (Time)			

Figure 6-1: A sample Project Optimization Matrix.

Depending on who's sponsoring your project, your level of flexibility in the project's scope, resources, and schedule can vary significantly. In the sample Project Optimization Matrix shown in Figure 6-1, for example, the project sponsor says flat out that the original project schedule is set. If that's the case with your project, don't even think about trying to negotiate the schedule and buy additional time.

If software development delays are significant, even the sponsor sometimes has to yield to avoid losing significant features in the product. The company can look at the experience as a learning one . . . albeit not to be repeated again!

The budget parameter, however, is the most flexible. So if you play your cards right (while you're down on your knees begging, or course), perhaps you can get your budget bumped up to what you need to meet your estimates. (In the sample shown in the figure, that's $50,000.)

If the project sponsor doesn't want to spot you for the full amount that you think you need, you can still try to wrangle some more resources. Maybe you can negotiate for, say, half what you think you need ($25,000 in the example in the figure) and thus add a few more live bodies to meet your estimates.

The bottom line is that you need to do some adjusting and figuring to make your project work, even at this young and tender stage of the game. The next several sections discuss how you can use the information in the Project Optimization Matrix to adjust the parameters of your plan within Microsoft Project.

Adjusting your project's scope

Chapter 3 provides overviews of the different meetings that you and your development team use to brainstorm and finalize the project scope and the Work Breakdown Structure for your project. The *scope*, in this case, is the total work you must perform to accomplish the project goals and objectives. The WBS describes how you break down the scope into discrete tasks.

You can also avoid affecting your current project's scope by proposing to marketing and the Change Control Board to consider deferring some of the features to the next product release. This approach may prove to be a more sellable compromise. For more information on the software change process and the CCB, you can refer to Chapter 10.

One way to try to optimize your project plan is to determine which tasks you can live without. The first place to look is your project's critical path. The *critical path* is a series of tasks that, taken together, define the overall duration of your schedule. If you delete a task that lies along the critical path, you shorten the overall length of your project.

You can also remove non-critical tasks if you want. These tasks are any that don't affect the overall schedule for the project, unlike critical tasks along the critical path. Anytime that you remove tasks, you reduce your amount of total work. Although removing these tasks reduces the scope (total work) of your project, their absence doesn't change the project's schedule in any way. Thus, you need to focus first on removing tasks that are critical in nature, as they most affect your project's scope.

You can sort the tasks that lie along the critical path in your project plan in Microsoft Project. To do so, follow these steps:

1. **Open your project in Project by choosing File➪Open from the menu bar or by clicking the Open button on the toolbar.**

   You can also open the CSSW6.mpp project file from the *Software Project Management Kit For Dummies* CD.

2. **Choose View➪Tracking Gantt from the Project menu bar.**

   You can also access the Tracking Gantt view by clicking on the Tracking Gantt icon on the left side of the Project window. In this view, you can easily see which tasks are critical (those that appear on the chart in red) and which aren't (those in blue).

3. **Choose Project➪Sort➪Sort by from the menu bar.**

   Project displays the Sort dialog box which enables you to sort the tasks in your project, as shown in Figure 6-2.

4. **Open the Sort by drop-down list and select Duration; then select the Descending radio button.**

   You want to sort your project so that the longest tasks appear at the top of the task list and the shorter ones follow.

5. Click the Sort button.

Project sorts your tasks. You are trying to identify the major tasks with the longest duration now appear at the top of the task list, and the shorter tasks follow. Within each major task, Project also arranges subtasks in descending order by duration.

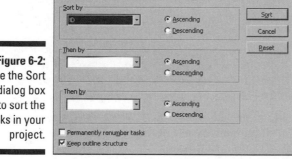

Figure 6-2:
Use the Sort dialog box to sort the tasks in your project.

As you work with your task list in this manner, you can easily determine which tasks most affect the overall schedule for your project. If you decide to delete some tasks and, thereby, reduce the scope of the project, simply select and delete them. (You discover how to delete tasks in Chapter 4.)

Playing with your project's schedule

Suppose that, after many hours of banging your heads against your project's preliminary critical path, you and your project team can't find even a single critical task that your project sponsor is willing to live without. Bummer city, dudes and dudettes!

The next place to look is the schedule. As you examine the scope of your project, you're often looking at the schedule as well. At that point, however, you're examining the overall schedule; now, you need to check through the schedule looking for individual tasks within the project that you can do without.

In looking at your schedule in such a manner, you're trying to determine whether you can decrease the duration of any individual tasks to save time on the schedule. As always, the tasks that most affect your overall schedule are those that lie along the critical path. (See the preceding section for information on how to view the critical path for your project.)

You can use a number of tricks in your managerial toolkit to trim a task's duration and, thereby, the overall project's schedule. Try, for example, the following ploys:

- ✔ **Talk with your development team members again.** They may have built some "fudge factor" time into the schedule.

- ✔ **Check availability schedules for your team members.** If they can currently devote only half-time to your project but you can get them to devote more time, you may shorten the duration of individual tasks. Again, focus on those tasks that lie along the critical path. Resources can be taken off competing (though lower-priority) projects.

- ✔ **Determine whether any of your tasks were already done in a different project.** If so, perhaps you can adapt the work on that project to your needs and, thereby, shorten durations. After all, you typically don't want to reinvent the wheel!

- ✔ **Revisit your task assignments.** Perhaps you'd be better off reassigning a certain task to a different team member? Perhaps a different team member can complete a given task quicker?

Going wild with project resources

You may notice that many of the ideas that you can consider in the preceding section (as you're trying to shorten schedule durations) actually involve resources (proof-positive that the three prongs of any project interrelate closely).

In many projects, the resources area is often the most flexible. This flexibility simply means that companies (or clients) usually prefer to throw more resources at a project than to bend on scope or schedule. (I want it *now*, and I'm willing to pay more to get it *now*!)

You can approach resources issues in several ways. First, you can physically assign more resources to a given task, and second, you can increase the pace of the work you're doing. The following sections cover these approaches.

Throwing more resources at a task

Suppose that you and your project team determine that your original duration guesstimates aren't very good. You can conceivably decrease a task's duration by putting more warm bodies to work on it!

You need to remain aware that more isn't always better. Have you ever heard the old truism that too many cooks spoil the broth? You can say the same for software projects — sometimes you can assign too many people to a task, and they get in each other's ways. Make sure that you carefully weigh the costs and benefits of assigning additional people to a task before you take such a step. By default, Project assumes that adding one resource cuts the time to accomplish the task proportionally, but this doesn't take into account additional communication time, time spent coordinating meetings, differences of opinion, and so on.

As you're selecting tasks for allocation of additional resources, you first want to look at those tasks that lie along the critical path. Looking at tasks that lie off the critical path, however, can sometimes be advantageous as well. Say, for example, that you assign Austin to several different non-critical tasks. Again, this label doesn't mean that these tasks are unimportant — just that they don't lie along the critical path.

You don't, after all, want to minimize Austin's power to contribute to the project — no way, baby. Perhaps if you assign additional resources to some of Austin's tasks, doing so may free him up to work on a different task — one that does lie along the critical path. The net result is that you can decrease the duration of the critical tasks by assigning additional resources to the non-critical tasks.

You can also consider pulling in outside resources for your project, such as independent contractors or consultants. Many companies decide to outsource noncritical tasks in a project to free up internal resources to focus on critical tasks.

By using Microsoft Project, you can assign additional resources to a task by using the same skills that I cover in Chapter 5. After you assign the additional resources, you can determine their effect on task durations and the overall project schedule.

Working the resources 24/7 — get a life!

If you have a hard time recruiting more warm bodies for your project or can't find the right people for the job, perhaps you can increase the number of working hours for your existing resources to try to shorten your project's overall schedule. As with other considerations, focusing your resources on shortening the overall duration of the critical path is the critical point.

Perhaps, for example, you can extend the schedule's workday from eight to nine or possibly even ten hours. Just be aware, however, that working 12- and 15-hour days for any sustained period is a sure way to burn out your personnel. Because of this potential for burnout, you want to use such a strategy only as a last resort.

If you do decide to extend the workday for the project, you can increase the working hours of a resource in Microsoft Project to accurately estimate task durations by following these steps:

1. **Open your project in Project by choosing File➪Open from the menu bar or by clicking the Open button on the toolbar.**

   You can also open the CSSW6.mpp project file from the *Software Project Management Kit For Dummies* CD.

2. **Choose Tools➪Change Working Time.**

   Project displays the Change Working Time dialog box, as shown in Figure 6-3.

Figure 6-3:
You can use this dialog box to change the length of workdays in Project.

Change Working Time								? ×

For: Standard (Project Calendar)

Set working time for selected date(s)

Legend:
- Working
- Nonworking
- Edited working hours

On this calendar:
- I   Edits to a day of the week
- 31 Edits to an individual day

Select Date(s):

February 2000

S	M	T	W	Th	F	S
		1	2	3	4	5
6	7	8	9	10	11	12
13	14	15	16	17	18	19
20	21	22	23	24	25	26
27	28	29				

Set selected date(s) to:
- ● Use Default
- ○ Nonworking time
- ○ Nondefault working time

From: To:
8:00 AM   12:00 PM
1:00 PM   5:00 PM

Help   New...   Options...   OK   Cancel

3. **Use the For drop-down list to select the resource for which you want to change the working hours.**

   The schedule for the resource appears in the Calendar area of the dialog box.

4. **Use the Calendar's spinner buttons to select the days for which you want to change hours.**

   If you're adjusting work schedules during a critical time of the project, make sure that you select all the dates for that time period.

5. **Adjust the work hours in the For Selected Dates area of the dialog box.**

   You want to change the starting and ending times for these dates, as appropriate.

6. **Repeat Steps 2 through 4 to adjust working hours for other resources.**

7. **Click OK after you finish making your adjustments.**

   The Change Working Time dialog box closes. As you can see, you can increase the number of working hours for your existing resources in an attempt to shorten your project's overall schedule.

Working overtime

Another way to try to shorten your project's overall schedule is to schedule resources to work overtime. You want to use this strategy only as a final resort — one to employ only if you can't convince your personnel to work 15-hour days at minimum wage or find any other warm bodies with the qualifications to complete the critical project tasks.

Normally, the criteria for authorizing overtime (paying people premium pay higher than their normal wages) is that the project is significantly behind schedule and/or is seriously at risk of failing. Getting authorization from your project sponsor before implementing this alternative is mandatory.

If you decide to use this strategy and obtain the necessary authorization, you can assign overtime to your resources in Microsoft Project by following these steps:

1. **Open your project in Project by choosing File⇨Open from the menu bar or by clicking the Open button on the toolbar.**

   You can also open the CSSW6.mpp project file from the *Software Project Management Kit For Dummies* CD.

2. **Make sure that you're using the Gantt Chart view of your project.**

   Click the Gantt Chart icon at the left of the program window or choose View⇨Gantt Chart from the Project menu bar.

3. **Choose Window⇨Split from the menu bar while in Gantt Chart view.**

   The Project window splits so that the Gantt Chart appears at the top and task information appears at the bottom (see Figure 6-4).

4. **Click anywhere in the bottom portion of the screen.**

   Choose one of the controls in the bottom portion of the screen.

5. **Choose Format⇨Details⇨Resource Work from the menu bar.**

   The bottom portion of the Project window changes to show the task and the resources assigned to the task.

6. **In the task list at the top of the Project window, click to select the task for which you want to assign overtime.**

   The resources for that task now appear in the bottom portion of the Project window.

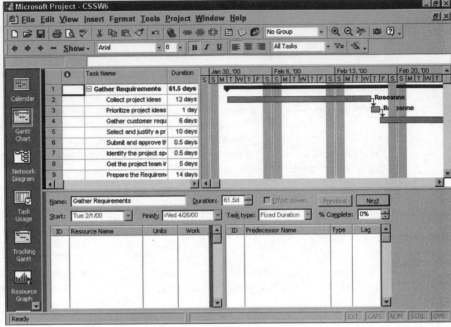

Figure 6-4:
Splitting the
Project
window
provides
more
information
on-screen.

7. **Change the overtime hours in the Ovt. Work column for the resources assigned to the task.**

8. **Click OK.**

   Project adjusts the duration of the task to reflect the overtime hours you enter in the Ovt. Work column for its resources.

9. **Repeat Steps 5 through 7 for any other overtime that you want to authorize.**

Optimizing resources

Earlier in the project management process, as I show you in Chapter 5, you can assign different tasks to different personnel. You then manually level the tasks to make sure that one particular person isn't overloaded with work as compared to another.

After you change working hours, allocate more resources, and assign overtime, you may need to level your resources again. Microsoft Project enables you to easily see which resources may need leveling. Simply click the Resource Usage icon at the left side of the program window or choose View➪Resource Usage from the menu bar. Project then displays information similar to that shown in Figure 6-5.

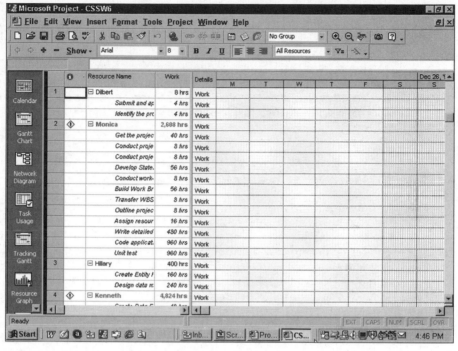

Figure 6-5:
Project can
show you
which
resources
need
leveling.

Notice in the figure that a small exclamation point appears to the left of some personnel names. (In Figure 6-5, such symbols appear to the left of Monica's and Kenneth's names.) Project calculates the usage level of each resource, in identifying which resources need leveling. This symbol indicates resources that, in the estimation of Project, you need to level.

Microsoft Project supports a number of resource leveling techniques, as the following list describes:

✔ **Manually delay tasks.** You can level over-allocated resources by manually adding delay time to the tasks one at a time. If you add delay time to a critical task, the critical path is lengthened, which will delay the overall project's finish date. For leveling a few tasks, manual delay of tasks is recommended over Project's automated task delay technique.

✔ **Automatically delay tasks.** If you have several over-allocated resources, you can use the automatic leveling technique by delaying a batch of tasks. The manual delay technique is recommended if you only have a few resources that need leveling.

✔ **Trimming a task's scope (amount of work).** Cutting down a task's scope is an alternative method of leveling resources when you are unable to delay the task.

> ✔ **Splitting a task into units of work.** Another way to level an overallocated or underallocated resource is to break a task's scope into smaller units of work, which you can then assign to multiple resources instead of just one.

A step-by-step discussion on identifying, assigning, and optimizing resources by using Project is a bit beyond the scope of this book, but you can refer to *Microsoft Project 2000 For Dummies* by Marty Doucette and published by IDG Books Worldwide, Inc. for helpful information.

Baseline? What Baseline?

After optimizing your plan in Microsoft Project, you should have a good idea of who needs to do what at what time in order to bring your software project to reality on time and on budget (be careful not to break any mirrors or walk under ladders for the duration of your project). Hopefully, the look in your eyes at this point is determination rather than resignation. Take several deep breaths (to avoid hyperventilating) before moving on to the next phase, setting the baseline for your project in Project.

So just what is this baseline anyway, and why is it important to your project? Good question, Grasshopper. In a word, a *baseline* is the standard by which you measure your project — the real, honest-to-goodness goal for which you're shooting. It's Exhibit Number One in either your promotion papers or your termination proceedings. In Microsoft Project, when you're confident in the definiteness of project plan, you can create a baseline project plan (file).

Aaaagggghhhhh! What? You don't *want* a baseline if it may end up getting you fired? Well, if it's any consolation, few first-time project managers are ever fired. (There — feel better?) Why? Because that just leads to more first-time project managers.

The reality is that you need a baseline. You can't measure your performance (and that of your team) without one. The baseline is a where-we-are-versus-where-we-planned-to-be snapshot of your project. In time, the resources, schedule, and milestones relating to your project may very well change, but your baseline doesn't. You can, therefore, make a comparison later on in the project to determine how good a job you did up front with your forecasting.

The following sections describe how to establish a baseline for your project. The trick, you see, is to make it the most accurate baseline project plan that you can — which is where optimizing your project's scope, resources, and schedule comes into play, as described in the preceding section.

Setting the Baseline Project Plan

I know, I know . . . if you're ready to set your baseline, then you've been steeped in the details of your project far too long. Everywhere you look you see resources, dollar signs, and tasks looming in the wings. You've met so often in negotiations with your project sponsor that you're a candidate for godparent at the project sponsor's next child's christening. And whenever you dream at night, giant calendar deadlines threaten to overrun you. Can't you find relief? Can no one help? Relax, oh, stressed-out one! Help is at hand.

In the preceding sections of this chapter, you study the critical path and shorten it as much as possible. In this section, I tell you how to set your project baseline as explained in the previous section. Here's where you cast your project in wet concrete and say, "We're valiantly ready to go forth and conquer the beast!" (You never knew software project management was so epic, did you?)

The following sections describe how you can set and use your baseline by using Microsoft Project.

You may notice that every time you save your project in Project, the Planning Wizard dialog box appears and asks whether you want to save a baseline for your project. In Chapters 4 and 5, I tell you to answer No to this plaintive query. Now, however, you're going to explicitly save the baseline. All you need to do is follow these steps:

1. **Open your project in Project by choosing File⇨Open or by clicking the Open button on the toolbar.**

   You can also open the CSSW6.mpp project file from the *Software Project Management Kit For Dummies.*

2. **Choose Tools⇨Tracking ⇨Save Baseline.**

   The Save Baseline dialog box appears, as shown in Figure 6-6.

Figure 6-6:
You can
control how
Project
saves your
baseline by
using this
dialog box.

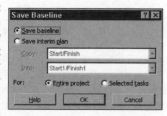

3. **Make sure that the Save baseline and Entire project radio buttons are selected. If they're not selected, then you need to select them.**

   You find out about the other choices in the dialog box later in this chapter in the section titled "Tracking Your Progress."

4. **Click OK.**

   The baseline is set. Easy as 1-2-3, huh?

In setting the baseline in Microsoft Project, you're setting your plan in stone. Your file becomes the standard against which you measure subsequent progress on your project. After Project takes its snapshot of your plan, you can't change it; it becomes the yardstick that you use to evaluate later progress for your project. Project actually saves the baseline to disk the next time that you save your project by clicking the Save tool on the toolbar or by choosing File⇨Save.

In versions of Microsoft Project prior to Project 2000, after you set a baseline, changing it was difficult. However, if you inadvertently set a baseline before you're completely ready in Project 2000, simply choose Tools⇨Tracking⇨ Clear Baseline. Your project baseline goes bye-bye.

Tracking Your Progress

As you go forward on your project, you change and refine your project file in Project on almost a daily basis. You make changes to reflect work that you complete or to modify tasks currently in progress.

Viewing actual versus baseline information

After you finish creating your newly built baseline project plan, you probably can't wait to see your handiwork. At such a relatively early stage in the project, however, you really don't have anything to see. Down the road, after you make a few changes and get past a couple milestones, what you can see at that point is probably quite a different story.

To view a comparison of your actual performance with your baseline, all you need to do is click the Tracking Gantt view icon at the left of the project window. This view enables you to see current performance as Project measures it against your forecasts. Figure 6-7 shows an example of such a comparison.

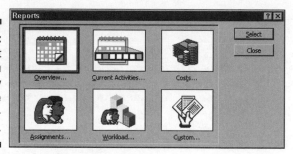

Figure 6-7:
Project
enables you
to quickly
compare
plan to per-
formance.

Setting an interim plan

As you achieve different milestones in your project, you may want to save additional snapshots of how the work is progressing. Project enables you to do so through the use of what it calls interim plans. Interim plans provide you with good, periodic benchmarks to measure against the original baseline plan to determine whether your project schedule is staying on track.

You can save an interim plan by following these steps:

1. **Open your project in Project by choosing File⇨Open or by clicking the Open button.**

   You can also open the CSSW6.mpp project file from the *Software Project Management Kit For Dummies* CD.

2. **Choose Tools⇨Tracking⇨Save Baseline.**

   The Save Baseline dialog box appears (refer to Figure 6-6).

3. **Select the Save Interim Plan radio button.**

   The Copy and Into text boxes become accessible in order to take a snap-shot (copy) of your baseline plan to create an interim plan. You use these text boxes to specify what elements of your project you're copy-ing, as well as to where you're copying them.

4. **Accept the default Copy and Into drop-down list box values, or select the desired values.**

   Normally, you can accept the default settings. If you want to base the interim plan on the baseline settings, however, you can select Baseline Start/Finish in the Copy text box.

5. **Make sure that the Entire Project radio button is selected, in order to create an interim (snapshot) plan of the entire project.**

   The other option is Selected Tasks, which you would use only if you were not creating an interim plan of the entire project.

   You want to save a snapshot of your entire project, don't you?

6. Click OK.

Project saves the interim plan.

By periodically saving interim plans during the various phases of your project, you obtain a series of snapshots of all your tasks' start and finish dates at certain points in time, which you can then compare with your baseline project to see if you're on or off schedule.

Reporting your project's progress

Building the baseline is unquestionably a big step toward managing a successful software project. Tracking *actual* project progress against the baseline, however, continues throughout the life of the project. Sound difficult? Actually, the process is quite simple. Microsoft Project puts valuable tracking information on your project's progress right at your fingertips! Earlier in this chapter, in the section titled "Baseline Project Plan," I show you how to set a baseline project plan.

The file CSSW6.mpp project file from the *Software Project Management Kit For Dummies* CD provides a final baseline project plan for a generic software project to give you a head start.

Looking at progress lines

You can measure your software project's success using Microsoft Project in a number of cool ways that include viewing your project's progress lines on your Gantt Chart. Progress lines connect tasks that are in progress. The lines either have peaks or valleys to graphically represent how far ahead or behind schedule the project is.

Ensure that your final baseline project is open in Gantt Chart view and follow these steps to display progress lines on the Gantt Chart:

Gantt Chart

1. Ensure that your file is open in Gantt Chart view.

Click the button that's displayed in the margin if not.

2. Choose Tools➪Tracking➪Progress Lines.

3. Click Dates and Intervals tab.

4. Select the Always Display Current Progress Line check box.

5. Click OK.

Reviewing your baseline

As your project gets a bit further along, you may want to go back and view your original baseline plan, chuckle, and say, "what was I thinking?" To review your project's baseline estimate after you have an idea of how the project is actually going, perform the following steps:

1. **Select the Tracking Gantt View button on the view bar.**

3. **Choose View⇨Table⇨More Tables.**

4. **From Tables list, select Baseline.**

5. **Click Apply.**

Checking your project's baseline variance

One of the advantages of setting a baseline plan is that doing so allows you to keep track of the progress of your project. Are you on time and on budget? To compare your project's baseline estimates against actual progress, just follow these steps:

1. **Click the Tracking Gantt View button on the view bar.**

2. **Choose View⇨Table⇨Variance.**

   You can now look at the percentage differences between your plan and the actual progress of the project.

Focusing on the schedule

Keeping your project on schedule requires eternal vigilance. Luckily, Microsoft Project understands this challenge and provides special views to help you. Check this information often.

You can verify whether your project's actual task start and finish dates are on schedule by following these steps:

1. **Select the Tracking Gantt View button from the view bar.**

2. **Choose View⇨Table⇨Variance.**

3. **Drag the divider bar to the right in order to view the variance fields.**

Project also offers way too many types of reports for me to go into them all here. For details, refer to a book specifically about Project, such as *Microsoft Project 2000 For Dummies* by Marty Doucette (published by IDG Books Worldwide, Inc.).

Printing out your tracking information

You can print any of Project's tracking information at any time that you want. Just follow these general steps to print any report in Project:

1. **Open your project in Project by choosing File⇨Open from the menu bar or by clicking the Open button on the toolbar.**

2. **Choose View⇨Reports from the Project menu bar.**

   Project opens the Reports dialog box, as shown in Figure 6-8.

Figure 6-8:
Project
offers sev-
eral cate-
gories of
reports you
can print.

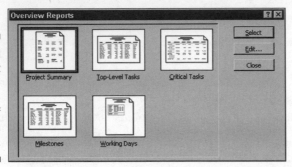

3. **Select the category of report by clicking on the desired icon that you want to print and then click the Select button.**

   Project displays the reports available in the category you select.

4. **Select the report icon you want to print and then click the Select button.**

Project pulls together all the information necessary for the report and then displays a Print Preview version of the report. You can then use the controls in the Print Preview view to examine the report, or you can click Print to actually print it to your printer. Or, you can go ahead and print the report without looking at the Print Preview window first.

Part III

Making Your
Software Happen

The 5th Wave — By Rich Tennant

"Why, of course. I'd be very interested in seeing this new milestone in the project."

In this part . . .

The old saying *all talk and no action* can apply to soft-ware projects too. Up to this point, you've spent a generous amount of time analyzing, brainstorming, head scratching, and generally meeting and discussing your customer's problem, your project's scope, the budget, and other such matters. But the goal isn't, of course, to create a great plan — it's to create great software. Your great plan is but a means to that end.

Part III gets past the smoke and mirrors. The time has come to focus your project team on *doing* the tasks that make your software project plan come together. Your team designs and builds the software and documentation required to deliver a successful Generally Available (GA) release to your customers as advertised.

Chapter 7

Analyzing Needs and Designing the Software

● ●

In This Chapter

▶ Designing software that you base on the Requirements Document

▶ Designing software by using the object-oriented design approach

▶ Reusing code

▶ Creating your project data model

▶ Designing the user interface

▶ Creating the prototypes and product demos

▶ Writing the Functional Specifications document

▶ Putting together a documentation plan

▶ Writing the Detailed Design Specifications document

▶ Writing the beta and SQA test plans

● ●

*W*henever I think of the analysis and design phases of a software project, I recall all the projects that fail because project managers short-change the rigorous demands of the requirements phase. Instead of thoroughly defining their customers' problem, they jump too quickly to designing and developing software solutions to the wrong problems. They become, in effect, captains of sinking ships, quietly going down with a project that they could save by investing a measure of hard work up front. (You can refer to Chapter 1 for an overview of the seven phases of the software development cycle.)

Sound scary? Good. If you're a project manager who hasn't yet thoroughly worked through the requirements phase of your project, I strongly suggest that you go back and work through Chapters 2 through 6 before reading this chapter. The extra up-front work that those chapters describe pays off in the long run.

This chapter covers two phases that work hand-in-hand: the *analysis phase* and the *design phase*. (You may think that spending five chapters on the requirements-gathering phase while devoting only one chapter to these two phases is a bit odd. It's not, however, if you realize that the majority of your management work is "front-loaded," meaning that you need to spend the majority of your time at the beginning of your project laying the correct groundwork for what follows. If you do, your chances of success greatly improve.)

Each hour that you spend making design decisions up front saves you and your team a day or more of last-minute changes and repairs on the back end of the project.

During the course of this chapter, your development team analyzes the needs of your software and creates several documents that pinpoint the development work that you need to do. In the following sections, you develop an *Entity Relationship Diagram (ERD)*, a *Data Flow Diagram (DFD)* and a *data dictionary*. You also perform an object-oriented analysis of your program needs. Based on this information, you can then proceed to the fun stuff: designing your program in depth.

Using the Requirements Document as Your Guide

Before beginning the design phase of your project, completing the Requirements Document and Project Scope Document (PSD) is absolutely essential. Chapters 2 and 3 explain how to put these documents together.

The *Requirements Document (RD)* is the single most important document your project team looks to as a roadmap for designing and developing all the other project deliverables for the remainder of the software-development cycle. As I describe in Chapter 2, the fundamental question to answer as you're writing the Requirements Document is exactly what *problem* is your customer trying to solve? What the software industry refers to as the "problem" is the actual or perceived software *needs* or *requirements* of your customers and target market.

The RD becomes the authoritative blueprint that everyone looks to in developing the project plan, Functional Specifications, data-model design, Detailed Design Specifications, and product's user publications, progressing through the actual coding of the software. You can trace the reason for this document's importance to its customer orientation. The customers' needs must always remain foremost in the minds of your project's team members, and the RD keeps the customers' needs squarely in focus. Whenever a dispute between project members arises about the vision of the project, you and your project team need to review the Requirements Document.

If the RD comprises your goal and vision for customer satisfaction with your product, the *Project Scope Document (PSD)* is your nod toward the speed component of the equation. Is, for example, a feature-complete product two years from now worth as much to your customer as an 80-percent-complete product next year? The PSD defines the scope of the project by identifying which of the customers' requirements that the RD identifies you need to include in your software release. (In Chapter 3, you sweat through the negotiations that comprise the creation of the Project Scope Document.)

These documents provide the input that you need for the analysis and design phases of your project. Together, these documents provide the strong foundation on which you build the detailed documents that describe what's going on under the hood of your project.

Understanding Object-Oriented Design

You may feel quite comfortable with all the talk about *object-oriented* gibberish you hear in the programming world. (If that's the case, feel free to skip over this section). Then again, you may be with the other 99.5 percent of humanity whose eyes glaze over at the merest mention of *classes objects* and *instances*. Yikes!

The good news is that, regardless of your expertise in the area of object-oriented programming, the programmers on your team are likely well-versed in the intricacies of object-oriented programming. The bad news is that you need to at least understand the fundamentals of object-oriented design to be effective in overseeing most of today's software projects.

Object-oriented programming may seem a bit more difficult to understand at first than procedural programming. But if you pick up even a basic understanding of how it works, you quickly find that using the design method actually simplifies the process of discussing and conceptualizing solutions to programming problems — and that benefits you greatly, Mr. or Ms. Project Manager!

Object-oriented programming (OOP) is a relatively new approach to programming. The approach enables you to create well-designed program modules that perform a particular task. Because you also design such modules to be reusable, your team can easily move the modules from one program to another.

In traditional (or non-OOP) programming, you keep the data that a program uses separate from the programming code that you use to manipulate that data. You store all data in one area of the computer's memory and all the programming code is in another. If the data must change (if, for example, you want to start tracking how many people instigate service incidents on your

Web site), the programs that access that data must also change. Such changes can prove troublesome, particularly if the program is quite large. If a class models a single database record, however, the information that these class instances access resides in a separate database.

Object-oriented programming attempts to solve this problem by changing the fundamental way in which you store programs and data in a computer. In OOP, you store the data along with the program module that you use to initialize, access, and process that data. If another program module needs a piece of the data, it requests it from the module that's responsible for that particular data, and that module then fulfills the request.

OOP inheritance enables you to make changes to the data within a module available to other modules simply by changing the module responsible for the data. Class-subclass inheritance enables you to change only the original module, which eliminates the need to change many references to the module in multiple locations, as you needed to do in earlier approaches to programming. The benefit to an organization of using an object-oriented approach, therefore, is that programs become easier to maintain and modify in the long run.

This method is an entirely revolutionary way of programming. Although object-oriented programming using languages such as Java, C++, and Visual Basic lies beyond the scope of this book (as you can find entire huge books on the topic), the following sections may help you understand some of the key concepts behind it. (These concepts may come in handy if you actually decide to glance at some of those huge books.)

Understanding classes

An important feature of object-oriented programming is the concept of *classes*. Object-oriented programming (OOP) categorizes objects into classes. Classes describe the characteristics and operations of a certain category of objects.

As an example of applying OOP concepts to a real-world object, consider how much more easily you can think of an automobile as a combination of its components and operations. The Ford Model-T automobile, for example, designates a certain class of automobiles that's different from other classes of automobiles. All Ford Model Ts share the following characteristics:

- Engine
- Transmission
- Steering wheel
- Brakes
- Tires

All Model Ts also share the same operations, as the following list describes:

✔ Starting or stopping the automobile

✔ Using gasoline as source of fuel

✔ Shifting of gears with a stick shift

Object-orientation enables you to back away from discussing the various minutiae that make up a Model T and just discuss the Model T itself as you and I see it, a Model T.

Understanding objects

The concept of an *object* is, of course, also fundamental to object-oriented programming. An object is an *instance* of a class. In the example that I provide in the preceding section, each Ford Model T automobile is an object (or an instance) in the class of Model Ts. Suppose that both your great-, great-, great-grandfather and grandmother each bought their own Model T. Both Model T units share the same characteristics and functions.

In the OOP world, objects are nothing but collections of data and the procedures that process that data. One advantage of objects for less-technically savvy project managers is that objects enable you to think about programs in terms of particular components. Conceptualizing programs in terms of their parts can help you discuss and think about the important parts of a program more easily.

You see the effects of creating instances (or *instantiating*, if you care to talk the talk) all the time whenever you use software. Every time that you click the New toolbar button in Microsoft Word, for example, Word creates a brand-new instance of the Document class, a blank document with a particular set of default properties. You then set about changing the properties of that instance. Although two instances of the Document class are exactly the same after you first create them, one may become a nasty letter to your noisy next-door neighbor and the other a love sonnet to your significant other — two sets of properties in wildly different states, as well as two wildly different states of mind!

Objects share certain characteristics in the OOP world that help you think about the object's data in some way, as the following list describes:

✔ **Methods:** *Methods* are the procedures that you can apply to an object. (Objects may or may not have methods.) You can, for example, apply the Start method to an Engine object to change its state in a number of ways.

✔ **Properties:** The state of the object is dependent on the values of the data in the object. These values are known as the object's *properties*. If you apply the Start method to the Engine object, the Boolean IsRunning property changes from False to True, the Temperature property moves from OutsideTemperature to 210 degrees, and so on.

✔ **Interface:** An object can contain information that defines its *interface*, which is its means for exchanging messages with other objects. This information exchange enables objects to communicate with one another. The Brake object, therefore, can communicate with the Wheel object via its interface to ask whether the Wheel object's RotationSpeed property is zero (while others are positive) and, if the answer is *yes*, to release pressure on that brake. This communication procedure creates an antilock brake system in your virtual car.

As an example of how objects work in the software world, suppose that the development team working on your Customer Self-Service Web project creates an object to which the team gives the name New Case. This object contains all the data relating to any service-related cases that you can generate from your Web site.

This data can obviously include names, dates, and other pertinent facts but may also include ancillary data, such as the department to which to route the incident. In addition, the New Case object may contain a collection of methods that you can use to manipulate the properties of the data — methods such as those to add a new instance (record) to the Case List form, remove a case, print out a list of open or resolved cases, and generate a count of the number of items (open or resolved cases) on the list.

Notice that, if you want to add an item to the new case list, all you need to do is pass that item to the method responsible for adding it to the case list. If you later want to retrieve a case from the list, you simply use the correct method for that task (for example, the Retrieve method). Object-oriented programming encourages programmers to start thinking about the environment in which the object functions and not just about the data that the object maintains.

Understanding inheritance

Classes are very important to the entire concept of object-oriented programming. They represent a huge advance in the concept of code reusability. *Inheritance* provides the software developer with the capability to create more and more specific examples of an object without importing the original code.

Inheritance refers to an object's capability to *pass on* its characteristics (both methods and properties) to any subclasses that you base on the object. In the example that I provide in the preceding section, New Case is a subclass of `Case List`. The `New Case` class inherits its capabilities from `Case List`. Similarly, the `Resolved` class can also inherit the capabilities of the `Case List` class. The main difference is that you may have some additional properties in the `Resolved` class, such as `Resolution` and `Resolution_Time` data members, which store the how and time of the case's resolution.

The Seven Steps of Object-Oriented Design

After you make the decision to use the OOP design method (or, more likely, the organization that you work for makes this decision for you), what comes next? You start to focus on designing your project by using a methodology known as *object-oriented design* (*OOD*). This approach works hand-in-glove with object-oriented programming.

The OOD process consists of seven identifiable tasks, each of which can help make your development tasks (which you face later) much lighter. The tasks of the OOD process are as follows:

- ✔ Determine whether you can reuse any of your software code.
- ✔ Design the project data model.
- ✔ Lay out your functional architecture.
- ✔ Write high-level Functional Specifications document.
- ✔ Write the software-documentation plan.
- ✔ Write the Detailed Design Specifications document.
- ✔ Write the project test plans.

You obviously need to examine each of these steps in detail. The following sections walk you (and your development team) through the step-by-step OOD process of your software — but without turning you into a full-fledged nerd!

Reusing Code Instead of Reinventing the Wheel

One of the major benefits of OOP is that you can reuse the programming modules that you create. Taking some time, therefore, to determine whether you can reuse any programming objects from other projects that your organization completed is definitely worth your while.

If this software project is your organization's first, however, you're going to be hard-pressed to find much software that you can reuse. If you're managing a software project for an organization that's made its way through the ups and downs of pre- and post-IPO, on the other hand, your chances of finding code from existing applications that you can reuse are quite good.

Have your development team check out any existing software modules for any candidates for reuse. Not only do you save development time by reusing code, but that code is already tested and debugged, which may save you even more time down the road.

If you can find in another project a class that does something similar to what you need (even if its application is fairly different), you can conceivably derive a subclass from that class that fits the bill perfectly for your project. Encourage your team to think outside the box in finding ways to reuse code.

Don't be afraid to suggest things yourself — even if you're not an experienced code writer by vocation. Perhaps you can draw analogies between objects and classes that the people who write the code may not see at first but that may prove applicable nonetheless. Even if you get only a that-can-never-work type of response, you pick up a bit more information about how object-oriented design works and, as a result, may become a bit better at doing your job.

Software design takes place on the following two basic levels:

- **Data-model design:** The structure of your data.
- **Functional architecture:** The structure of the program modules or application code.

Besides reusing individual programming objects, you also may find that you can locate and reuse data models and architectural frameworks from past projects. Heck, if you hit the mother lode, maybe you can shave weeks or even months off your development cycle!

Designing the Data Model

The data-model design defines all the schema requirements of the Relational Database Management System (RDBMS) for the software project. This model includes domains, data elements, tables, table relationships, and so on.

You may ask: *What language are you speaking, anyway?*

DBAspeak. It's all relative, is my Orwellian voice's reply, emanating through your interactive PC.

Relative to what? you wonder.

Good question, Grasshopper. Before you can snatch the pebble from my hand, you must understand a bit of terminology. . . .

Database terminology

As in any other branch of information technology, database concept and design has its own specialized lingo that many people speak as their native language. In fact, some of your team members may seem quite accomplished at bandying about database terminology. Unless you have a database background, you may feel a bit overwhelmed.

Now, don't go thinking that this section can teach you the entire database dialect right away. No, that process can take months or years. Settle back and buckle in for a crash course in the most rudimentary of terminology. (For a couple detailed primers, check out *Oracle 8i For Dummies,* by Carol McCullough, and *SQL For Dummies,* 3rd Edition by Allen G. Taylor, both published by IDG Books Worldwide, Inc.)

You probably already know what a database is but may have trouble explaining it to someone else. A pretty good working definition is an organized collection of data that relates to a particular topic.

Deciding against flat files

Before databases came along, the only way to organize data was by using a *flat file,* which is nothing but a sequential group of records. A flat file isn't a database at all in that no metadata about the structure of the database is included in the file. You get the data, the whole data, and nothing but the data. You have to program your application to understand the structure of the file. Flat files have one benefit: They tend to be compact in size. Their significant drawbacks, however, far outweigh their lone benefit. These drawbacks include the following:

✔ **The application code must be tied to the database structure:** The only way to find information in a flat file is to hard code into your application the method for finding and retrieving the data. For example, the simplest flat file would be one in which you code a certain number of characters for each field (such as 20 characters for the first name, 25 characters for the last name, and so on). To retrieve the last name requires you to code into the program instructions such as the following: (1) move to a particular record in the flat file, (2) move to the 21st position in the record, and (3) copy the next 25 characters.

✔ **Flat files are inflexible:** If you decide late in the process to change the structure of your database, a flat file is unforgiving. Continuing the example from the previous bullet, suppose that you need a field to store a title (such as Mr., Ms., or Dr.) to precede the fields storing the first and last names, you would then have to recode the data-retrieval algorithms that retrieve the last name, perhaps starting at 25th position to get the last name instead of the 21st position. (In fact, you probably have to recode all the data-retrieval algorithms.)

✔ **Flat files require redundant data entry:** All the data in a flat file must exist within that file, which requires redundant storage of data. For example, in the Customer Self-Service Web application, the same customer is likely to create multiple help case entries, which you would want to store as separate cases. Rather than enter the customer's contact information only once, however, the flat-file structure calls for entering that information *every time* that the customer calls for help. The customer's contact information hasn't changed, however, so reentering information is inefficient. The information that is different is the new support need of the customer. Entering data multiple times also greatly increases the likelihood of data-entry errors.

Discovering why relational databases reign supreme

Databases store information about their structure (called *metadata*) that your program can access. Databases advanced through three different models: hierarchical, network, and finally to the relational model. Because the hierarchical and network structures don't adequately solve the problem of redundant data storage, however, the real winner is the *relational database management system (RDBMS),* which refers to a relational database and the software interface that allows you to access the data through an external program. Some of the common RDBMS products on the market include: Sybase, Oracle, Microsoft SQL-Server, Informix, and DB2.

The easiest way to think about the information in a table is to think of a spreadsheet in which each row of data is a record and each column is a field. The intersection of a row and column represents the unique data that a particular field stores. In fact, you typically hear database designers talk about rows and columns rather than records and fields.

Relational databases allow data stored in one table to refer to data stored in another table. Such references are called *relationships.* In the Customer Self-Service Web project's database, for example, you would want to have separate tables to store the customer contact information and the customer help-desk cases. That way, when a customer already in the database creates a new case, no one has to reenter that customer's contact information. Instead, the new case data merely refers to the existing customer contact information that's stored in another table.

When the database structure changes, such as when you add a new data field (or column), the application programs still work, because the relational database's metadata allows the program to find the column regardless of its location within the table. (Of course, you would need to add some more code to access the new data, but you would only need to add code to access the new field rather than changing all the data retrieval codes, which is vastly less work than is necessary when you make such a change to a flat file.)

A relational version of the Customer Self-Service Web database, for example, may contain a table for case information, another table for contact information, and yet another table for software change requests. These tables refer to one another by using *keys,* which are codes that uniquely identify the records in a table. For example, in a contact information database, a sequence number column (containing numbers such as 101, 102, and so on) could uniquely identify each company, and other tables could refer to that sequence number.

When you add a new column to a relational database, the application code still works because the relational database structure (the table structure and the relationships between the tables) is stored within the database itself as metadata and available via the RDBMS rather than being hard-coded into the application code. This concept is really cool stuff or *RCS* as a computer geek may tend to call it. With the benefits of a flexible structure and ability to reference data in only one place in the application code, relational databases have become the standard in the software industry.

Dealing with database jargon

After you understand the basics of relational databases, everything else is effectively jargon that confuses the issues and keeps the salaries of database administrators high (a trick they may have picked up from lawyers). Some of the more obfuscating terms that you may hear include those in the following list:

- **Data dictionary:** A best-selling book that defines all goofy database terms (just kidding). Really, a *data dictionary* is a table that defines the data elements (objects) in a database, along with the range of data that can exist in a field (see Figure 7-1). Every data element of the data dictionary needs to be unique. Data dictionaries often contain metadata.

- **Domain:** The set of all values associated with a specific table column (or field), as the data dictionary defines it.

- **Keys:** *Keys* are fields that you use to index the information in a table. You use two types of keys in relational database-management systems (RDBMSes): *primary* and *foreign (secondary)* keys. Keys are typically unique, and you often use them in large or complex tables to enable the quick retrieval of information.

A *primary key* is a column or combination of columns in a database table that uniquely identifies each row in the table. The `Case_Number` column for example, is a primary key serving as the unique identifier for each row (record) on the `Case_Reports` table in the Customer Self-Service database application.

A *foreign (secondary) key* is a column or combination of columns in a database table that references the primary key of another table in the database. The `Customer_Number` column for example, is a foreign key on the `Customer_Profiles` table, which is a primary key on the `Case_Reports` table.

✔ **Metadata:** A fancy name for data that describes the data structure. Some databases include metadata that describes the layout and relationship of tables in the database.

You store the metadata in the data dictionary, which defines what the tables, columns, indexes, constraints, and so on in the database look like. In the Customer Self-Service Web project, the drop-down list boxes on the New Case form are examples of metadata that describe how the database displays the data from the columns on the tables.

✔ **Schema:** This term is simply another word that you can use for structure or data model. A database *schema* is the structure of the database.

Defining your data dictionary

Almost all software projects have at their hearts a database that stores and retrieves the data that the software manipulates. A well-defined database provides you with swift access to the information that you need and saves each piece of information only once and in a manner that maximizes data access. The *data dictionary* acts as a single repository for the various data elements that you store in your database.

You keep a data dictionary for the following reasons:

✔ **Central repository:** Having a central store for the data elements of the database can avoid finger pointing if half the team thinks that you need to make a data element 11 characters long and the other thinks that you need to make the element 12 characters long. A data dictionary can break such ties. The database administrator needs to take due diligence, therefore, in creating this document. Errors in the data directory can cause much work for everyone involved.

✔ **Database-design tool:** A well-designed relational database stores each piece of information only once and relates that information to other tables (instead of storing a customer's name in multiple tables, for example). Having a list of the various data elements ensures that two different elements aren't saving the same information.

Reference this number in your data model

**Data Dictionary: Customer Self-Service Web
Case Report Form Sample**

Number	Data Element	Type	Size	Edit Mask	Edits/Validations
1	CustomerID	NUM	3	9(3)	Not Null
2	CaseNumber	NUM	10	9(10)	Display Only
3	Customer_Name	CHAR	30	X(30)	Not Null
4	Contact_Name	CHAR	30	X(30)	Not Null
5	Address	CHAR	40	X(40)	Not Null
6	Telephone	NUM	12	999 999 9999	Not Null
7	Email	CHAR	20	X(20)	Optional
8	Product_Mix	CHAR	50	X(50)	Not Null
9	Release_Level	NUM	5	9 9 9	Not Null
10	Server_Hardware	CHAR	20	X(20)	Not Null
12	OS	CHAR	15	X(15)	Not Null
13	DBMS	CHAR	15	X(15)	Not Null
14	Web_Server	CHAR	20	X(20)	Not Null
15	ODBC	CHAR	15	X(15)	Not Null
16	Browser	CHAR	15	X(15)	Not Null
17	FAQ_Number	NUM	10	9(10)	Optional
18	CR_Number	NUM	10	9(10)	Optional
19	Report_Date	DATE	10	99/99/9999	Not Null
20	Issue_Summary	CHAR	200	X(200)	Not Null
21	Issue_Detail	CHAR	1000	X(1000)	Not Null
22	Resolution	CHAR	1000	X(1000)	Not Null
23	Response_Time	NUM	5	99:99	Not Null
24	Resolution_Time	NUM	5	99:99	Not Null
25	Outside_Assitance	CHAR	3	X(3)	Not Null

You can also include whether data element is a primary or secondary key

No hyphens in phone numbers here

Figure 7-1: Every data element of the data dictionary needs to be unique.

✔ **Parallel programming processes:** The creation of a data dictionary enables the team members designing the middle code (which transports the information from the UI to the database and manipulates the data) to create their code at the same time that the database folks are creating the database. Thanks to the data dictionary, they all know the names and size constraints of the database already.

The *Software Project Management Kit For Dummies* CD contains the document Data Dictionary Example.doc. This document provides a sample data dictionary for the Customer Self-Service Web project. Figure 7-2 shows this document. You can use this sample to give you ideas of the types of information to store in the data dictionary for your project.

The fields in the sample data dictionary perform the following functions:

✔ **Number:** This field is a unique number that you use in the data model to quickly cross-reference the information in the data dictionary. You use numbers as unique identifiers of metadata, such as each data element in the data dictionary. (Please refer to the definitions of data model, data dictionary, and metadata in the preceding section.)

✔ **Data Element:** This field contains the name of the element as it appears in the database and to which you can made external calls.

✔ **Type:** This field describes the data type of the database field, such as numeric, string, Boolean, and so on.

✔ **Size:** This field describes the maximum field length as a measurement in characters.

✔ **Edit Mask:** This field contains special entry information for the UI designers. Notice, for example, that the telephone number in the sample doesn't store the hyphens. The UI designers provide the hyphens in the UI, but everyone agrees that the database doesn't store these characters.

✔ **Constraints:** You use constraints to make sure that the data you enter into your database is valid. Constraints are restrictions on the data before you add it to your database. A common practice, for example, is to define a `Not Null` constraint on those columns (fields) that you determine must contain data. A `Null` value is a data type that you leave undefined.

A field containing no data contains a `Null` value. Keep in mind, however, that a null value is not the same as a blank or zero value. The `Case_Number` column on the New Case form for the Customer Self-Service Web project is a column that you want to define as `Not Null` so that you must always include a data item for each `Case` record.

Data Model for Customer Self-Service Web Project

Database Tables: *There are three tables in data model for the Customer Self-Service Web: Customer_Profile, Case_Reports, and KnowledgeBase_Solutions.*

Table #1: Customer_Profile: Stores basic customer profile data including the following data:

CustomerID: ***Primary Key (PK)***

CaseNumber: ***Secondary Key (SK)***

Name

Address

Telephone

Email

Table #2: Customer_Environment: Stores customer software and hardware environment information including the following data:

CustomerID: *Primary Key (PK)*

Product_Mix

Release_Level

Server_Hardware

Network_Config

OS

DBMS

Web_Server

ODBC

Browser

Back_Office

Figure 7-2: A sample data dictionary for the Customer Self-Service Web project.

Although you can use the form on the CD as a basis for your data dictionary, the needs of your individual project must guide you as to how much information to store in your data dictionary. You may, for example, want to add a field to identify primary, secondary, and foreign keys.

Data-model design

Almost without exception, your data-model design (sometimes known as your *database schema*) serves as the foundation for your application's overall architectural design. Your data-model design is a major source of input for the completion of your software's Functional Specifications and Detailed Design Specifications documents. (I explain these documents in the section "Designing the Data Model," earlier in this chapter.)

As project manager, you probably need at least a high-level understanding of the tasks involved in designing your software's data model. You can leave the detailed design to your development team's database administrator (DBA), who possesses the specialized skill.

The following list describes some high-level tasks that your project team can consider during your meetings:

- ✔ Brainstorm all possible alternative data-model design solutions to the problems that the RD defines.

- ✔ Evaluate the top data-model design proposals that you come up with.

- ✔ Determine which database objects to include in your design by reevaluating the problems and scope as the RD and the PSD define them.

- ✔ Determine the data structures and operations that you need to perform on the data within those structures.

- ✔ Develop a data dictionary for your project.

- ✔ Decide which objects and relationships (the ones that you identify in the third paragraph of this list) you need to define as tables and which you need to make columns and rows.

The *Software Project Management Kit For Dummies* CD contains the document Data Model Example.doc, as shown in Figure 7-3. This document provides a sample data model for the Customer Self-Service Web project example. Use this document as a guide for building a data model for your project.

Data Model for Customer Self-Service Web Project

Table #3: Case_Reports: Stores cases (issue reports) received from Customers.

Case_Number: Primary Key (PK):

FAQ_Number : Secondary Key (SK)- Establishes relationship between the Case_Reports and KnowledgeBase_Solutions tables.

Report_Date

Issue_Summary

Issue_Detail

Resolution

Priority

ChangeRequest_Number

Table #4: KnowledgeBase_Solutions: Stores solutions to previously reported known issues including summary of the solution.

FAQ_Number: Primary Key (PK)-Establishes relationship between the

Case_Reports and KnowledgeBase_Solutions tables.

Case_Number: Secondary Key (SK)

CR_Number (SK)

Issue_Summary

Issue_Detail

Resolution

Table #5: Change_Requests: Stores reproduced product defects and product enhancement requests.

CR_Number: Primary Key (PK)

Case_Number (SK)

Issue_Summary

Issue_Detail

Resolution

Priority

Assigned_To

Status

Figure 7-3: A sample data model for the Customer Self-Service Web project.

After you put your data-model design on paper, you're ready to create the final output for this design stage: the Entity Relationship Diagram (ERD). This diagram depicts the data model graphically so that designers can understand at a glance how you use and retain data within your program. You can create this diagram by using software tools such as Power Designer or Visio Professional, or you can use a simple tool such as Microsoft Paintbrush.

You use the ERD as a basis for later documents that you create in the design stage, as well as for the actual implementation of your program by the developers.

Laying Out the Functional Architecture

As you go about designing your project's functional architecture, you focus on three components: the *user interface (UI)*, the *information-flow model,* and the *prototype*. The following sections describe these three components.

Modeling the user interface

The user interface (UI) is the "look and feel" of your software as far as concerns the end user. It's also the program element that your customers use in comparing your software with that of any competition's. As the sales-and-marketing department demos your product to potential customers, the user interface gives customers their first impressions of your product — and goes a long way toward determining whether they want to buy it.

Depending on your own company's priorities, however, you may not perform any fine-tuning on the user interface in its late beta stage. For some companies, a spiffy looking UI isn't really a high priority; they'd rather you spend your project time increasing the application's functionality than merely making it look nice.

Your goal in this part of the design phase is to make the best first impression possible, enabling your product to outdistance the competition. Your user interface can include anything from screen and form colors to frames (for Web-based applications), graphics, icons, drop-down lists, radio buttons, menus, and workflow processes.

A major selling point particularly with the recent explosion of Web self-service and e-Commerce applications are workflow processes that you build into the UI. You design these processes to model improved business practices that you can customize to your particular customers' needs. The Customer

Self-Service Web application, for example, includes workflow processes and steps for escalating "hot" customer issues through a customer-service organization for efficient and effective resolution.

Your tool for modeling your user interface is known as a *user-interface model*, which describes the flow of data and the screens that the user sees. In many ways, the user-interface model is what separates a good application from a bad one.

You typically create a user-interface model first as a series of drawings that describe screens, dialog boxes, menus, and so on. You often depict these elements in some hierarchical fashion so that team members who later use the model can see the normal progression of the user through the interface. A well-designed user-interface model can greatly speed up later development of your application.

You and your team can create your initial user-interface model as sketches on paper, but after that, you may want to get a professional graphic artist to create the final, color interface model.

Entire books cover the issue of designing user interfaces, so, as you can imagine, the coverage of the topic in this book isn't comprehensive. An excellent reference book on this GUI subject is *GUI Design For Dummies,* by Laura Arlov, published by IDG Books Worldwide, Inc. I can, however, pass along the following guidelines for you to keep in mind as you oversee the development of the user interface:

✔ Match the interface to your customer's expectations.

✔ Plan a logical menu structure.

✔ Create multiple ways to accomplish tasks.

✔ Utilize familiar conventions.

✔ Develop an uncluttered interface.

✔ Be consistent.

✔ Design your interface so that the user can customize it.

The following sections explain these important considerations and what they can mean for your interface.

Meeting customer expectations

Your customers have expectations about the interface you develop even if you fail to uncover these expectations during the research, analysis, and design stages of your project. They probably base their expectations on two elements: the type of operating system they use and the perceived genre of your software.

If you spend any amount of time working on different computer systems, you're probably well aware of the differences between operating systems. Mac users do things a bit differently than do Windows users, and UNIX users do everything differently (nothing against UNIX users, of course).

The point is that if you're developing a program for use on a Windows system, the interface needs to include many of the same characteristics as do other Windows programs. These characteristics probably include the use of menus, tool bars, context-sensitive menus, and dialog boxes. Your design also needs to take into account items such as a two-button mouse. If you're designing the program for Mac users, it can contain some of the same elements but may also include Help balloons, command keys, and items for a single-button mouse. You get the idea, right?

As for the software genre, your user interface needs to reflect what users expect in programs that they may view as similar to yours. If your program involves entering financial data, for example, you may want to include elements similar to those that other financial software interfaces use. Similarly, if your program includes some sort of word-processing feature, you want the interface to mimic popular word-processing interface features.

The reasoning behind mimicking popular interfaces and features is that doing so enhances the chance that your customers are immediately comfortable with your software. Attaining such a level of comfort is a very good thing — it decreases the amount of training time necessary and makes the customer more immediately productive.

Developing a logical menu structure

Although you may provide different ways to access the same commands, your menus comprise the black-and-white roadmap to your program. If your users don't understand what a toolbar button does, they're going to look through the menu to find out how to accomplish a command. You need to spend sufficient time with your menus, therefore, to make sure that you lay them out in a logical structure.

Make sure that you group similar functions in a series of top-level menus. Users of particular operating systems expect to see certain top-level menus. Most Windows users, for example, expect to see File, Edit, and Help menus in every program. Depending on the program, you may also need to include a Format menu and others. Take time to study your commands and create a simple, logical menu structure.

The Customer Self-Service Web application's UI may, for example, include a top-level Case Reports menu with submenus for adding, updating, and deleting case reports. You also may incorporate a top-level menu for Case Reports, with several submenus for the various case-management reporting metrics, including daily total cases that a customer-service representative opens/closes, total escalated cases, average response and resolution times, total number of complaints, and so on.

A user-friendly UI design enables the user to intuitively navigate from the appropriate top-level menu down to the appropriate Web input and listing forms to perform the desired transactions.

Another important point is to make sure that the user doesn't need to navigate through too many menu levels. If your user must navigate through more than three levels, your menus need restructuring. Take the time to do so right up front.

If you're developing a Web-based application, your "menu" structure isn't the same as in non-Web-based applications. Instead, you replace the menus with a *navigation sequence*. The sequence of pages through which the user navigates is critical, because it defines the entire user experience with your program. Make sure that you divide your application into a logical series of pages through which the user can navigate easily and quickly. Again, the three-level rule still holds: Make sure that the user can accomplish any task or reach any desired information in no more than three clicks.

In using the Customer Self-Service Web application, for example, I've optimally designed the UI so that I can accomplish the task of adding a new customer case-report task in only *three* clicks instead of *23!*

Establishing multiple ways to the same feature

Every program includes a series of commands, and those commands differ according to the needs of the program. You may include commands to create a new document, copy information, transfer data, connect to a network, or delete expired data. The list goes on and on.

Don't underestimate the necessity of devising different ways to accomplish the same command. You may, for example, make the same command accessible through a menu, a toolbar button, and a shortcut key on the keyboard. Some commands you may also make accessible through different dialog boxes.

The reasoning behind this "multiple-door" approach to commands is quite simple: You're making allowances for different work styles in your users. Some people feel comfortable using menus, while others want to use the keyboard. By providing different methods of accessing a command, you leave the decision on which method to use up to your customers. Because they can access the command by using the methods that they prefer, they're happier with the user interface. (And you come off looking like a thoughtful developer.)

Using familiar paradigms

Which way do you prefer to enter information to appear on a computer-generated check: in a dialog box or on a form that looks like the final check? (Oh, I forgot. You're flexible and can easily adapt to either input paradigm.)

Well, even if *you* don't have a preference, your customer probably does. You need to use familiar symbols, such as icons on a menu or toolbar (for example, a printer icon on the toolbar) in designing your user interface. Why? Because if you do, the user's immediately familiar with that portion of your interface and feels more comfortable using it. Greater comfort translates to greater satisfaction.

Understand, however, that you tread a fine line here. If you're gathering information that's going to end up in a custom report, for example, your input form needn't look like that report. Your users probably aren't familiar with how the report is supposed to look, and the design is thus lost on them.

You also don't want to make your UI too "cute." You don't want to implement certain conventions if the overall perception of professionalism in your interface suffers as a result. Adding inconsistent fonts, for example, offers an unprofessional first impression to your customer-user community. Oh, and Microsoft Bob — need I say more?

You need, therefore, to develop a keen awareness not only of the symbols that the user is likely to recognize (for example, the printer icon on a toolbar), but also of how you expect the user to perceive your application's UI. Throw these two elements into a blender, and you can probably come up with a user interface exhibiting just the right mix to enhance the user's experience.

Uncluttering the interface

Have you ever used a program that bombards you with on-screen information? Overwhelming people with information and thereby making your program difficult to use is all too easy if you're not careful.

Good user-interface design dictates that you strike a fine balance between too little information and too much. Keeping such a balance can prove difficult at times, but the rewards of doing so are well worth the effort.

So how do you handle excess information that you can't put on-screen? If the information is important to the user, you may want to make it available in a separate dialog box or accessible through a menu option. Or you can divide up the information in a single dialog box by placing it on different tabs (common in Windows environments) or separating it into a series of steps that present in different dialog boxes (such as you do with a wizard).

Creating a consistent interface

Consistency is key to a successful user interface. The best guideline that I can give you here is to use the *principal of least perplexity* — that is, never, ever surprise the end user. Always assume that your end user is uncomfortable with technology. No matter how cleverly you design a particular screen, if it doesn't fit seamlessly with other screens in your application, the screen ultimately detracts from the product.

As you develop the user interface, make sure that different interface elements (such as screens, dialog boxes, and prompts) display the same look and feel throughout the application. Present queries for user input consistently and treat capitalization and punctuation in a consistent manner. Even the fonts that you use in the interface best serve the user if you keep them consistent.

Consistency is one of the biggest elements that contributes to a sense of simplicity. If your design is consistent and well executed, the user gets the feeling that your program is easy to use. If your program is inconsistent — even if other design elements are well done — the user becomes confused while using the application, and productivity suffers.

Customizing the user interface

Understanding that every user is different, many program designers enable users to customize what they see on the interface. Users can add tools to or remove them from the toolbars, move the toolbars around the screen, change or delete menus entirely, and size windows to any dimension imaginable.

I grant you that only advanced users typically customize a user interface. But you're sure to have a certain number of such users in your customer pool. After they use your program for a time, they may question why they can't put their toolbar tools in a different order. Be careful to caution your customers not to give every Dick or Jane User update authority to change the UI at will — and to document that warning. Those engaging in any customization of the UI need to undergo extensive adaptation training and must possess the requisite skill set for such a task. Giving full rein to the entire customer-user community to change the UI just opens up the high-risk situation of jeopardizing your software's integrity and stability! This freedom may end up proving very expensive to support as well.

Depending on how you approach it from a developmental standpoint, however, building into a program a certain level of customizability (hmmm, is that a word?) can prove relatively easy. Instead of "hard-coding" your menus and toolbars in your application code so that the users can't customize, say, the order of icons on your toolbar, construct them to use information in a configuration file from the metadata in your database. Your program reads the file that accesses the configuration file that the data dictionary defines and builds the menus and toolbars on the fly rather than statically from code that you cast in stone.

All you then need to do is provide a way for the user to modify the configuration file. The next time that your program reads the file, it reads the customer's modified configuration file.

Whenever you build customization into your interface, you need to provide a way for the customer to reset everything back to its default condition. You can do so by including a simple button in a dialog box that, after the user clicks it, rewrites the configuration files to their beginning state. Such a button can save you tons of support time if any users accidentally screw up their interfaces completely.

If you're on a tight development schedule, you may not want to build interface-customization capabilities into your program in the first version. Although you may plan such a feature for a future release, you can at least start planning for it early on in the project so that the job of creating the feature later is easier. You still may use configuration files to create menus and toolbars, for example, but you may not give the user a way to change the files in the first version of the program. As you add on that capability later, you don't need to make huge changes to your main program; you simply must add the user configuration module.

Designing the information-flow model

Another task that you need to complete during the design phase is to design the *information-flow model* (sometimes called the workflow model). This model lies at the center of your software's architectural design process. It details the flow of information (data) through the program, focusing on all points of input, process, and output. You model the workflow model in the Data Flow Diagram (DFD), as shown in Figure 7-4.

An information-flow model that replicates some theoretical data flow that you and your programmers visualize in a vacuum is insufficient. This model must also reflect the requirements of an implementation of your software at a typical customer's site. Thus you and your team need to again review the RD and PSD to make sure that your model reflects what the customer wants the software to do.

Another requirement to consider in designing this model is that you need to integrate your application with the rest of your company's application suite (if applicable). You want also to model any potential interface and integration opportunities for your software with third-party applications. Doing so may mean bringing in people outside your normal development team — even external consultants — who are experts in the other software that your own program may affect. If your software is to interface with other programs, make sure that you spend a good deal of time on the interface between your program and the other systems. Pay particular attention to how and in what format the data is to flow through the interface.

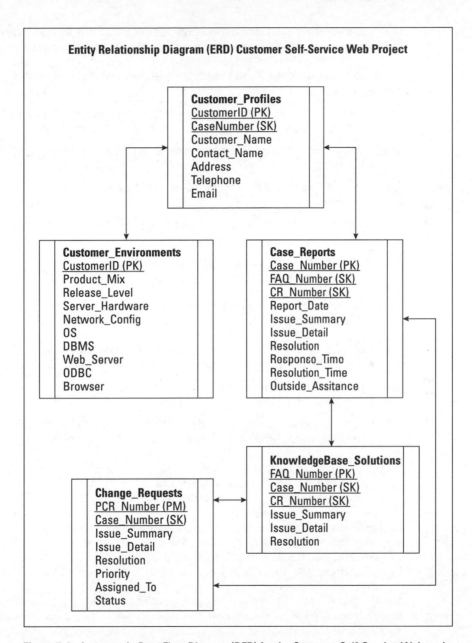

Figure 7-4: An example Data Flow Diagram (DFD) for the Customer Self-Service Web project.

In putting together the information-flow model, you want to make sure that it contains several different elements, as the following list describes:

- **Input information:** Data items that the user enters in the software application.

- **Processes:** The software activities of transforming input information into the form of output information.

- **Output information:** The processed information that your application creates.

- **External entities:** An information source that's external to your application.

- **Internal entities** An information source (typically a program module) that's a part of your application.

- **Data Stores:** A holder of information (data) that you store for future transformation by one or more processes of your application.

The following are some high-level tasks that your development team can accomplish during your meetings in relation to the information-flow model:

- Brainstorm all possible alternative information-flow-model design solutions to the problems that the RD, data-model design, and ERD define.

- Evaluate the top information-flow-model design proposals to determine the best one for your project according to the PSD.

- Determine which input and output information, processes, internal and external entities, and data stores to include in the model.

As you create your information-flow model, you also create a *Data Flow Diagram (DFD)*. This diagram is a graphical representation of your information-flow model. Figure 7-5 shows an example of the DFD.

Feel free to check out the document Data Flow Diagram Example.doc on the *Software Project Management Kit For Dummies* CD. I used Microsoft Word to prepare this document, but you may want to consider using a specialized flow-charting program such as Visio to create complex Data Flow Diagrams.

Notice that the DFD shows each component of the information-flow model and indicates in which direction information flows through the component. You want to make sure that your DFD reflects exactly how you anticipate data flowing in your project, because you use this information as a basis for development and testing of your software's overall design, prototype, and final general availability (GA) build going forward.

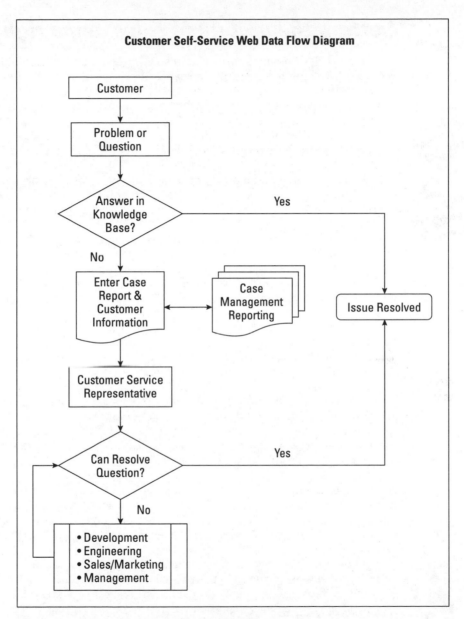

Figure 7-5: An example Data Flow Diagram (DFD) for the Customer Self-Service Web project.

Getting the prototype sales demo right

Because the development of the actual software typically takes months or decades, developing demo prototypes is critical. (Just kidding about decades. Everyone knows that software projects don't take longer than a year or two — unless you work for the government.)

To give you an idea of where to start with a prototype, check out the early prototype example for the Customer Self-Service Web project on the CD.

One possible source of the prototype's generation is your research and development department, if you have one. R&D can create the prototype and also lay the foundation for the software architectural design going forward.

The major advantage of creating a demo now — in the design phase instead of waiting until the development phase — is the opportunity to obtain feedback from your sales team. Members of your sales-and-marketing department are typically in close contact with your customers and can, therefore, demo your software to customers.

You then can receive customer feedback as to whether you're on the right track before you waste a lot of time developing the wrong solution to the customer's problem. This way, by the time that your team's ready to begin developing the actual software, many of the kinks are already worked out.

The objective of your prototype design is to determine whether your project's overall architectural design satisfies the demands of the RD. To meet this objective, you needn't create every field and button on the application's screens. You instead want to focus your prototyping effort on the most complex and user-*un*friendly areas of the software.

Alternatively, alpha or beta releases may need to serve this demo function instead of a separate prototype. Creating a prototype may not be feasible if resources are relatively limited (such as in a company where developers are working on different versions and for different operating systems).

You gain more by finding out which elements of your prototype *don't* meet your customers' needs early in the process — while you can still fix them — than you gain by attempting to get your customers' heads to nod. So show your customers the areas that you and your team are the least sure of. Painful as it may be, you're really better off making the decision to scrap a project early and cheaply rather than later and expensively if you can't devise an adequate solution to your customers' problems.

Start with storyboards before doing any actual coding. Storyboarding enables your team to lay out prototypical screens and fields, as well as to model the flow of information via the screens and workflow processing. The storyboarding process is where you are creating a "cardboard" model of what the final software UI, data model, and information model is suppose to look like.

Think of how architects carefully model a scale mockup of a complex office building prior to beginning construction. Your team members must be certain that they understand all the technical and functional issues of the project before moving to the development phase, in which they actually build the various parts of the software.

If you have sufficient time and resources, then you want to ensure that the entire team, including sales and marketing, have carefully considered the customer's requirements prior to building the prototype and beginning development. You should carefully plan how you intend to deal with any design issues that may arise.

Be sure to document the detailed components of your prototype design (for example, its submenus, buttons, toolbars, forms, fields, online Help documents, fonts, and so on) in a working version of the Functional Specifications document. Continually update this document as your plan progresses.

Keep in mind that at the time that you initially draw up the Functional Specifications, you may be facing quite a few unknown design issues that you can often flesh out later. This practice enables your team to review smaller chunks of the prototype frequently — before the prototype design gets out of control!

Following are some recommended questions to ask during your team's meetings concerning the prototype's design process:

- How difficult is adding additional software components to this design?
- Is this prototype's design consistent with your organization's development processes and procedures?
- Does the prototype work well enough for a sales demo?
- How simple is the design? (Is it user friendly?)
- How easy does the information (data) flow?
- Does the prototype design solve the customer's problem that the RD describes?
- Are your customers eager to buy your software after the sales demo?

Writing the Functional Specifications

The *Functional Specifications document* is a high-level design document. You use the Requirements Document, the Project Scope Document, and the on-going feedback from the prototype as your primary input in creating this document. The Functional Specifications document serves the following functions:

- **Explains explicitly how you're meeting the customer's requirements:** You provide this explanation in much greater detail in the Functional Specifications document than you do in earlier documents, such as the RD and PSD.

- **Documents which requirements of the RD are within/outside the project's scope:** You can take this portion of the Functional Specifications almost directly from the PSD.

- **Describes how you intend to build the product:** You can use an amalgamation of the information that you develop in earlier documents to create this description.

- **Defines the specifics of the user interface of the product:** You can accomplish this portion of the document simply by including the user interface model, as you develop it in the section "Laying Out the Functional Architecture," earlier in this chapter.

- **Defines consistent user interface rules and recommendations:** Again, you can provide this information by including the user-interface model.

- **Explains how users can access information and navigate throughout the software's functions:** This is another element that you can pull from the user-interface model.

You may wonder how these elements in the Functional Specifications differ from those in the earlier documents such as the Requirements Document and Project Scope Document that you create for the project. In truth, they don't differ that much. Instead, they represent a "final version" of the documents and models that create to this point. The Functional Specifications document becomes a one-stop information source for those wanting to see the final high-level specifications for your project.

The Functional Specifications document provides a high-level design of your software's feature set. Thus they're for the "bottom-line" managerial types in your organization. Although the document can get quite voluminous, it's still not at the level of technical detail that your developers require for use. You leave those smaller (technical) design details to the Detailed Design Specifications document, as I describe in the section "Compiling the Detailed Design Specifications," later in this chapter.

In some cases, the Functional Specifications document serves as a contract and warranty between you (the software vendor) and the customer. It becomes the formal document that describes what you're doing and how you plan to go about it.

If you aren't quite sure where to start with your Functional Specifications document, you may be very happy to discover that a template for such a document (Functional Specifications.dot) appears on the *Software Project Management Kit For Dummies* CD. Create a new Microsoft Word document by using the template, and you're ready to hit the ground running.

In reality, you want the Functional Specifications to contain any high-level information that you feel is pertinent to the development and completion of your project. The following are just a few of the many different items that you may consider including on such a document:

- Project overview
- Primary functions
- Component descriptions
- Publications
- System requirements
- Installation procedure
- System integration and migration compatibility
- Support and maintenance
- Security
- Contract terms and conditions
- Sign-off sheets

The Functional Specifications document can become quite long. Figure 7-6 shows just the beginning of a Functional Specifications document — in this case, one for the Customer Self-Service Web project.

The Functional Specifications document requires both a technical and a functional sign off. Typically, the functional architect (if you have one), product-marketing manager, project manager (you), project sponsor, and a customer representative are responsible for signing off on this document.

Customer Self-Service Web Documentation Plan

Publications List

Instructions: *The documentation set for a software project can include many items. Select which of the following items will be included in your documentation. Make your selections in the provided boxes in the "Printed" and "Online" columns.*

Printed	Online	Publication
☑	☑	Release Notes
☑	☐	Installation Instructions
☐	☐	New Product Enhancements
☐	☐	Fixed Bugs
☐	☐	Known Issues
☑	☑	User Guide
☐	☐	Administrator Guide
☑	☑	Implementation Guide
☑	☑	Adaption Guide
☑	☐	Customer Acceptance Test Procedure

Publication Standards

Instructions: *Specify which standards will be followed in the development of each publication in the documentation set.*

- All publications will be designed and developed according to the requirements and detailed design specifications specified in the Requirements Document.

- Internal writers will be utilized, but copy editing and technical editing will be done by external freelancers under non-disclosure agreements.

- Standard in-house word processing templates will be used to standardize format of text files.

- All writers, reviewers, and editors will use the latest edition of *Chicago Manual of Style* as their basis for writing and editing. In addition, a project style guide will be developed to handle special needs of this particular project.

- All writers, reviewers, and editors will use a standard glossary of technical terminology.

Figure 7-6: A Functional Specifications document for the Customer Self-Service Web project — page 2 of 14.

Writing the Documentation Plan

Every good piece of software includes some sort of documentation. Documentation can make or break your product's success, as it offers your customers their first impression in evaluating the quality of your software — and, of course, the successful installation and implementation of your software at customer sites rely on the clarity and thoroughness of its documentation.

For some software, you provide the documentation online; for other programs, you provide it in a printed manual. Either way, the documentation is an absolutely essential component of the product. Superior documentation can make the difference in having a highly educated customer-user community, while also decreasing your tech-support load.

Before you begin writing the documentation for your product, you need to develop what's known as a *Documentation Plan*. This plan needs to accomplish several important functions, as the following list describes:

✔ It provides an overview of the product to document.

✔ It lays out a proposed approach to the documentation.

✔ It defines the document review and editing process.

✔ It lists the documentation deliverables to create.

The approach you take to documentation necessarily varies, depending on the needs both of your project and of the end user. A typical Documentation Plan may include the following deliverables:

✔ **Release Notes:** A summary of the software release's functionality, new features, enhancements, and bug fixes.

✔ **Installation Instructions:** Step-by-step installation directions, including any known issues, bugs, and work-arounds. If you intend your software for multiple hardware platforms, you need to develop installation instructions for each platform.

✔ **User Guide:** General product information for the end user. This part of the documentation is where you step users through each of the functions of the software and describe how to use them.

✔ **Implementation/Adaptation Guide:** Instructions and/or guidelines on how to integrate the software into a normal work routine. If the user can customize the software, this section also includes instructions on how to do so.

✔ **Online Help:** As a supplement and/or substitute for the preceding components, mature software companies often provide customers with an electronic medium of documentation accessible via a software menu item. Sometimes this supplement is simply an electronic version of any print documentation that you provide.

✓ **Customer Acceptance Test Plan:** A series of steps that the customer can follow to confirm that the installation is successful. The sole purpose of this test plan is to enable your software company to justify customer revenue on the basis of successful installations. This test is not a substitute for a complete Software Quality Assurance (SQA) system test, which occurs before you release the software to the customer.

Understand that this list of deliverables is not exhaustive. Feel free to add and omit items as applicable to your software project.

You can begin writing your documentation plan by using a template (Documentation Plan.dot) on the *Software Project Management Kit For Dummies* CD. An example of a completed documentation plan is shown in Figure 7-7.

Compiling the Detailed Design Specifications

A Functional Specifications document alone usually isn't enough for programmers to use as a guide in creating a new program, because the Functional Specifications document is such a high-level software design document. I strongly recommend that you also create a *Detailed Design Specifications* document. You may find that thinking of the Functional Specifications document as a high-level outline and thinking of the Detailed Design Specifications document as the detailed outline clarifies the difference between the two in your mind.

You use most of the documents that you create up to this point as your basis for creating the Detailed Design Specifications document. Primarily, this document consists of the Functional Specifications, along with the following components:

✓ User-interface model

✓ Data model

✓ Data dictionary

✓ Entity Relationship Diagram (ERD)

✓ Information-flow (workflow) model

✓ Data Flow Diagram (DFD)

✓ Project prototype

✓ Documentation Plan

✓ Training curriculum

Development Procedures

Instructions: *Indicate the general development process that will be followed by each publication in the documentation set. If there are different development paths for different elements, be specific for the elements that are different.*

- Writers receive basis materials from development team

- Writers create first draft

- In-house review of first draft

- Technical edit (external)

- Copy edit (external)

- Copy editor prepares second draft

- In-house review of second draft

- Writers prepare documentation for beta test of software

- Writers prepare online version of documentation set for beta test

- Writers receive feedback from development team on beta test changes

- Writers revise documentation based on changes

- Copy edit (external)

- Copy editor prepares final draft

- In-house review of final draft

- Writers send documentation set to production for manufacturing

- Writers prepare final online version of documentation set

- Writers send online documentation set to development team

Figure 7-7: A sample Documentation Plan for the Customer Self-Service Web project.

I explain each of these documents at some point earlier in this book, many of them in this chapter. In addition to these existing documents, the Detailed Design Specifications also contain a number of unique elements that are essential to the programmers completing their work, as the following list describes:

- ✔ **Tools and conventions:** A listing of the different software tools (development packages, and so on) that the development team needs. This section also contains a list of the standards and conventions that the team is to follow on the project. You can often cull these standards from the best practices that a corporation develops over time.

- ✔ **Reuse analysis:** In the section, "Reusing Code Instead of Reinventing the Wheel," earlier in this chapter, you examine the objects that earlier programming projects created. This document is where you list those objects that you plan to reuse. You want not only to list the object, but also to include any location data for the latest versions of the objects, interface specifications for the objects, and perhaps a listing of their coding. You can also list here any objects that you're going to use from third-party sources.

- ✔ **Files and tables:** You can develop the information in this section primarily from the data model. Here you specifically list the files and data tables that you're going to create for your software application.

- ✔ **Error handling:** This section lists any special error-handling considerations for your project. You want to take special care to detail the conditions that may arise and how you intend to handle them.

By the time that you finish compiling the Detailed Design Specifications, the document can end up very long. Fortunately, most of the document consists of existing documents you already created. The purpose of compiling these existing documents (and the new sections) is that you then have all the details about creating your project in one place.

If you want a template for your own Detailed Design Specifications, you can find one on the *Software Project Management Kit For Dummies* CD: Detailed Design Specifications.dot. You can also look at a sample document that I completed.

As project manager, you need to ensure that the Detailed Design Specifications document contains enough detail to enable the actual development of the project to begin. As an example, Figure 7-8 shows an acceptable level of detail for information on a user-input screen.

Notice that the table shows the prompts the user must face, along with guidelines for what constitutes an acceptable response and other comments that may affect development. You may develop similarly detailed tables for every other object in your design.

Customer Self-Service Web Case Entry Form

Company:

Contact Name:

Email Address:

Phone:

Fax:

Issue Summary: [Provide one-line summary of issue, i.e. **Ask Questions/Define Problem**.]

Issue Detail: [Provide detailed description of issue, including exact steps to reproduce problem and specific error message(s).]

Release: [1.0, 1.1, 2.0, 2.1, etc.]

Liscensed Products: Problem Module: [Choose from Marketing's list of Licensed Products]

Hardware: [Pentium 4, Sun Sparc, etc.]

Network Platforms: [Ethernet 10MB (100MB, or 1000MB)]

Operating System (OS): [NT 4.0, Sun Solaris 2.5.1 (2.6), HP-UX 10.1, etc.]

Web Server: [Netscape Enterprise Server 3.0, Microsoft Internet Information Server (IIS) 4.0, O'Reilly WebSite, Other CGI-compliant HTTP Server (e.g. Apache, etc.)]

ODBC Drivers: [NT - Oracle 2.5.3.1.0, Sun Solaris - Intersolv 3.0 (3.01), HP-UX - Intersolv 3.0, Sybase - Intersolv 3.x, Informix - Intersolv 3.x]

DBMS (Server): [Oracle 8.1.x (7.3.4), Microsoft SQL Server 7.0 (6.5), Sybase 12.xx (11.xx), Informix, other ANSI-compliant ODBC-accessible Database]

Source System:

Priority:

       1 - Critical - Production Down (Resolved w/in 8 business hours)
       2 - Seriously Impaired - system slowdown (Resolved w/in 1-3 business days)
       3 - Normal - Development/Implementation (Resolved w/in 1 business week)
       4 - Low - Information Request (Resolved w/in 1 business week)

Solution: [HOW to fix problem, work around – if known.]

Change Request (CR) Number: [Development/Engineering Problem Report# – if duplicable bug or Enhancement Request]

Response Time: [For Customer Support Center's internal use only]

Resolution Time: [For Customer Support Center's internal use only]

Outside Assistance: [Y/N] [For Customer Support Center's internal use only]

Figure 7-8: An example of Detailed Design Specifications for the layout of a user-input form.

Writing the Test Plans

Testing is, of course, an integral part of any software development project. As you're designing your software, you generally need to concern yourself with two test plans: the *beta-test plan,* and the *Software Quality Assurance (SQA)* test plan.

Beta-test plan

As you discover in Chapter 8, *beta testing* occurs after your software is complete enough and stable enough that you can release it to external personnel for testing. During the design phase of the project cycle, you need to create a detailed beta-test plan. This plan needs to include the following elements:

- **Indication of who's participating in the beta test:** This element is either a list of customers or external testers or some other method of indicating how many "general-public" testers you intend to seek. If the latter is how you plan to beta-test your software, you also need to include some criteria for beta testers to meet.

- **Customer test matrix:** This element is nothing more than an indication of which customers are to test which features. This test matrix is particularly important if you know at plan time exactly who are your beta testers.

- **Beta-tester agreements:** This element includes all the legal documents that your company requires beta testers to sign. Typically, it's a statement of what you expect the testers to do, along with a nondisclosure agreement to prevent testers from giving away copies of the beta.

- **Documentation:** This element consists of the actual documentation that you're including with the beta release. This set of documents can be a subset of the final documentation that you plan to include with the actual product. You also want it to include instructions that you expect the beta tester to follow, along with information on how your beta customers are to report software bugs that they discover and their test results to your team and/or customer-support department.

- **Beta-distribution plan:** You need to determine how your beta-release software gets into the hands of the testers. This element provides that information.

- **Resources the test requires:** This element specifies the resources that the beta test requires. These resources include not only personnel, but also phone lines, e-mail accounts, response packets, and perhaps a Web site.

- **Beta-support plan:** This element indicates how your group plans to support beta testers if they experience problems.

✔ **Reporting and tracking procedures:** This element serves as a framework for testers to follow in making their reports to your group and for you to follow up on those reports.

✔ **Schedule:** The beta plan needs to include some sort of schedule that you expect beta testers to use — for example, how long do you expect testers to take in finishing their base tests? When do you need them to return their responses to you?

✔ **Exit criteria:** This element is a checklist indicating benchmarks that testers must meet during the beta-release period. After the checklist is complete, the beta testing is over.

Software Quality Assurance test plan

A *Software Quality Assurance (SQA)* test plan is a suite of test cases that you use for testing the quality of your software so that the product meet certain level of quality before the release finally becomes available to your customers. An SQA test plan typically includes the following elements:

✔ **Functions and features to test:** Notice that this element is just a list of functions and features and not step-by-step instructions on how to test them. You want to rely on the testers to come up with the "how," just as end users do.

✔ **Hardware, software, and data test requirements:** The hardware and software components need to match, very closely, the final system requirements for your software. The data test requirements may actually comprise the benchmark data that you want the testers to use with the software.

✔ **Setup instructions:** Tell the testers how to install the software and configure it for their testing purposes. You may, for example, have special monitoring software that runs in conjunction with the software they're testing. The testers need to know how to install and configure not only your software, but also the monitoring software.

✔ **Entrance and exit criteria:** Indicate when the SQA tests are to start and how to tell that they're complete.

✔ **Types of testing to conduct:** You want to include a list of specific tests for the SQA testers to complete. If your software processes transaction records, for example, you may specify that you want them to test the software at intervals of 100 transactions for loads between 100 and 10,000 transactions. You may also want testing of other elements, such as installation; documentation; functionality; compatibility; recovery characteristics; performance, security, multi-user, multitasking, and interface standards; and automation.

✔ **Defect-reporting procedure:** How are testers to correctly log and submit any defects that they encounter?

✔ **Defect-resolution procedure:** How is your development team to handle defects that the testers report?

I cover the process of developing an SQA test plan in detail in Chapter 9.

Chapter 8

Developing the Front End, Middle, and Back End

*A*fter you finish the requirements gathering, analysis, and design phases, you're finally ready to start the coding of your software's front, middle, and back end. The start of this phase marks the moment your project team most anxiously awaits, having patiently endured the three most grueling phases of the software-development cycle. You're now ready to dive into the deep end of the pool and begin your actual coding, the part of the process in which your project plans become reality!

Your software's *front end* consists of the *user interface (UI)* or *graphical user interface (GUI)*. The only technical difference between these two types of interfaces is that one is graphical . . . and the other may not be (though in most software circles, you refer to all user interfaces, graphical and otherwise, as the UI). Most software development these days, however, includes some sort of UI, which defines your application's look and feel. In the PC environment, the UI includes the Windows menu bars, graphics, buttons, and much more. The *middle* of your software is the *software code* and *information model*. The middle incorporates everything hiding under the covers of the UI. The *back end* is the *data model* — the database, tables, columns, domains, and so on that you use to make your software work.

In this chapter, you begin work on the development phase of your project, which is the fourth in the cycle of the seven phases that I present in Chapter 1. You may think that beginning the actual hands-on coding so late in the process is a strange way to organize your project, but the hard work (and the time) that you put into the phases prior to this one should significantly reduce the amount of time that you need to complete this phase.

The work that you do in the development phase builds on all your work up to this point. Your development team still needs to intimately involve itself with the Requirements Document (see Chapter 2), the functional requirements (see Chapter 7), and the Detailed Design Specifications (also see Chapter 7).

In essence, this phase is when you buckle down on the assembly line and start cranking out the code. I'm not saying that you want to create a cyber sweat shop and work your team to death. (Kathie Lee would never approve!) You just need to begin thinking of the development of your software in terms of the assembly-line model that Henry Ford used in the production of the first Model-T automobiles. The development of software follows a series of iterative steps, just as the automobile assembly line does.

So get all your anxious developers on the starting line: On your marks; get set — code!

A Common-Sense Development Approach

To minimize your project team's sweat during the development phase, this chapter presents a series of 12 steps that you can view as a common-sense approach to software development. In many ways, these steps parallel the steps that you follow in designing your project. This similarity makes sense, of course, because your design is part of the planning phase, and coding is the implementation of that plan.

These 12 general steps of software development are as follows:

- Revisit the project specifications.
- Evaluate your resources, processes, and environment.
- Plan for effective integration of your software.
- Update the detailed development tasks in Microsoft Project.
- Develop your software modules.
- Unit test your software modules.
- Integrate your software modules.
- Test all levels of integration.

- ✔ Develop the documentation.
- ✔ Perform SQA system testing.
- ✔ Conduct the beta test.
- ✔ Develop your training curriculum.

The following sections describe these steps in greater detail.

Just because I choose to divvy up the work among 12 different steps, however, you don't need to limit yourself to those particular ones. Heck, no — be flexible! Just make sure that the well-thought-out plan that you implement really *is* one that you think through thoroughly. You're free, of course, to add or omit steps from the list that I offer here, as appropriate to your organization's processes and procedures and to the specific needs of your project.

Step 1: Revisit the Project Specifications

Before you create a single line of code or table, I recommend that you conduct a JAD meeting that you dedicate to identifying any changes in your software's original design specifications.

The only people who really need to attend this meeting are your development team members, although you may find that including the project sponsor is helpful. (In fact, your project sponsor may insist on coming.) The purpose of the meeting is to make sure that everyone's on the same page in developing the software.

Remember that your development team is working with documents that you create earlier in the management process. At this point, you may very possibly find differences between the Requirements Document and the Functional Requirements document.

Although the Functional Requirements document represents the "latest and greatest" version of the project, your development team needs to fully understand how and why any changes occur. If they don't, they may think that someone inadvertently left something out of the Functional Requirements and add it back in on their own. This type of situation can negatively affect both your schedule and your resource budgets — bad news for the project manager!

The bottom line is that your software, testing, documentation, and training must rigorously follow the final software blueprint as your Functional Specifications and other design documents embody them. If everyone is working from the same set of plans and using the same assumptions and vision for the project, your job becomes easier.

Step 2: Evaluate Your Resources, Processes, and Environment

Before your project team actually starts coding your software, you, as project manager, need to reevaluate whether you have sufficient resources, appropriate development processes, and an adequate development environment for this phase of the project. The following sections describe how to evaluate these factors.

Evaluating your resources

You've most likely already evaluated your project resources quite well. After all, this process is what you focus on beginning in the phases that I describe in Chapter 5. If a significant amount of time has lapsed between your resource evaluations and the present, however, you may want to again review your resources to make sure that everything's still in line with your original project plan.

A common problem that many project managers share is a tendency to take for granted the availability of human resources. Project managers often include only the best technical people in their project plans. Such planning is great, except that these in-house experts may be working on ten other projects of higher or equal importance to yours. A final check to make sure that those resources are actually available doesn't hurt in the least — and may save you a headache later on.

Whether you're managing a small, medium or large software project, make sure your team is trained to accomplish their tasks. If your project is ongoing or has a huge scope over a wide range of time, you may have more time available to schedule your team members for training opportunities that keep them in top form for your project. Smaller, less-complicated software projects with shorter schedules often don't afford you such a luxury.

Evaluating your development processes

If you work in a well-established company, you probably already have a set of development processes in place. Typically, the Research and Development group plays a pivotal role in the software architecture, development environment, and programming language selection.

Your developmental processes often dictate the intricate details that a company or client requires. The processes may specify, for example, that you conduct all your development work in a *clean room* that unauthorized

Safety in an unsafe world

Your developmental processes need to provide a safety net to recover from things that go wrong during development. You can, for example, specify backup procedures (including a plan for rotating your backups) in your processes. If something goes wrong with a hard drive on a development system, the backups provide the safety net.

Established software organizations have a formal disaster recovery plan in place, which includes uninterrupted power sources (UPSs), daily server backups, and off-site backup storage. UPS software and hardware are implemented to keep the servers up and running in the case of power outages.

Daily backup tapes are created of the critical development servers containing the code, documentation, and sensitive company intranet information. The backup tapes are stored in an offsite fire/earthquake proof facility a distance away from your company's operations. In the event that vital code or information is lost and needs to be recovered, you would pull the latest backup tape from the offsite storage facility to restore the lost code or information on your servers.

personnel can't enter. They may require you to develop projects for online use on an isolated network to avoid public exposure of the project. The development processes may even require adherence to a rigid backup schedule and specify the media for you to use.

The point here is that you need to understand the development processes by which you must live — and you need to make sure that your development team understands and obeys the practices. The processes are generally in place for a reason, and adhering to them saves the project manager unnecessary explanations from a corporate perspective.

If your company doesn't have developmental processes in place, you may want to invest some time into developing them. If no external source (such as the corporation or your client) is imposing guidelines on you, you're free to draw on your own experiences and those of your team members in creating your development processes. Managers who put effective processes into place are often on a fast track up the corporate ladder, so don't hesitate to identify the need for such standards and to start a conversation about them. Be prepared to do the hard work to put them into place, too.

The function of the development process is to define standards that provide your project team the best chance for success and that provide means for useful communication regarding each project's status. The development processes that you ultimately put into place — whether your own or the company's — should provide the necessary framework for measuring and reporting the day-to-day progress of your project and identifying problems as they emerge.

Evaluating your development environment

Your development *environment* is simply that — the daily environment in which your team must perform its work. Some companies may set up special development labs for your work, whereas other companies may expect development to take place at team members' regular workstations.

Regardless of the approach your company or client uses, you (as project manager) must make sure that the environment is conducive to high-quality work. I can't overemphasize, for example, the importance of an automated configuration management system and tightly integrated defect tracking system, processes, and procedures. These tools ensure that code changes and bug reports and fixes are tracked, merged and reconfigured into a clean baseline build for each release iteration.

The development environment can include everything from rooms, heating, ventilation, and lighting to desk height, monitor sizes, and keyboard placement. The environment also includes such intangibles as the programming languages and development tools that your team uses.

One way to determine whether the development environment is adequate is to simply ask your team members. Because they must do the work, they are intimately aware of what they need. Take their recommendations to heart and make the decisions necessary to balance their needs with the needs of the organization as a whole.

Step 3: Plan for Effective Integration of Your Software

The *integration process* is known by different names, depending on the development tools that you use. You call the integration process *assembly* if you're using assembly language, for example, and you call it *compilation* if you're using C++. In any case, integration refers to one of the most basic concepts in software creation — the process of building complex projects by making simpler, individual modules play nicely together. You integrate these pieces, known as *modules,* into a whole that's, you hope, a whole lot greater than the sum of its parts.

The result of the integration process is known as a *build.* Creating a build involves configuring all the project files, objects, and so on that comprise your software product so that they function together correctly — each performing specific duties that the project as a whole needs. During the course of the development cycle, you typically go through the process of configuring new builds several times (possibly even *hundreds* of times) before the ultimate release of your general availability (GA) software.

As you begin the actual development of your software, you need to have an *integration plan* in hand. You use this plan to indicate the different builds of your software that you intend to create. You then release each build to testing, the results of which you then use to help formulate the next build.

In some environments, you use the terms *release* and *build* almost interchangeably. In reality, however, they're a bit different. Releases can include alpha, beta, and GA releases and typically form more of a milestone than a build does. Not every build constitutes a release, but every release consists of a build. Builds include every configuration of your software project from the beginning of development to the integration build to the final GA candidate build that you ultimately release to the customers. For the full skinny on releases, check out the next section.

Understanding software releases

In the software world, different releases often serve as milestones in the development of software. Over the years, developers have given to these milestone releases special names that are now commonly recognized. In general, each release name refers to the level of development of your software code.

The following sections describe some of the more common release names that you use in software development. You may recognize some (or all) of these names depending on any testing in which you've participated. Now, as project manager, you're responsible for determining when each of these same releases happens for your own project.

Pre-alpha release

Technically, the *pre-alpha* "release" isn't a software release at all. This term describes the condition of the software at any point prior to its availability for a primary testing release.

During the pre-alpha stage, many of the necessary software modules are probably complete, but several of the individual modules may still need further development. Additionally, you may need to work out a few kinks in the integration of the individual modules (that is, some modules, like spoiled children, may not play nicely with others at this stage).

Alpha release

An *alpha* release is the earliest actual testing release and reflects code that you use primarily for internal testing. The software may still include a few incomplete modules and the code may not yet be feature-complete, but it's nonetheless ready for a first complete build. (In other words, the modules appear to work with each other.)

The alpha release is ready for submission to your Software Quality Assurance (SQA) testing team for integration testing. Your technical writers can also begin developing the documentation for the software according to the documentation plan.

Pre-beta release

Again, the *pre-beta* "release" is not so much an identified release as it is a stage through which the software passes on its way from alpha to beta.

The software industry's general criterion for determining whether software has truly evolved from alpha to pre-beta is that all the beta requirements are complete, but the software's still not quite ready for beta release. The software may be waiting, for example, on completion of the beta agreements, identification of the beta testers, or some other non-software element.

Beta release

A *beta* release is a bit more complete than an alpha (although still not totally complete) and is what you release to a limited population of beta testers for evaluation. These beta testers are independent testers that your organization doesn't employ. This release represents the first stage at which people outside your company see your project.

Many software projects also refer to a *beta phase*. This term recognizes the fact that software stays in a beta release state until such time as it's ready for general release. (You ship no code before its time.) You may, therefore, have one, two, three, or even more actual beta releases, each undergoing testing in sequential order to assure that the next beta version (build) of the software is getting closer to completion of final GA release for the customers.

Some common criteria for a true beta release may include the following:

- All core features that the Requirements Document and the Functional Requirements identify are complete.
- The major defects that testers identify in the alpha release are eliminated.
- The software is presentable to customers, meaning that the user interface is complete.
- A working first draft of documentation is available to assist users in the use of the major functions of the software application.

Your product-marketing manager probably identifies some of your customers to participate as beta testers, as well as specifying the *beta-exit criteria* (which is what you use to determine when the beta-release phase is complete). An example of beta-exit criteria may be that the software is that the beta testing must include the testing of every major function in the software, before the beta testing is considered completed at a particular beta customer site. You want to identify and plan for beta sites early in the project-management cycle — ideally, during the design phase. (See Chapter 7 for more information about this phase.)

Exceptions do crop up where not all software projects go through a defined beta release. You often skip beta tests in the following situations:

✔ **If you need to rush the software because of market constraints:** Your competition may already have released their software, for example, and you may suffer drastic economic duress if you don't get your software out the door. If forgoing a beta release becomes a detriment to your company's reputation, however, you need to weigh the possible negative publicity resulting from a release that you rush to market against the short-term cash-flow disruption that competition causes.

✔ **If extensive design and development occur:** If the scope of your project is very limited and you take your analysis and design stages very seriously, you can sometimes skip a beta release. You can make this decision early in the planning process in consultation with your development team and project sponsor.

✔ **If you can't identify any particular beta testers:** If the software fills a brand-new niche, you may not have a mature market for it. This situation makes identifying external beta testers difficult. It also means that the internal testers face a heavier burden to identify and isolate all potential software problems.

GA release

GA is an abbreviation for *general availability*. This term describes the condition of your software after your SQA test group and beta testers determine that the software is at a level of quality where you're ready to release it to the community as a whole.

The criteria for GA releases are much more stringent than for alpha or beta releases, including the fixing of all identified bugs that haven't been explicitly relegated to a maintenance release or to the next version. Other components also must be ready and in place for the GA release, including your documentation, packaging (if any), and any internal organizations to support the release.

Integration planning approach

Exactly how you go about creating your integration plan depends, obviously, on the unique nature of your software. By this point in the project management cycle, you usually have a pretty good idea of your software project, as well as the people the project involves (both your development team and those for whom you're developing the software).

By this phase in the project, for example, you can probably determine how many release *milestones* you expect the project to entail. There are seven phases (milestones) to a software project that are provided in this kit, which are introduced in Chapter 1. Within each milestone (phase) you can have a series of *benchmarks*. In completing the Development phase, for example, your benchmarks may include development of the following: units (modules), alpha build, beta build, and integration build.

You can probably also determine whether you can bypass the beta benchmark (stage) entirely. With this knowledge in hand, you want to sit down and figure out a "path" that your software is to follow as it makes its way toward completion. This path is your *integration plan*. The following is an integration plan for a generic software project:

1. **Develop a software module.**

2. **Unit test the software module.**

3. **Identify defects in the module.**

4. **Fix the most urgent and severe bugs that prevent the module from functioning.**

5. **Repeat Steps 1 through 4 until all modules are completed.**

6. **Integrate all modules in a first pre-alpha build.**

7. **Submit the integrated pre-alpha build for integration testing when the alpha build is ready.**

8. **Identify defects in the pre-alpha build.**

9. **Fix bugs to make the pre-alpha build alpha ready.**

10. **Repeat Steps 7 through 9 until the pre-alpha build is ready to be classified as a alpha build.**

11. **Approve the alpha build.**

12. **Integrate all modules into the alpha build.**

13. **Submit the alpha build for Software Quality Assurance (SQA) testing.**

14. **Repeat Steps 1 through 13 for pre-beta and pre-GA (Generally Available) releases.**

These steps are flexible; you want to adapt them to your own specific needs.

Step 4: Update the Detailed Development Tasks in Microsoft Project

By this point, you probably understand that project management is one continuous series of planning, evaluating, replanning, and reevaluating. During all the management phases that I discuss in previous chapters of this book, your team is constantly evaluating the status of different tasks, their schedules, and the resources that you assign to them. As you make any changes in the project, you need also to make sure that you continually update the plan that you develop in Microsoft Project with any new information.

In fact, you may want to make changes in Project before making a final decision. Making these changes in Project enables you to quickly see the effects of a potential change before you commit to it. You can see, for example, what a one-week delay in completion of a particular task does to the final schedule. In fact, the actual result may surprise you — the final effect may take much more than that simple week (or even nothing at all).

The point is that you want to consider Project a tool that you can use in your project management. Don't make the mistake, however, of having Project make your decisions for you (although Microsoft Project's just-a-click-away answers can inform your decisions). You still need to make the final decision for any project changes, basing it on your knowledge of the overall needs of the organization and your development team.

Keep in mind that last-minute changes in the scope of a project inevitably affect what software modules you ultimately develop. Nevertheless, good software-development practice requires you to look to the approved detailed design-specifications document as your final authority. Chapter 7 explains how to develop your Detailed Design Specifications document.

Step 5: Develop Your Software Modules

The development phase of the software project management cycle is often known in high-tech circles as the *implementation phase* or the *construction phase* because your team implements (or constructs) the software from the blueprints that you create during the design phase.

The blueprints for your software's development include the Functional Specifications and Detailed Design Specifications, which you base on input from the Requirements Document. I discuss these documents in Chapters 7 and 2 respectively.

Your project team is developing four primary components: the *data model (schema);* the *information model (workflow);* the *user interface (UI);* and the underlying application *code.* The following sections discuss these components in more detail. Each of these documents is covered in detail in Chapters 7 and 8.

Implementing the data model

In Chapter 7, you find out how to design the data model for your project. This model defines all the Relational Database Management System's (RDBMS) schema requirements that you may need, including domains, data elements, tables, table relationships, demo data, and so on. Most (but not all) software projects include a data-model component.

During the development phase, your database administrator is most likely building your software's data model, basing it on the specifications that you create in the design phase. As project manager, your job (as always) is to make sure that the database administrator builds the model according to the detailed design specs. Your team is likely to stumble across problems as they build the data model. You need to stress that no one can make changes to the model without your knowledge and authorization.

Coding the application

As you develop your software project's application, you focus on each of your program components in turn. Your blueprint is the Detailed Design Specifications that you develop in Chapter 7. As your project's development team codes each portion of the software application, your project evolves from a prototype demo to a real application!

The following several sections detail a few of the major considerations that you face during the actual coding.

Developing the user interface (UI)

The user interface is just that — it defines how the user interacts with your program. You need to realize that, to your users, the UI *is* the program. They're not aware of what goes on behind the scenes, away from their viewpoint, except for a general feeling about whether the program performs quickly or slowly and whether the program performs its functions accurately.

The UI is extremely important to gaining the user's buy-in to your program. The user's first impression of your software comes from whether they can quickly and intuitively get around your program's interface.

Despite the fact that the user interface is important to the user's experience with the program and deserves time, effort, and research in its design (as I describe in Chapter 7), don't fall into the trap of believing that a good interface is a good software program.

If you follow the advice that I offer in Chapter 7, you spend quite a bit of time designing your user interface. Your emphasis should be on functional richness first, then worry about making it pretty later. Developing that interface, therefore, is likely to go much more smoothly.

The interface is also likely to require less reworking later, after the various testing phases, simply because many flaws that users refer to as "bugs" in the program may actually result from a poor design in the user interface. If the interface isn't clear and understandable, it may cause faulty user input and, therefore, a greater chance of erroneous results. The user thinks he's dealing with a bug, but in reality the problem's nothing more than a poorly designed or developed user interface.

If you work in a company that develops object-oriented programming procedures, developing the user interface may prove quite easy. Many of the objects necessary to develop features on the interface may already exist as the result of earlier company projects. If a previous program includes a toolbar, for example, and your design calls for developing a toolbar, you can perhaps reuse the programming objects from the earlier program. Make sure that you take a look through the inventory of such objects available for your use and select the ones that make your job easier.

At the beginning of this section, I state that, to the user, the interface *is* the program. Because of this fact, you can find many programming books about how to develop elements of a user interface. You may not find a book with the title *User Interfaces For Dummies* on the shelf, but you can find books on writing programs in C++ (or whatever language you're using). These books very often include sections on creating a menu system or displaying graphics and icons in toolbars. Look through such books to determine how to actually code the elements of your user interface.

As you're developing the user interface, don't worry about the final function of each command that users can access through that interface. Say, for example, that your program enables the user to create a new data file. To initiate this command, the user must choose File➪New from the menu bar. In developing the user interface, however, you need to concern yourself with the correct operation of the menu structure.

Make sure, therefore, that the File menu not only appears on the menu bar, but that it also contains a New option. During your own developmental testing (you know — your personal testing as you're writing the code), you can then set up the program simply to open a dialog box that reads `New file created now` whenever you choose the File➪New menu option. This dialog box acts as a placeholder for the actual work that the program does later on, after you complete it. (The placeholder is necessary during these early stages because you may not yet have developed the modules that actually create the file.)

After you finish creating the user interface, you essentially have an "outer shell" for your program. You can click toolbar buttons, choose menu items, and display dialog boxes. You can access data-input forms and sample output screens. Although you may see a lot of activity on-screen at this stage, you add the actual "guts" of your program later, as you move closer to your alpha-release stage.

Implementing the information-flow model

You often refer to the third element in coding your module as the *information-flow model* or the workflow. This term represents nothing more than a fancy way of referring to the actual workflow that the user follows in putting your program through its paces.

To develop your information-flow (workflow) model, refer to Chapter 7, where I discuss the design of the information-flow (workflow) model. This model lies at the center of your software's architectural design process. It specifies the information (data) flow and data transformations during all points of input, process, and output.

If you perform the required design work according to the detailed design specifications, Entity Relationship Diagram (ERD), and Data Flow Diagram (DRD), as I cover in Chapter 7, developing the information-flow model is relatively painless. Very few questions should remain unanswered at this point concerning how the program acquires, processes, and uses information.

Remember that the primary result of designing the information-flow model is the *Data Flow Diagram (DFD)*. Figure 8-1 shows an example of a DFD for the Customer Self-Service Web project, as you can design in Chapter 7, and the accompanying template on the CD.

As your development team is coding the application, team members can refer to the DFD to make sure that this diagram accurately represents what they're actually creating. In fact, from this point forward, you want to refer to this diagram quite often, to make sure everyone who is developing and testing the software's information model (workflow) understands the intended design specs, to ensure that the correct product is ultimately developed.

As project manager, you need to understand the DFD. It's your tool to keep your developers on track in developing the information-flow model. At times, members of the development team may approach you, asking whether they can alter the program's data flow. They may, for example, discover an easier way to accomplish a particular function.

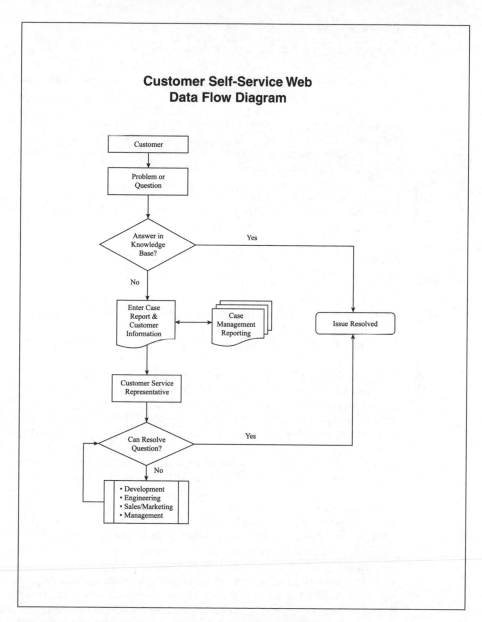

Figure 8-1: A sample DFD for the Customer Self-Service Web project.

Or during development, they may discover that moving a certain command from one menu to another makes more sense than keeping it at its original location. You must act as the arbitrator in such situations, deciding what team members can change and what they can't, basing your decisions on the DFD. If you don't understand the DFD right up front, therefore, you can't make particularly informed decisions about such changes.

Checking the code

As your development team put together the prototype for your program, it was probably far from finished, which is covered in Chapter 7. In fact, the prototype may not even use the same programming language that you're using for your final software coding.

As your programmers execute the plans that the detailed design specifications describe, you see program lines start to grow and modules start to proliferate. At this stage, someone must act as the chief orchestrator to make sure that everything fits together as it needs to.

If you're working on a large project, you may have a lead programmer or analyst whom you charge with this responsibility. On other, smaller projects, you may act as the one leading the orchestra.

Typically, software project managers are former programmers; however, exceptions do exist. Knowing how to at least read program code is essential for you to carry out your duties. You can then check up on your programmers by spot-checking their code to make sure that they're doing their job correctly. If you are having difficulties reading some of the program code, ask the programmers to do a code walk-through with you, and make sure that they fully document their code to make it easy for anyone else to understand.

You need to receive reports either directly from your programmers or from the lead person you select to coordinate the programming efforts for the project. If many programmers are working on the project, you may need them to generate such reports daily. If you're working with a smaller number of programmers, weekly progress reports are probably sufficient. You want these reports to detail exactly what modules the programming team completes and what it still needs to finish. You want to make sure that you understand at least the purpose of each module and how it fits into the overall jigsaw puzzle.

If the modules that the programmers are producing appear to work correctly and all the pieces are coming together, you probably don't need to personally check every line of code. You do want to conduct spot-checks, however, to verify the following conditions:

- ✔ **Are your programmers following in-house programming conventions?** You need to make sure that you state such conventions clearly in the early development team meetings and in design documents for the project. Make sure that your programmers follow these conventions closely so that the project may prove useful to developers working on future projects going forward. I cover the project team meetings and design documents in detail in Chapters 3 and 7.

- ✔ **Is the code understandable?** Can you understand what's happening in the code? (Here is where an ability to read program lines comes in *really* handy.) As software project manager, you're assumed to have enough technical knowledge to read software code.

If you're having difficulties reading some of the program code, however, ask the programmers to point you to the design documents, including the Data Flow Diagram, Entity Relationship Diagram, and Detailed Design Specifications, to try to explain the program logic of their code and how it fits into the overall software design.

✔ **Are your programmers using common-sense variable names?** Make sure that the programmers are using variable names that describe the purpose of the variable. Of course, you need to make sure, too, that variable naming always is in accordance with in-house conventions.

✔ **Does the code contain sufficient comments?** Program comments or remarks don't slow the execution speed of the final program, but they do make maintenance much easier. Make sure that the code lines include sufficient noncode comments that you can understand what the programmer is doing and why.

✔ **Are the programmers working from a common set of objects for their programming?** Working from a common set of objects is very important, because doing so removes redundancy in the code. If one programmer needs a module that performs some transformation on data, for example, and another programmer needs the same set of objects for a similar function, make sure that each one doesn't come up with his own separate version. Make sure instead that they use a common version, thereby keeping everyone using the same code baseline for good version control.

Step 6: Unit Test Your Software Modules

After your programmers complete the coding of a module or unit, they need to test it out, just as a customer does under real-world conditions.

The project developers are the ones who perform the *unit testing* for a module (which is sometimes also known as *glass-box testing* because you can actually see the code).

You need to distinguish such testing from an integration test (which your programmers also perform), a system test, and *black-box* testing (when you're testing from the functionality in the dark, without seeing the actual code). Independent Software Quality Assurance (SQA) engineers usually perform the system test and black-box tests. For a detailed explanation of white-box and black-box testing, you can refer to Chapter 9.

Unfortunately, developers often skip unit testing, a situation that occurs most typically if programmers are under tremendous pressures to reach unrealistic deadlines. (Your organization may, for example, impose unrealistic deadlines to meet quarter-end results for investors or the stock market.) Regardless of the pressures you're under, unit testing every module so that you can identify and fix all major bugs is imperative. Unit testing helps to ensure that your software matures into true alpha and beta releases and increases its likelihood for success as an eventual product for the public.

Because you share many the elements of software testing among different types of tests, I devote an entire chapter to this topic. See Chapter 9 for more information about conducting unit tests and other tests.

Step 7: Integrate Your Software Modules

After you construct and unit-test the individual modules, you create the first integration of all the program modules. You then *freeze* this integrated build, meaning that the newly accepted code replaces the baseline code. Because you create this build early in the development process (generally, right after you complete the critical individual modules), the build obviously isn't yet fully functional. Heck, you aren't even to the alpha stage yet (as I define it in the section "Step 3: Plan for Effective Integration of Your Software," earlier in this chapter).

This frozen baseline build does prove helpful, however, in giving you a glimpse of how far you've come in arriving at this point and by providing you with an idea of what you still need to do on the project.

At a minimum, you want the build to contain the data model, information flow (workflow), and UI software components, based upon the following design models:

- ✔ Data model
- ✔ Information-flow functionality model
- ✔ User-interface (UI) model

I describe each of these models in detail in Chapter 7 and provide some software development guidance in the section "Step 5: Develop Your Software Modules," earlier in this chapter. If you include these elements in the baseline build, you at least have a program that you can get up and running so that you can start some integration testing. Integration testing involves testing against a software build that contains two or more modules, with the objective of seeing if these modules work together. I discuss Integration testing at length in Chapter 9.

If you have other modules that don't fit into the models that I mention in the preceding list but that are available (in other words, you've unit-tested them and they passed), go ahead and include them in the baseline build. Doing so can save you some testing time later. Suppose, for example, that during the first phase of the Customer Self-Service Web project, your Marketing group and project sponsor are requesting that you integrate defect-tracking modules. After taking a cursory look at your data model, information-flow (workflow), and UI model, you realize that the new defect-tracking modules don't currently fit into the Customer Self-Service Web case-reporting models.

Step 8: Test All Levels of Integration

After you freeze your baseline build, the build is ready for testing. Your development team conducts the integration testing, because they have the expertise to troubleshoot problems with the integration.

The objective of executing an integration test is to determine how well the modules "get along with each other." During the earlier unit tests of each individual module, your development team doesn't get the opportunity to see whether the modules can work together. The integration test becomes crucial in determining whether the individual modules work together as a whole system for the software to have a chance of becoming a GA (general availability) release candidate to the customers.

Assuming that, if modules pass their individual unit tests, they can work correctly with other modules is dangerous. Keep in mind that your database administrators, application developers, and engineers are often developing modules in their "own little worlds." The mark of a final release candidate is one in which all levels of its integrated modules can pass the integration test successfully.

Step 9: Develop the Documentation

At the point that you, your project team, and the project sponsor agree that your software's at the level of a true alpha release, your technical writer (or writers) is probably eager to begin some serious writing.

The documentation is a critical component of your software product. Your technical writers develop the product's documentation according to the *documentation plan,* which I describe in Chapter 7.

If you examine the suggested documentation plan that I mention in Chapter 7, you notice that the process of developing documentation is a collaborative effort. In other words, you don't just leave it to the technical writers on your team. Instead, you need to involve most of the members of your team, as well as many outside specialists. The following list describes the people whom you need to involve in developing the documentation:

✔ **Technical writers:** Typically, these are people on your staff, although you can outsource technical writing. If you decide to outsource this position, make sure that you examine representative samples of the author's writing before making your decision on whom to use.

✔ **Internal review committee:** Think of the documentation as a component of your overall software product. Just as with the SQA system testing of your software by an independent SQA testing group, you need to choose a small number of people from your development team to sit on a documentation review committee to review the quality of your documentation. Your documentation review committee typically includes a representative from the SQA organization, development, engineering, and customer support.

If you're using in-house writers, you don't want those writers to sit on this committee. The purpose of this team is to provide an independent forum for reviewing the technical accuracy and thoroughness of the documentation. (The team also needs to make sure that the documentation is on target and doesn't betray any proprietary information or trade secrets.) You generally call on this committee several times during the documentation development cycle to review the publications you're creating.

✔ **Copy editor:** You want to outsource this position rather than use someone on your own team. Having no prior familiarity with the project enables the copy editor to come at the material from a fresh angle. Don't make the mistake of assuming that if someone can write, they can also objectively and effectively edit their own material. After the initial writing is complete, the copy editor is key in making sure that your publications go from a first draft to final, publishable material.

✔ **Technical editor:** A technical editor checks your publications to make sure that they're technically correct (no surprise here). This person doesn't look for punctuation, grammar, and style issues; that's the job of the copy editor. Instead, the technical editor must be conversant with the technical issues that the audience of your software faces and then edit the documentation from that perspective. In effect, a technical editor is to your publications what a beta tester is to your software.

✔ **Proofreaders:** Ah, the job of proofreader! This person possess a completely different skill set and mentality than any of those that I mention elsewhere in this list. The proofreader's job is to read through your publications, typically very late in the development cycle, and make any final touches, including grammar, spelling, vocabulary, and any other omissions or additions. Using construction-trade terms, a copy editor is analogous to a rough carpenter and a proofreader to a finish carpenter. (And the technical editor is the building inspector.)

As you schedule time for completing your documentation, you optimally want it to be close to complete at the time that you send out your software for beta testing. Having documentation during the beta cycle enables the beta testers to see the software "package" in much the same condition that the end users see it and provides an opportunity for feedback about this component from independent sources.

Step 10: Perform SQA System Testing

After your software's integration build reaches sufficient maturity by successfully meeting SQA's *Entrance Testing*, which includes undergoing rigorous unit and integration testing, and you've fixed all the major bugs, you need to execute the SQA System Test cases, as the SQA Test Plan prescribes. (I introduce the SQA Entrance Test Criteria and how to conduct SQA tests in quite a bit more detail in Chapter 9. The SQA Test Plan in Chapter 7 is an integral part of your detailed design specifications.)

An SQA Test Plan references a suite of test cases that you can use for testing the quality of your software so that it meets a certain standard before the final release becomes available to your customers.

Step 11: Conduct the Beta Test

You typically conduct your beta test in parallel with the systems testing that I describe in the preceding section. Independent beta testers, who (by definition) your organization doesn't employ, are the people who test your beta releases at designated customer sites. Your marketing manager is likely to already have identified some of your customers to participate at beta sites, but the task of locating the beta testers may also fall to your development team.

Your beta sites provide a good sampling of real-life production environments at a number of customer sites. Your beta customers provide invaluable feedback to your project team, which goes a long way in helping you catch critical bugs before the final release goes out the door — which is too late. Tech support is also happy not to receive as many of those dreadful telephone calls from screaming customers and embarrassed consultants wondering why you sent them an alpha or beta product instead of the promised GA release.

I provide detailed information on understanding beta releases of your software in the section "Step 3: Plan for Effective Integration of Your Software," earlier in this chapter. In Chapter 7, I introduce you to the concept of a beta test plan, which is essential to your detailed design specifications document. In Chapter 9, you find out exactly what goes into your beta test plan and how to conduct a beta test in general.

Step 12: Develop Your Training Curriculum

Training your customers at the beta sites, your regular customers, internal developers, system integrators, and customer support staff is critical for a successful software GA release. For the complete scoop on training, take a look at Chapter 12.

Part IV
Testing 1,2,3. . .

The 5th Wave   By Rich Tennant

"And tell David to come in out of the hall. I found a way to adjust our project budget estimate."

In this part . . .

I think of the software development process in the same way that I think of any other manufactured product. When the Pinto automobiles all crashed and burned during the '70s, consumer advocates urged consumers to insist on a little more quality-assurance testing before the little flaming ponies were allowed on the streets of San Francisco. After so many Pintos fueled the torch of freedom, the U.S. government finally forced Ford Motor Company to do a recall of the pony show. The total recall of Pintos introduced a major change and risk in the overall research and development plans and financial health of Ford. Drastic change/risk control processes were enacted to assure the quality of the future products that Ford released for customer consumption.

In Part IV, you find out how to test for quality throughout, test, and test again. I guide you step-by-step in developing comprehensive software quality assurance (SQA) plans, change control, and configuration management strategies and tools.

Chapter 9

Software Quality Assurance Throughout

• •

• •

*A*fter the development effort sends the code to the test engineers, you may think that testing a few builds of the software assures a high-quality product to the customers. The reality, however, is that the system testing is only one component falling under the all-encompassing umbrella of Software Quality Assurance (SQA) testing. Assuring the quality of your software cuts through all the phases of the development cycle.

You want to make SQA your development team's focus and obsession during each phase of your project's development. From the moment that marketing conceives the product idea to the software's actual rollout, quality is always the name of the game. The software's quality isn't merely a function of your SQA team's processes, but the shared responsibility of virtually everyone involved with the project.

This chapter focuses on the different testing approaches that you can take. Wherever possible, I use a step-by-step approach so that you know exactly what you need to do. If your project team follows all the steps in this chapter, you can be confident in delivering high-quality software to your customers.

Understanding the Big Picture

As you may guess, you can conduct many different types of testing while also tracking those bugs and enhancement requests, throughout the development your software. In reality, the names by which the types of tests are known are pretty standard — the implementation of those tests is what varies, depending on the type of software you're developing and change (defect/enhancement) management system you are using. The tests can even vary depending on the customer you're trying to satisfy!

For the purposes of this book, I focus on the following fundamental software quality assurance (SQA) tasks:

- **Unit testing:** The development team performs this type of testing on modules before they integrate them with other modules.

- **Integration testing:** The development team performs this type of testing on each build of the software as the team creates the build from the individual modules.

- **Entrance testing:** The development team or the Software Quality Assurance (SQA) team performs this type of testing on the integration build of the software after unit and integration testing have been completed. Regardless of which team performs the entrance testing, the SQA team generally provides the *entrance criteria,* which are a series of tests performed against the integration build that must be executed successfully before SQA accepts the build for system testing.

- **System testing:** You carry out this type of testing in simulated live conditions in-house. Sometimes you call this type of testing *alpha testing* (although you can actually apply that term to any pre-beta testing).

- **Beta testing:** You conduct this type of testing in live conditions by using external customers or testers.

- **Defect and enhancement reporting:** During the course of the development cycle of your software, your project team reports defects and potential enhancements in your change management (defect/enhancement) tracking system. Make sure that your system provides for rating the importance of each bug fix and enhancement.

  Developers, SQA engineers, and other team members can use the change management system to track the provision and regression testing of product enhancements and bug fixes. For more information on developing a change/risk management (CR/M) plan and Change Management Board, you can refer to Chapter 10.

  In the "Reporting Defects and Enhancements" section, later in this chapter, you can find detailed definitions of defect/enhancement categories and priority classifications. You can also refer to Chapter 10 for everything you ever wanted to know about software change management but were not afraid to ask.

Michaels

Made by you™

MICHAELS STORE #1266 (847) 380-2309
MICHAELS STORE #1266
2411 W SCHAUMBURG RD
SCHAUMBURG, IL 60194

8-9341-1365-8659-9704-6138-1182-1259-0457

4075938   SALE   8319 1266 040 5/25/22 17:50
WM RLX JRSY SS V   884913392656 1 @ 12.99   12.99
GHIRARDELLI C   747599409943 1 @ .99   .99 N
                 SUBTOTAL   13.98
           Sales Tax 10%   1.40
                    TOTAL   15.38
ACCOUNT NUMBER   ************9419
     Visa   15.38
     APPROVAL: 715205 CHIP ONLINE
       AID: A0000000031010
       TVR: 0000000000
       TSI: 0000

This receipt expires at 60 days on 07/23/22
Click. Buy. Create. Shop michaels.com today!
Get Savings & Inspiration! Text* SIGNUP to 273283
     To Sign Up for Email & Text Messages.
        *Msg & Data Rates May Apply
    You will receive 1 autodialed message
    with a link to join Michaels alerts.

                Aaron Brothers
               Custom Framing
New! Now in Over 1,200 Michaels Stores & Online
   THANK YOU FOR SHOPPING AT MICHAELS

            Dear Valued Customer:
Michaels return and coupon policies are available
   at michaels.com and in store at registers.
*** Please be advised, effective April 15th, 2021
Michaels will be moving from a 180 day return policy
 to a 60 day return policy from the date of purchase.
 Please see a store associate for more information.

                5/25/22 17:50

✔ **Debugging:** After a product bug is reported to the change management (defect/enhancement tracking) system, the developer or programmer attempts to isolate and debug the cause of the defect, beginning with those that are rated the most severe.

Not all system problems identified through testing are actually product defects. The debugging process often points out that what appeared to be a bug was due to user error, the environment, or improper data.

✔ **Customer acceptance testing:** Your customers do this testing after the initial delivery of your software. This type of testing determines whether the software meets your customers' predefined requirements.

All these tasks are fundamental to ensuring the overall quality and success of your software project. In this chapter, I cover the methods that you use for implementing four of these tests. The only type of test that I don't cover in this chapter is beta testing, which I cover fully in Chapters 7 and 8.

Unit Testing

You perform *unit testing* at the *module* level of your software. In programming circles, the *module* is the basic software unit (or component). Thus you can often hear developers referring to unit testing as *module testing*.

Ideally, you schedule enough time for both developing and unit testing the software modules to assure the modules work as you intend. Too often, however, teams develop the module but fail to unit test it for any of several reasons — in the interest of saving time, because of too heavy a workload or shortened project schedule, and so on.

As a result, the SQA testers who handle the code later in the development cycle may end up conducting additional testing. The later in the process that you find and fix a bug, the more expensive and detrimental to the schedule is the repair process. Try to test as early in the development cycle as possible to catch those darn bugs!

Before your developers can run unit tests against their modules, the development team needs to create a series of unit-test cases to exercise the modules. If your team develops the modules and accurate test cases based on the Requirements Document, Project Scope Document, Functional Specifications, and Detailed Design Specifications for the project (which they certainly should be doing), then those unit tests provide the means to perform the following key measurements:

✔ Determining whether the software contains major design or functional defects as measured against the specification documents.

The timing of unit testing

Ideally, your developers conduct unit testing in concert with the actual coding of the module. Make sure that your developers write down what sort of tests they conduct on the modules and how the modules perform on those tests. This information can prove invaluable later if you're trying to track down a problem in a group of modules that are already integrated into the program as a whole.

For example, with the Customer Self-Service Web project, your developers would ideally unit test the creation of a new customer case record via the Web-based input form and verify that the knowledge-base search engine is working properly.

Typical programmers dread unit testing because of lack of time in the schedule, boredom with its tedious nature, and so on. Ask your SQA group to help the Development team by providing templates and functional test scenarios that can simplify the development of unit tests.

> ✔ Determining when the software is ready to move into integration testing, entrance testing, and ultimately into SQA system testing.
>
> ✔ Determining whether the software performs correctly on the test environments (such as network, hardware, operating system, relational database management system, and so on) that are necessary for your potential customer base.

The testing that your development team does at the unit level is generally informal in nature, where programmers devise whatever tests they deem necessary to fully exercise their modules. In a perfect world, unit tests will be formally written and consistently executed by development for all software units (modules).

One of the surest ways to destine your software project to failure is to short-change the time available for unit testing. You want to avoid uncovering significant problems at a time when debugging requires a complex regression testing cycle even as the customer expects the code any minute. Convince your project sponsor that the schedule must take unit testing into account!

A great way to encourage unit testing is to have junior developers start out as SQA testers before writing a single line of code. By working in the SQA department, young developers quickly come to appreciate the need for sufficient unit and integration testing up-front, rather than identifying problems late and having to delay the release of the GA product to your customers.

Junior developers with a background in SQA testing develop the mind-set and tools to develop and execute unit test cases in a timely manner. Such tests are an essential ingredient to successful integration, entrance, and SQA testing, as well as to the overall success of the project. In addition, junior developers on the SQA team can work with the development team early in the project to help write the code for good unit tests.

Integration Testing

After your modules are complete and pass the necessary unit tests, you need to start putting the modules (units) together. Amazingly, perfectly sound modules can start acting in perfectly unsound ways after you combine them with other perfectly sound modules. Perhaps "mob frenzy" or some other phenomenon of program mentality is the culprit.

Who knows? The fact that bugs tend to crop up at integration time means that you, as the project manager, are responsible to ensure that your Development team conducts integration testing on your software. Here's where your SQA test group can provide an Entrance Test Plan (ETP) that provides criteria for determining whether an integration build is ready for acceptance for SQA testing. The ETP can also serve as the beginning of an in-depth integration test suite. You can refer to the next section for more details on developing and executing Entrance Test Plans.

If your project is large enough, your team may even include a specialized development member who functions as your *configuration manager* or *integration manager*. This person is responsible for overseeing the integrated builds of the software, tracking any problems, and making sure that your team solves those problems.

Two levels of integration testing

You want your tests to focus on two things at integration time. First, you want to test to make sure that the new module still functions as you expect. In other words, the module needs to provide the same results on the integration tests as it does on the unit tests.

The second aspect of these tests, however, is even more important: *regression testing*. Regression testing is a thorough battery of tests designed to uncover detrimental effects of adding new code to the functionality of a previously tested code. This is a common practice after code fixes have been reconfigured into a new software build.

For example, you conduct regression tests on an integration build to make sure that, as you add new modules, those modules previously created and tested still work together correctly (that is, they function together in the same way both before and after you add the new module). Sometimes the addition of a module can introduce errors in the interactions of seemingly unrelated modules elsewhere in the program. (This situation is *very* frustrating and, without regression testing, exceedingly difficult to debug.)

As an example of how integration testing can work, suppose that you're developing the Customer Self-Service Web project and you're ready to combine the first three modules of the program. These modules represent your user interface, the New Case module, and the Resolution Knowledge Base module.

The New Case module performs the under-the-covers processing each time a new customer case (issue report) is added via the Web input form. The Resolution Knowledge Base module performs the under-the-covers keyword searching and retrieval of customer case solutions.

You put these three together and run them through their paces to make sure that everything works as you expect. You may run into a problem or two, but you can easily fix such snags at this stage — you still don't have that many areas to check for the problems. After you finish the testing, you place the tests that you perform in the checklist of tests that you intend to use for your future regression tests.

Next, you're ready to add another module to your Customer Self-Service Web integration build — perhaps the Update Case module enables the customer to make changes to an already existing case record. You add this module and perform a series of tests to make sure that the new module also works, just as you expect it to.

You find, in fact, that you really *can* pull up an existing incident and edit it on-screen. You now want to set this series of successful tests to the side, where you can lay your hands on them later.

You're now ready to conduct regression testing. You pull out the tests that you previously used — you know, the ones you did on the first three modules. These tests form the basis of your regression testing. You want to run through the regression testing to make sure that the older modules still work as you expect, even with the addition of the new edit-incident module to the mix.

Unfortunately, the old modules don't always work correctly — for example, the addition of the edit-incident module may introduce an error in the new-incident module. Regression testing uncovers this error and enables you to fix it right away.

After the newly integrated software finally passes the regression testing, you can pick up the tests you did on the edit-incident module and then add them to your regression checklist.

In the process that I describe here, you're always performing new tests and adding to your stable of regression tests. This cumulative approach to integration testing helps you create the best product possible in the shortest possible time. (You may question my assertion concerning the shortest possible time, but it really is true.) If you procrastinate about testing until later in the process, tracking down the bugs becomes a much more overwhelming job and can easily swamp a tight schedule.

Looking into the box

The type of testing that your developers or programmers typically do at both the unit and integration levels is often known as *glass-box testing*. Your developers typically conduct glass-box testing during the program's unit testing, although sometimes your team may conduct it during integration testing.

I'm not, however, saying that glass-box testing and unit testing (or integration testing) are the same thing; they're not. Indeed, the terms *unit testing* and *integration testing* describe the level at which you're doing the testing. *Glass-box testing,* on the other hand, describes the perspective of the tester, as follows:

✔ **Glass-box testing:** Glass-box testing (or white-box testing) refers to the concept that the programmer has a good idea exactly what the input, processing, and output of the tests is to involve and can provide specific tests of the data.

   Because the programmer knows so much about the program code and its design, she can view test results through the transparent glass box and immediately understand the meaning of the testing efforts. Glass-box testing is often performed directly in the debugger by forcing various values into variables and seeing if the program code can handle all possible error cases.

✔ **Black-box testing:** Black-box testing involves testing *after* unit and integration testing is complete. Black-box testers (generally Software Quality Assurance (SQA) engineers or offsite beta customer users) have no knowledge of the program logic. Black-box testers typically only test the installation and functionality via the user interface.

   The functioning of the program is a black box to these testers. Black-box tests may uncover problems that glass-box tests miss, because the black-box testers can't subconsciously tailor their tests to the known needs of the program code. Because the testers can't see in the box, they may test the code in ways that the programmers haven't conceived.

If your Customer Self-Service Web project contains code for a New Case form, then the form may contain input fields for customer profile information, a description of the issue, and so on. To insert a New Case record into the back-end database, the programmer may structure the program to validate the data that the user inputs, such as whether the data matches the particular numeric, character, or date format of a particular field and whether the program can ensure that invalid data generates an appropriate error condition.

Now suppose that the program logic constrains the Effective Date value to be a date no more than one year in the past or future. If this condition isn't met, then the following error message should appear: `Insert failed—Case Effective Date too far in the past/future. Enter a different Effective Date...`

A glass-box test of the program's data-validation algorithms on the New Case form may include testing a boundary of the Effective Date field by entering a date way in the future or way in the past. If the incorrect date is accepted by the system, then the glass/white box unit test failed, and the programmer should open a defect report in the change management system and correct the code before performing the integration test.

A black-box test of the program's data-validation algorithm could also identify such an error (based on an SQA tester checking the constraints on different fields described in the Detailed Design Specifications document), but the black-box tester would only know that the incorrect data was accepted for some reason as opposed to the actual logical error in the programming.

Even if your developers can fix bugs that they identify right away, make sure that they understand the importance of logging and tracking the bug anyway. You have two good reasons for doing so:

✔ **Logging each bug ensures that the updated version of the module is reconfigured into the next build.** If someone fails to log a bug, then the need to integrate a new version of the module into the next build may be overlooked in the QA department. Accurate defect tracking avoids finger-pointing exercises due to a bug fix missing the next build.

✔ **Keeping an accurate accounting of all bugs allows each new code module to be double-checked for its operation and regression checked by QA during later testing phases.** Remember that an undiscovered bug is a bug nonetheless, and nobody writes error-free code. It's better to discover as soon as you can that a bug fix may not handle a certain unforeseen situation (you know, the kind that only an end user could dream up) or that the new code may uncover an error in another module.

Loops, methods of performing a set of instructions multiple times, are another area that glass-box testing rewards. The glass-box tester needs to test the function of loops to see that they take place the correct number of times and that the code provides the desired result.

For example, a programmer may have coded the Resolutions Knowledge Base search engine to extract a listing of resolutions for the keywords *installation problems* into an array that enables the user to display, sort, delete, and further filter the results of the query. The loop would repeat the same process of storing each result that met the query's search criteria *installation problems* into the array.

During the glass-box testing of the Resolutions Knowledge Base search engine loop, the programmer looks closely to see that the program correctly dimensions memory for the array so that it can store every instance of the *installation problems* keyword and that the loop correctly stores each result in the array (paying special attention to the last result because a poor exit condition often affects the last iteration through the loop).

The programmer could further test whether the `display`, `delete`, `sort`, and `filter` methods work correctly for the class and whether the program handles invalid data types elegantly.

Conducting numerous glass-box tests against the various program modules (such as the user interface and engine) and testing the various design document specifications (such as the data model and data-flow diagram) is a good practice for developers to employ during the development of a project.

You want to run these tests both before and after you integrate a given combination of modules, for two reasons:

✔ To verify that each module works as designed as a stand-alone component.

✔ To verify that two or more modules get along together, without breaking the other's designed functionality.

After completing a rock-solid unit-and-integration test suite, your integration build is ready to undergo entrance testing for entry into SQA system testing and a step closer as a possible release candidate to your customers.

Entrance Testing

Another excellent software quality assurance practice is to develop an Entrance Test Plan (ETP). The objective of the ETP is to perform a quick test that exercises the basic functions of the integration build of the software functions to determine whether or not the build is ready for the QA Test Cycle. This entrance test should not take longer than 1–2 hours. The test also serves to verify, of course, the successful installation of the product — without which no further testing could take place.

Be sure to check off the items in the following list before an integration build undergoes entrance testing:

- ✔ **The *demo data* (the test data that the demo uses) is current:** For example, the data would have to test for Y2K date–compatibility and a ten-digit zip code to be current today. You don't want the data to present any issues in preventing customers' acceptance testing.

- ✔ **The entrance test is platform-neutral:** In other words, the entrance test is a high-level test of the overall software's functionality, not environment specific, and therefore should pass on any customer-supported environment. Ideally, you want to formulate entrance test criteria that are generic, not specific to a particular platform.

- ✔ **The Technical Publications team has finished the software's Release Notes:** SQA testers can also ensure that the information in this document allows the customer to install the software successfully.

- ✔ **Unit testing is complete:** First things first. If unit testing isn't complete, then system testing shouldn't begin.

- ✔ **Integration testing is complete on a formal build configured by the configuration manager (CM):** If the development team hasn't finished the configuration testing, then system testing shouldn't begin.

Typical Entrance Test Plan criteria for the Customer Self-Service Web project may include:

- ✔ Successful installation of software with no errors.

- ✔ The correct integration build (that is, configured by the CM in the CMS) is installed.

- ✔ Successfully add, update, and delete of customer cases (incident reports).

- ✔ Successfully searching and retrieving of case resolutions from the Knowledge Base search engine and database.

The assumption is that if development turns over a build that has passed the SQA entrance criteria, then the build is an SQA candidate for system testing. If system testing is successfully completed, then the software becomes a potential release candidate.

If a Priority 1 (Fatal) defect is uncovered during Entrance Testing, the SQA Team Lead will notify you, the Project Manager, that the build failed the Entrance Test, and the tester will log the defect in the change management system. For more information on defect priority codes, check out the section titled "Reporting Defects and Enhancements," later in this chapter.

System Testing

System testing refers to a focused effort to test every aspect of the program in an attempt to anticipate as many user errors as possible. You begin system testing only after the software has undergone thorough unit and integration testing and has passed the SQA entrance test criteria. System testing is the type of testing in which you're likely to find the majority of problems in your software.

System testing is most fruitful if you do it in-house under simulated live conditions. Your testers try to rip apart the software and make it fail. Earlier tests try to make sure that the software lives up to design specifications, but during the system tests, the testers really *are* trying to break the software.

Your testers don't try to break the code maliciously; in fact, attempting to trip up the code serves an important function for the software. If the software's going to break at all, you want it to break in-house, before people outside the organization run into problems.

You typically conduct system testing at the same time as beta testing. If you refer to the discussions of beta testing in Chapters 7 and Chapter 8, you can identify important differences between system testing and beta testing. First of all, you conduct system testing in-house, while beta testing occurs out house (er — make that out-*of*-house).

The biggest difference between system testing and beta testing, however, is that system testing is extremely structured and methodical while beta testing is very unstructured. When your SQA engineers develop test plans, test cases, and test-automation scripts, almost everything is planned and scripted, which makes for a very structured system-testing environment. With structured and scripted system tests, the results are very predictable — either the software works as designed or it doesn't.

After all the positive tests are completed against your customer-supported platforms, then, if you have time in your often rushed test cycle, you begin thinking creatively about potential *negative* test cases. The tester says to himself, *How might an end user stress or break the system?* The tester goes about trying to anticipate all the goofy ways that end users may blunder that have little or nothing to do with the design of the program. *(Hmmm. What happens if I try to store a full-motion video in the address field?)* Negative tests are often very spontaneous (informal rather than in writing), developed by the tester on the fly, just as end users often do silly things on the fly.

Often, the positive test scenarios are scripted so that the tester doesn't have the opportunity to do negative testing, which includes tests such as entering bogus data, trying every which way to break the system, and conducting test scenarios that are unscripted and unpredictable. Nevertheless, negative testing may uncover the bugs that may only be uncovered by a prospective customer. In the best case, positive and negative testing is combined into a hybrid testing process that uncovers bugs from both angles.

You may wonder why the distinction between system testing and beta testing is important. Primarily, system testers and beta testers must focus on different criteria. In system testing, you want a methodical, structured approach to testing that exercises every area of the program and theoretically runs through every line of code. In beta testing, you want your program to undergo testing in the wild away from any preconceived notions or constraints that you place on it.

Customer off-site beta testing for the most part is very unstructured; therefore, the customer beta site is a great place to uncover bugs that only show up during negative testing. Your project team may be amazed by the number of ways your customers will uncover bugs that went undiscovered during unit, integration, entrance, or system testing.

Picking unbiased system testers

Typically, established software vendors have an in-house SQA team that normally conducts system tests — because this group is completely independent from the development group's unit- and integration-testing efforts. Another excellent source of SQA system testers may be drawn from experienced SQA contractors and from third-party consulting firms.

Having independent testers perform a different battery of tests than those performed by the development group is crucial to ensure that the testing is bias-free. Because programmers and developers have already tested the program in every way that they can imagine, this group may not be as effective in making the software hiccup as a group who hasn't worked with the code from Day One. Therefore, during system testing, the development team's role is to track down and fix bugs that the SQA testers may uncover.

Your SQA testers may have been programmers at one time or they may have analytical and critical abilities to find clever ways to break the system. They need, however, to enjoy working on their own and paying excruciating attention to detail. You want people who love to pick nits as your system testers.

 Because system testers often try to break programs, animosity often develops between these people and your programmers. Part of your job as project manager is to manage that tension and make sure that it doesn't get out of hand. Your most important contribution during system testing is to ensure that the situation doesn't get personal.

Think of the different responses that are likely based on the following statements:

- ✔ *This code was obviously written by someone who doesn't understand the Data Flow Diagram.*
- ✔ *This code doesn't follow the Data Flow Diagram in this area.*

The first statement is going to cause hard feelings and an unhealthy work environment; the second statement is more likely to elicit a fix to the code. Make sure that you clamp down on the tone and tenor of comments without stifling the eagerness of the system testers to find problems in the program. If you feel that someone is out of line, you should pull that person aside and tell him to remember to keep his comments professional.

Model the appropriate attitude and tone at all times when you're questioning a team member's thinking or work. Try to keep everyone who works on the project focused like a laser beam on the needs and experience of the customer.

Ideally, you want to include primarily SQA engineers who have years of test case design and execution experience to perform your system tests. However, you may not want to choose experienced testers *exclusively,* because inexperienced testers sometimes blunder upon defects that experienced testers may overlook.

System testing provides an excellent opportunity for your programmers and developers to review the change management system for any reported defects and to observe the testers. Developers should watch testers carefully and try to reproduce the defects or stumbling blocks that the testers encounter during the testing process. This process can help refine the software and lead to breakthroughs in usability that your developers may not have conceived previously.

Developing the SQA system-test plan

You want the *system-test plan* to pick up where integration and entrance testing leaves off; your objective at this stage is to test all modules and components of your software as a fully integrated system.

You write this plan during the analysis and design phases, as soon as you complete the Project Scope Document (PSD) and get approval for it. The guidelines that you follow for putting together the system-test plan comes from both the PSD and the Requirements Document (RD).

You follow these general steps in creating a series of system tests:

1. **Specify the scope of the testing that you need to do.**

   This step is usually pretty easy, as system tests normally cover every nook and cranny of your software. If you're working on a large project in which you divide the work between your team and others, however, your scope may be more limited.

2. **Define the test environment.**

   Include all the hardware and software that you need for test equipment, as the minimum requirements section of the detailed design specifications defines these needs. You can also indicate any test data requirements if your project requires large data files.

3. **Break down System testing effort into major testing categories.**

   Here is where you indicate the various types of tests you intend to run. You may, for example, decide to run all or some subset of the following tests:

   - **Stress testing:** This system test involves multiple testers and/or automated test machines that issue an inordinate number of transactions in order to simulate a high-volume customer environment. This test attempts to max out the software's limits. The objective is to find out whether the system can handle peak-volume activity. Stress testing is often run in parallel with performance testing.

   - **Functionality testing:** This system test exercises the various software components (functions) when the testers process various transactions. For example, to test the functionality of adding a new case record via the New Case form, the tester would enter the required and/or optional data and see whether the data properly inserts a new record in the back-end database.

   - **Integration and compatibility testing:** These tests exercise the combination of software modules to determine if they can work together or not.

   - **Recovery testing:** This is the system test that forces the software to fail under a variety of conditions, and tests how well the software properly recovers from the failures, and handles exceptions. An important test of a software's recovery system is to measure its ability to trap error messages necessary for the user's debugging and recovery of the system from the failure condition.

   - **Performance testing:** This is a system test with the objective of measuring the integrated software modules' processing quality (performance) at run time. Performance testing may be done in conjunction with stress testing. A good measure of software performance is to check the server's resource utilization before, during, and after a given test. Performance testing is also performed during unit, integration, and entrance testing.

- **Security testing:** Testing the software's security involves setting certain .ini file parameters, encrypting critical system files and user passwords, and similar actions to make sure that legitimate users can log into the system, have appropriate file access rights, and so on. The objective is to verify that the software provides sufficient safety to thwart illegal access and potential harm to the system.

- **Boundary testing:** These tests check the minimum and maximum data input ranges (boundaries) of the software. In testing the Zip_Code field on the New Case form, the number of digits has a minimum boundary of 5 and a maximum of 9 (not including the dashes). The tester would enter 4 or less, or 10 or more digits to see if the appropriate user error messages are generated and that the record insertion fails. (Note that the error message alone isn't enough!)

- **Concurrency testing:** This system test assesses how well the software handles multitasking, communication, and synchronization between tasks (transactions). For example, Concurrency testing may involve verifying how the Customer Self-Service Web handles the multiple users trying to simultaneously add a New Case record while another user attempts to update the exact record with address changes and a third user tries to delete that record.

  Some questions you may ask during concurrency testing may be: Which of the three users will have first dibs, and which users are locked out? Or is the system smart enough to put transactions on hold in queue on a first-come-first-served basis?

  The range of system tests that you run depends on the exact nature of the software you're developing, the practices of your organization, and the specific business needs of your customers.

4. **List all the test cases that you intend to test.**

   This list can become quite detailed. Figure 9-1 shows an example of such a list. Notice that each potential test area includes a number for later reference.

5. **Write the individual test cases.**

   I cover how to write test cases in the following section.

Writing the SQA System test cases

In getting ready for your SQA system test plan, you put together a list of test cases to fully exercise the overall functions of your software. This list represents the major functions and sections of the software you're testing. This stage is when you get down and dirty and define *exactly* how you're going to test each of those cases.

Customer Self-Service Web SQA Test Case List

ID	Test Case Description		ID	Test Case Description
0100	Verify sign-on page		1700	Review user information
0150	Login		1750	Change user information
0200	Add new customer profile		1800	Log off process
0250	Review customer profile			
0300	Delete customer profile			
0350	Print customer profile			
0400	Add case			
0450	Edit case			
0500	Update case			
0550	Delete case			
0600	Search and find case			
0650	Escalate case			
0700	Generate full case report			
0750	View full case report			
0800	Print full case report			
0850	Generate limited case report			
0900	View limited case report			
0950	Print limited case report			
1000	View case history			
1050	Print case history			
1100	Generate case tracking summary			
1150	View case tracking summary			
1200	Print case tracking summary			
1250	Generate case aging report			
1300	View case aging report			
1350	Print case aging report			
1400	Generate case metrics report			
1450	View case metrics report			
1500	Print case metrics report			
1550	Generate staff schedule report			
1600	View staff schedule report			
1650	Print staff schedule report			

Figure 9-1: A list of test cases for the Customer Self-Service Web project example.

In creating your system test cases, you can use the template (SQA Test Case.dot) that I include on the *Software Project Management Kit For Dummies* CD. Load it up and start creating to your heart's content! Figure 9-2 shows an example of a blank SQA Test Case form that I base on this template.

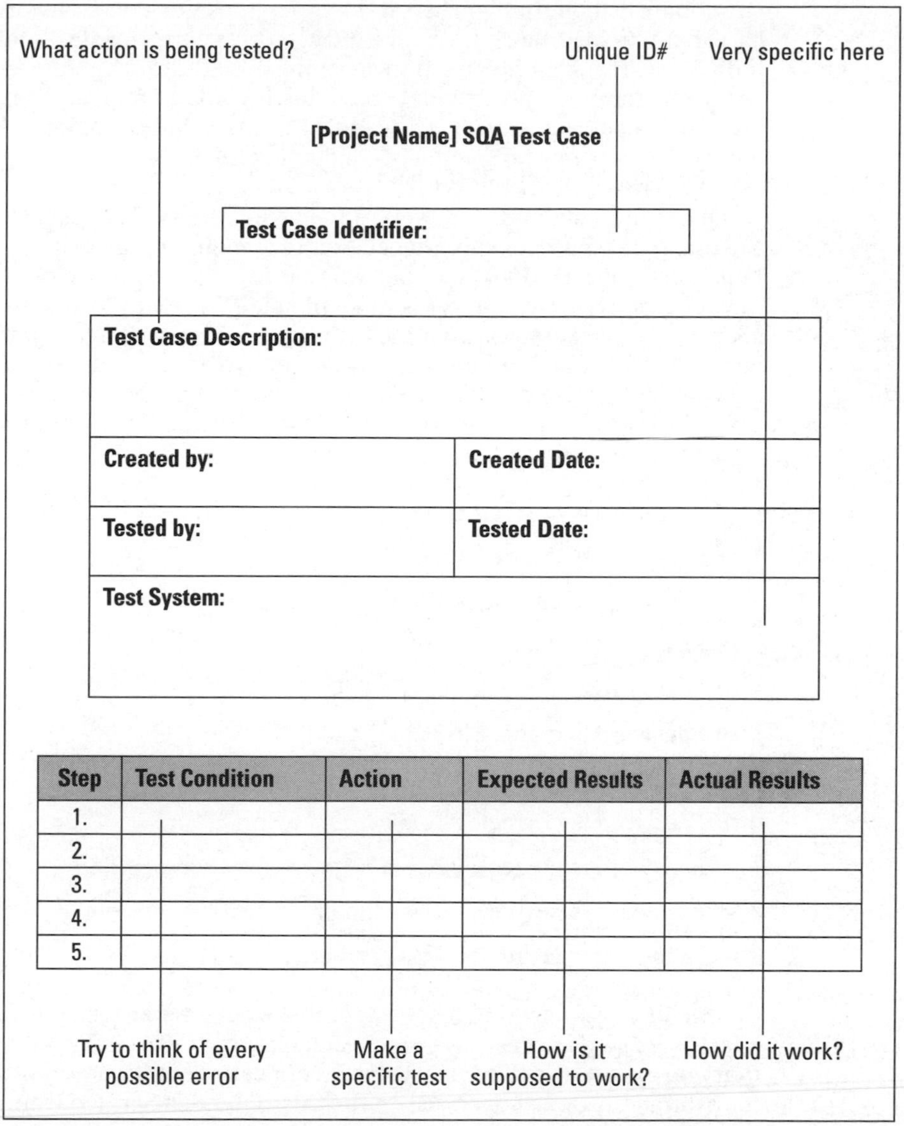

What action is being tested?   Unique ID#   Very specific here

[Project Name] SQA Test Case

Test Case Identifier:

Test Case Description:

Created by:	**Created Date:**
Tested by:	**Tested Date:**

Test System:

Step	Test Condition	Action	Expected Results	Actual Results
1.				
2.				
3.				
4.				
5.				

Try to think of every   Make a   How is it   How did it work?
possible error   specific test   supposed to work?

Figure 9-2: A blank SQA Test Case form.

As you start filling out the SQA Test Case form, notice that the very first thing that you enter is the test case identifier. This item is the tracking number that you attach to each test case in Step 4 of the steps in the preceding section (refer to Figure 9-1). These numbers are completely arbitrary, although you want them to be unique. You use them to track a test case through the entire testing process.

Other information that you see at the top of the SQA Test Case form is self-explanatory. You then come to the nitty-gritty, where you start indicating individual steps that you need to accomplish to thoroughly test a given case. For each step, you specify what you're testing, what actions you need to take, and what result you expect. The Actual Results column you leave blank for use by the person who's actually conducting the tests.

As an example, suppose that you're specifying the system tests for the Customer Self-Service Web project. You're working on the test case for the Login function (ID 0150). You may wonder exactly how much detail you want in your test case. The answer is "a lot of detail." You must do more than simply say, for example, "Test the login screen." Such a vague statement leaves way too much open to interpretation. You need to know exactly what aspects of the login screen to test to prove that the login process works. In thinking about the process, you may identify the following conditions that need testing for logins:

- Password is correct; PIN is incorrect.

- Password is incorrect; PIN is incorrect.

- Password is incorrect; PIN is correct.

- Password is blank; PIN is correct.

- Password is correct; PIN is blank.

- Password is blank; PIN is blank.

- Password is extremely long; PIN is correct.

- Password is correct; PIN is extremely long.

- Password is correct; PIN is a negative number.

- Password is correct; PIN is alphanumeric.

- Password is correct; PIN is correct.

Get the idea? You need to test each of these circumstances. You also need to specify the steps necessary to test each circumstance, along with the results that you expect. (In this case, you expect every condition except the last one to result in the denial of access to the Customer Self-Service Web.)

With your different testing steps in hand, you're ready to completely fill out the SQA Test Case form. Figures 9-3 and 9-4 show an example of a filled-in SQA Test Case form for the login function (ID 0150).

[Project Name] SQA Test Case

Test Case Identifier: 0150

Test Case Description:

Login

Created by: Kenneth	**Created Date:** 2/17/2000
Tested by: S. Mitchell	**Tested Date:**

Test System:

System 17: Intel, Windows NT 4.0, SR 5, 128 MB RAM, Netscape Navigator

Step	Test Condition	Action	Expected Results	Actual Results
1.	Password is correct, PIN is incorrect	Type in password "Testy" Type in PIN of 56812 Click on Login button	User login blocked	
2.	Password is incorrect, PIN is incorrect	Type in random password Type in PIN of 8731 Click on Login button	User login blocked	
3.	Password is incorrect, PIN is correct	Type in random password Type in PIN of 3812 Click on Login button	User login blocked	
4.	Password is blank, PIN is correct	Enter no password Type in PIN of 3812 Click on Login button	User login blocked	
5.	Password is correct, PIN is blank	Type in password "Testy" Enter no PIN Click on Login button	User login blocked	
6.	Password is blank, PIN is blank	Enter no password Enter no PIN Click on Login button	User login blocked	

Figure 9-3: A completed SQA Test Case form. Page 1 of 2.

7.	Password is extremely long, PIN is correct	Type in random password of at least 75 characters Type in PIN of 3812 Click on Login button	User login blocked	
8.	Password is correct, PIN is extremely long	Type in password of "Testy" Type in PIN of at least 25 digits Click on Login button	User login blocked	
9.	Password is correct, PIN is negative number	Type in password of "Testy" Type in PIN of −12 Click on Login button	User login blocked	
10.	Password is correct, PIN is alphanumeric	Type in password of "Testy" Type in PIN of A1B2C3 Click on Login button	User login blocked	
11.	Password is correct, PIN is correct	Type in password of "Testy" Type in PIN of 3812 Click on Login button	User logged in	

Figure 9-4: A completed SQA Test Case form. Page 2 of 2.

Notice that the actual test cases can get very long and involved. This level of detail is the only way for you to ensure that you fully test every aspect of your program.

Administering system tests

With the SQA test cases in hand, you're ready to start your tests. (Of course, you must have the software itself in hand as well.) You need to set up your test environment in a secure area, preferably away from the development team. (You don't want programmers wandering through, innocently telling a tester what to do or not do.)

Each system that you use for testing needs to match the different platforms for which you're designing your software. According to its detailed design specifications, for example, you're designing the Customer Self-Service Web project for the following systems:

✔ **Operating System:** Windows 95 or later; Windows NT 4.0 or later; Linux; or Sun Solaris 2.6 or later.

✔ **Web Server:** Netscape Enterprise Server 3.0 or later; Microsoft Internet Information Server 4.0 or later; or Apache Server.

✔ **Web Browser:** Microsoft Internet Explorer 4.0 or later (Windows 95, 98, NT); or Netscape Navigator 4.0 or later (Windows 95, 98, NT, Linux, Sun Solaris).

✔ **Database:** Oracle 7.3.4 or later; Sybase 11.51 or later; or Microsoft SQL Server 6.5 or later.

In addition, you want each system to use the following minimum hardware:

- Pentium 3
- 128 MB RAM
- 1 GB hard-drive space

These specifications can lead to quite a few permutations of systems. You want to set up a computer for each permutation, which means, in the case of the Customer Self-Service Web example, you set up two different types of systems in your testing lab: servers and browsers. I detail the different servers that you need in Table 9-1.

Table 9-1   Servers that You Need for System Tests of the Customer Self-Service Web Project

Operating System	Web Server	Database
Windows NT 4	Netscape Enterprise Server 3.0	Oracle 7.34
Windows 2000 Server	Netscape Enterprise Server 3.0	Oracle 7.34
Windows NT 4	IIS 4.0	Oracle 7.34
Windows 2000 Server	IIS 5.0	Oracle 7.34
Windows NT 4	Netscape Enterprise Server 3.0	Sybase 11.51
Windows 2000 Server	Netscape Enterprise Server 3.0	Sybase 11.51
Windows NT 4	IIS 4.0	Sybase 11.51
Windows NT 4	Netscape Enterprise Server 3.0	SQL Server 6.5
Windows 2000 Server	IIS 5.0	Sybase 11.51
Windows 2000 Server	Netscape Enterprise Server 3.0	SQL Server 7.0
Windows NT 4	IIS 4.0	SQL Server 6.5
Windows 2000 Server	IIS 5.0	SQL Server 7.0
Linux	Netscape Enterprise Server 3.0	Oracle 7.34
Linux	Apache Server	Oracle 7.34
Sun Solaris 2.6	Netscape Enterprise Server 3.0	Oracle 7.34
Sun Solaris 2.6	Apache Server	Oracle 7.34

The system examples that I provide here are minimal in nature, although at first glance, they may seem quite extensive. Windows NT 4, for example, has at least six different service packs. If you want to be thorough, you need to conduct your Windows NT 4 system tests by first using a base system with no service packs installed and then one with each of the six service packs. (You never know what your customers may have installed.)

If you look at the information in Table 9-1, you see six systems that use Windows NT 4 — and none of them specify service packs. Take those six systems and multiply them by the six service packs, and you quickly see that you end up at 36 systems — just for Windows NT 4. If you do the same thing with different versions of your Web servers and your databases, you very quickly can run into hundreds of permutations of base system software — and that's just for the servers!

On the client side of the fence, you want to set up 10 systems, as I detail in Table 9-2.

Table 9-2	Client Systems Needed for System Tests of the Customer Self-Service Web Project
Operating System	**Web Browser**
Windows 95	IE 4.0
Windows 98	IE 4.0
Windows NT 4 Workstation	IE 4.0
Windows 2000 Workstation	IE 4.0
Windows 95	Navigator 4.0
Windows 98	Navigator 4.0
Windows NT 4 Workstation	Navigator 4.0
Windows 2000 Workstation	Navigator 4.0
Linux	Navigator 4.0
Sun Solaris	Navigator 4.0

You want to carry out each test case on each test machine in your stable of test systems. In this example, you need to conduct the same tests on each client system as you connect the clients to each and every server in your setup. Thus you run each test case 16 times on each client system (once for each server) for a total of 160 total iterations of the test case. That's a lot of testing!

Now perhaps you can see why some organizations try to skimp on their testing. Conducting tests on every possible system is both expensive and time-consuming. If you don't do this testing, however, you're playing Russian roulette with your organization's image and integrity in the market. Don't take the chance; make sure that you conduct all the necessary testing — doing so is much cheaper in the long run.

Reporting Defects and Enhancements

Your project team, and potentially everyone in your software organization, will be reporting software bugs (defects) and enhancement requests (new features) in your change-management system (defect/enhancement tracking system). The objective of a change-management system is to provide a mechanism for tracking and managing requested changes to your software.

I use the term *change requests (CRs)* to include both software defect and enhancement reports. CRs can originate during any of the seven phases of your software's development cycle. Some common defects can originate due to following causes:

- **Insufficient or erroneous requirements:** Deficiencies in the requirements document (RD), project scope document (PSD), functional specifications, and/or detailed design specifications can lead to defects.

- **Deviation in coding from design specifications:** Your development team's coding of software that unintentionally (or possibly intentionally, if you have a slacker on board) deviates from the original design specifications.

- **User documentation defects:** The end-user documentation includes incomplete, misleading, or erroneous information, which may involve release notes, installation guide, administration/user manuals, courseware, and so on.

- **Insufficient or erroneous testing:** Defects may arise due to insufficient or erroneous unit, integration, entrance, system, or customer-acceptance testing.

- **Incorrect configuration and reconfiguration of software:** Defects can arise from incorrect configurations and/or reconfigurations of modules, integration, or system build candidate. Developers sometimes fail to check in or reconfigure their code changes into the configuration management system, resulting in fixes missing the next software build.

Defects and enhancement requests are typically reported using priority classifications similar to the following:

- ✔ **Priority 1 - Fatal:** The entire system is adversely affected and is completely inaccessible.

- ✔ **Priority 2 - Critical:** A major part of the system or critical functionality is affected and no reasonable workaround is available.

- ✔ **Priority 3 - Medium:** A moderate part of the system or critical functionality is affected. However, a reasonable workaround is available, but it requires a tremendous effort on the part of the user. Furthermore, the solution can't be postponed forever.

- ✔ **Priority 4 - Minor:** Functioning of system is not adversely affected and users are able to complete their transactions despite the problem.

- ✔ **Priority 5 - Enhancement:** A change request to add a new feature to the software requirement in a future release that was not previously identified in the original software Requirements Document and Project Scope Document.

The change management system is useful to everyone involved in your project. Developers, SQA engineers, and other team members can use the change management system to follow up on providing and testing fixes for defects and enhancements. After releases of your software, your customers and consultants in the field can begin reporting bugs and file enhancement requests to your customer-support department. When such reports pop up, your Customer Support team needs to know how to handle them.

If the report is not a bug, then it should be considered an enhancement. Enhancement requests are a great thing for a company to collect because it gives them a gauge for what customers are seeking. How you handle enhancement requests is up to your organization. Some companies enter enhancement requests directly into their in-house change-request tracking system. Others let them pile up until such time as they are ready to consider upgrading the software. Check with your company to see what has been done in this regard for previous projects.

Uncovering and reporting of bugs and potential enhancement change requests typically involves the following steps, depending upon your organization's processes and procedures:

1. **Perform a valid test against the shipping version of the software.**

   Before entering a defect change request (CR) in the change management system (CMS), the tester needs to verify that their test environment is a system that's installed right out of the box (often referred to as a *vanilla* system). Vanilla systems contain no customizations or customer data.

The importance of staying vanilla is that doing so allows for effective problem isolation. You can tell whether the problem is inherent in the delivered software or due to user error, data-related problems, or customizations.

2. Isolate whether problem is actually a bug in the vanilla software.

During any test cycle (that is, unit, integration, entrance, system, or customer-acceptance testing), if a tester uncovers what they think is a bug in your software, you need to isolate the cause of the problem, whether it's a defect in the delivered (vanilla) software, a user error, a data-related error, or a customization error.

3. Enter only a legitimate change request for a defect or enhancement into the change management system.

If you've isolated that the problem is truly a defect or limitation in the delivered software, then you have a legitimate CR that's been screened for entry into the change management system. The last thing your development team wants to report back to the tester who didn't do their homework are the all-too-familiar responses: "This is not a bug, but a feature . . . ;" or better yet, "This is data related . . . ;" or even, "This is due to user error . . . ."

4. Submit CR for review by the Change Control Board (CCB).

Not every CR (defect or enhancement) automatically goes to a developer or is targeted for a future release. Established software organizations have CCB's who accept, defer, or reject CR for possible inclusion in a future release, assignment of resources, and tasks. For detailed discussion of the Change Control Board, check out Chapter 10.

5. Write documentation — including installation instructions and release notes.

Typically, you have a number of fixes included in a patch, service pack, or maintenance release. You need to provide documentation to your customers on how to install the software fixes and release notes that include a list of defects and fixes included in the release.

In established software organizations, technical writers specialize in writing documentation. They seek input from the developers and SQA engineers on what exactly needs to be documented.

6. Unit and integration test the fix or enhancement.

Just as with a full release of a new product, developers and programmers need to perform complete unit and integration tests on their new code fixes and enhancements to verify everything actually works and that nothing new is broken.

7. **SQA regression tests the fix or enhancement and documentation.**

After the Development team finishes unit and integration testing they send the code to the SQA team. SQA regression tests all areas of the system's functionality that are determined to be at risk from the particular fixes. By fixing even one area of functionality, you always run the risk of breaking a number of other areas.

8. **Deliver the Fix or enhancement to your customers.**

After the fixed or enhanced code passes SQA testing, the software is SQA certified for release to customers. FTP and Web-based software download sites are a common delivery medium of choice in the brave new world of e-Commerce.

Debugging Those &%$# Bugs!

After a product bug has been reported in the change-management (defect/enhancement tracking) system, the developer or programmer attempts to track down the cause of the bug and fix the error. Not all system problems identified through testing are actually product defects. The debugging process often points out what appeared to be a bug, ended up being due to user error (procedural), an environment-specific problem, or a data-related error.

Three debugging techniques are widely used in the software industry, and the following sections describe these methods.

Problem isolation

The programmer or developer narrows down the source of the defect through a process of elimination, as follows:

1. **The programmer arrives at a hypothesis of the cause of the program errors related to the defect.**

2. **The programmer designs test-case scenarios using various test data that are closely related to the error messages.**

3. **The programmer executes the test scenarios one-by-one, entering various data input values until the error message is isolated to a particular set of data and test conditions.**

4. **Fourth, the programmer begins designing and coding a fix for the defective code.**

An example illustrating the use of this debugging approach can be seen with the Customer Self-Service Web. Suppose there is a defect change request entered in the change management system reporting that user cannot add a new case via the New Case form, resulting in errors.

The programmer first would examine the error message, which reads `Add New Case Insert failed - abnormal date format...` From the error message and trace of output from the New Case form, the programmer can formulate a hypothesis that the cause of the error is likely data-related, in particular, an abnormal date format where the date entered was too far back in the past.

Next, the programmer will develop test case scenarios and data designed to test the boundaries of the date functionality of the add New Case form. Then the test scenarios will be executed one-by-one by entering various data input values, until the error message stating `Add New Case Insert failed - abnormal date format...` is isolated to a particular set of data and test conditions. Finally, the programmer begins designing and coding a fix for the defective code.

Leave it to the Beav — I mean the computer

The second debugging method starts with gathering as much information as possible and is the most popular and conservative approach used by programmers. The mindset here is that the error the tester reports from the surface of the user interface (UI) isn't enough information to debug the software problem. Instead, you need to collect more data. How much more? Everything — including the kitchen sink.

Most operating systems, including Windows 9*x,* Windows NT, and Unix provide various information when errors occur, including database transaction/error log files, Web server and open database connection (ODBC) traces and dumps, stack register dumps, and so on. You want your customer service folks to receive training in how to get this information from customers and end users.

After you collect this data, you and your development team can sift through the information in search of the error message or strange value that unlocks the mysterious cause of the defect, even though it wasn't readily apparent from the errors reported by the tester.

Source code backtracking

Another technique programmers and developers use to debug erroneous code in small scale software projects is to manually trace back through each code change, retesting along the way to determine exactly what piece of code introduced the defect in question.

In the Customer Self-Service Web example, you are getting the error `Add New Case Insert failed - abnormal date format...` when you try to add a new case via the New Case Form. The programmer will manually "backtrack" through the Html, JavaScript, and SQL code to see what piece of code introduced the defect.

 A helpful tool you can use with Windows products is *Windiff* to identify all the files that have changed in a given software build from your prior build. Windiff is the counterpart to *Grep* in the Unix world, which identifies the file differences from your last build.

After the programmer identifies the changed files, then it's a matter of going through the tedious process of manually examining each and every line of code that has changed. Because this approach is so labor-intensive, it's not recommended for medium or large-scale software projects.

Customer-Acceptance Testing

Whether done formally or informally, your customers perform some degree of acceptance testing by the sheer fact that they install, configure, and start to use the software. If the software doesn't install properly, an early-morning phone call will roust your customer-support engineers out of bed earlier than normal to respond to the customers' needs.

For large software deployments at customer sites, you may also require a formalized acceptance procedure known in the software development industry as a *Customer Acceptance Test Procedure* (*CATP*). The objective of running a CATP at the customer site is to head off giving an unready product to the customer. You run this suite of tests as part of the process of delivering the software at the customer's site.

All the other test activities to this point are academic if the implementation of a particular customer's software implementation can't pass the CATP. If you're managing an internal project that doesn't involve an off-site customer implementation, you still need some form of an internal CATP. *Customer acceptance* is, of course, the operative term whenever you're talking about a CATP.

The typical scenario for a CATP occurs right after you release your software to the customers. The consulting arm of your organization embarks on an entire new series of implementation projects at the customers' sites.

One redeeming factor is that you don't really expect the CATP to test every nook and cranny of the software's functionality — as your SQA test team had to go through during system testing before the release. For more information on SQA System testing you can refer to the "System Testing" section earlier in this chapter.

The CATP exercises only those functions that you and your consulting team promised to deliver. Until your customer signs off on the CATP, however, your consultants may remain held as hostages in Siberia doing bug fixes until Hell freezes over!

In many ways, the CATP is very similar to a limited system test. Thus you can use a subset of your SQA System test as your starting point. The customer must sign off on the CATP, typically just before the system is ready to "go live" into production.

Your customer's implementation project is a completely new project beginning after the general availability (GA) release of the vanilla (out-of-the-box) version of your software, which repeats a slight variation of the seven phases of software development undergone for the GA release.

The implementation project at the customer site involves customizations that often go far beyond the functionality of the vanilla product. The detail and thoroughness of the CATP varies according to how extensive the GA code has been customized at the particular customer site.

As a general rule, every piece of code that touches a particular functional component of your original GA software can potentially break. Therefore, each customized component deserves thorough regression testing. For additional information on implementing the software at a customer site, refer to Chapter 12.

Automating Your Testing

After working on a number of software projects, team members realize the pressing need to automate their testing wherever possible. In a perfect e-world, your testing automation efforts begin early in the development cycle and affect all aspects of your development cycle. A number of testing automation tools is currently on the market.

Creating an automated test plan and scripts

To have quality automated testing, you must also have quality manual test plans and test cases as input.

By using the manual test plan and test case development processes and SQA Test Plan and SQA Test Case templates that you find on this book's CD-ROM as your guide, your team can set off solidly down the path to a successful automation effort.

After you have a manual test plan in hand, you can begin creating your automated test plan using your automated software. After you have created your automation test plan and have your manual test cases in hand, you can begin creating your automated test cases using automation software tool.

Chapter 10

Controlling Risks, Changes, and Scope Creep

Controlling the ever-creeping scope and other risks affecting your software project is one of the biggest challenges that you must face as a project manager. As soon as your marketing department presents you with the Requirements Document during the project kickoff meeting, your team can respond with a Project Scope Document. In the PSD, your project team identifies which RD features you can include in — or must exclude from — the project's scope.

Your mission is to negotiate the final terms of the PSD with the project sponsor and the marketing department as reasonably as possible so that you can keep your project scope from becoming a constantly moving target. During the analysis phase, you also need to identify and prioritize any potential risks that can jeopardize your project's success.

Your Change Control Plan is where you focus on controlling project change (risk) instead of merely planning.

This chapter and the accompanying kit templates on the book's CD-ROM can give you an edge in controlling risks, changes, and preventing "scope creep." So focus your rifle scope and sharpen your sword so that you can stop those creeps from running amok!

Understanding Types of Changes

If you're currently taking your first crack at being a project manager, you may wonder why you can't just rule with an iron fist and refuse to make changes in the software. ("Changes? Changes? We don't need no stinking changes!") In an ideal world, refusing to make changes is great. In the real world, however, things aren't always so easy.

You can make two kinds of changes in project management: necessary changes and "nice" changes. Putting off "nice" changes is easy — most managers shrug them off, intending to implement them later.

Necessary changes are those that usually crop up as you're developing and testing software. You may discover, for example, that two modules don't work together properly. This situation may happen because of poor planning or poor programming, but you definitely need to change something. You need to decide how to best make the change and what that action means for the project as a whole.

Experienced project managers know that necessary changes are both inevitable and carry potential risks. The mark of a good manager is to handle and deal with those risks with a cool head — balancing the needs of your company from a schedule standpoint and the customer from a quality standpoint.

Developing a Change/Risk Management Plan

Although you may go to great lengths to nail down every element of your project by creating and reorganizing a Work Breakdown Structure your project can still fall victim to change. (Refer to Chapter 3 for more details on creating the WBS and the critical path.) Because change is inevitable, you need to devise a change/risk-management plan for your project. A good C/RM plan encompasses the following easily identifiable facets:

- **Identification:** Change can come from many different places, both internal and external. You can experience a "scope creep" of requirements, objectives, design, technologies, markets, staffing levels, and other project resources.
- **Assessment:** After you identify a change in scope, the key to keeping your project on the critical path, on schedule, and under budget is to identify the effects those changes have on the project.

- ✔ **Aversion:** Changes don't normally occur singly; they come in bunches. After you identify and assess one change, you can often determine how to avert others that may come from the same source.

- ✔ **Monitoring:** You need to determine how to monitor your project so that you can continue to make sure that changes don't sneak in the back door.

See the section, "Handling Project Changes," later in this chapter to find out how to execute a project change plan that addresses these facets.

Laying out the plan

The C/RM plan doesn't need to be big and fancy. It does, however, need to describe the following items:

- ✔ **Key project documents:** These documents include your Requirements Document, Statement of Scope, and detailed design specs. You use these documents as a measuring rod to determine whether to make a particular change. The C/RM plan also includes a copy of a blank Change Request form, as I discuss in the section, "Working with a Change Control Board," later in this chapter.

- ✔ **Baseline project plan:** This item is your Microsoft Project plan, which I tell you how to put together in Chapter 4 and how to baseline in Chapter 6. You use this plan to determine how changes affect your schedule.

- ✔ **Change control board composition:** You use the Change Control Board to rule on the disposition of any proposed changes. I discuss this board in the following section. This portion of the plan describes who sits on the CCB.

- ✔ **Change control board processes:** This portion of the plan describes how the CCB does its work, describing when meetings occur and what decisions the board can reach.

The *Software Project Management Kit For Dummies* CD includes a template (CRM Plan.dot) that you may find helpful as a starting point for developing your own C/RM plan. Figures 10-1, 10-2, and 10-3 show parts of the C/RM.

Working with a Change Control Board

Early in your project management cycle, you put together a change control board. This group can consist of members of your development team, but you definitely also want to include a customer representative and possibly the actual project sponsor.

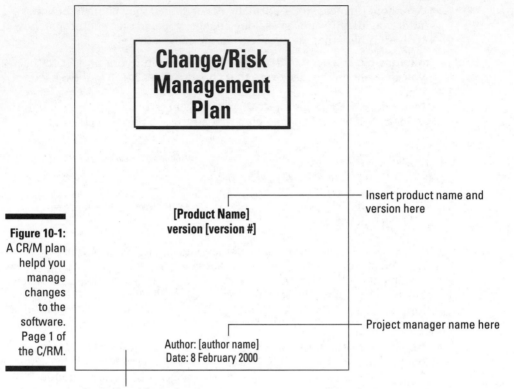

Figure 10-1:
A CR/M plan helpd you manage changes to the software. Page 1 of the C/RM.

Change/Risk Management Plan

Insert product name and version here

[Product Name]
version [version #]

Project manager name here

Author: [author name]
Date: 8 February 2000

Pages 2 and 3 not shown

Figure 10-2:
The CCB composition form. Page 4 of the C/RM.

CCB Composition

Instructions: *Provide the names and titles of each member initially assigned to the Change Control Board (CCB).*

Name	Title	Date Assigned

Consider including yourself, the project sponsor, and a representative from customer service in the CCB

CCB Procedures

Instructions: Indicate the procedures to be followed by the CCB in its considerations of proposed changes.

1. Change request submitted to CCB on Change Request form

2. Board meets to consider request

3. Board considers nature of change (critical, feature enhancement, etc.)

4. Board considers impact of request on schedule and resources

5. Decision is rendered

6. Project scope, schedule, or resources changed, as necessary

Potential Decisions

Instructions: Indicate the potential decisions that can be reached by the CCB. The following are provided as basic decisions. Changes should be made to reflect standards for your organization.

* **Approval.** The change should be adopted in the project. This approval may or may not result in a change in project scope. For instance, the change may only result in a change of how a particular project goal is implemented in software.

* **Deferral.** The change has merit, but will adversely affect the current project scope, schedule, or resources. The change is tabled until some future date or software version.

* **Field Fix.** The change has merit, but only limited applicability. It is approved to be made in a particular customer implementation of the software, but not in the general release.

* **Refusal.** The change is rejected, and does not warrant future consideration. The basis of the refusal can either be made public or not, based on common practice in your organization.

Figure 10-3: Sample CCB procedures and potential decisions. Page 5 of the C/RM.

The Change Control Board considers and makes decisions on each change that the project requires. In effect, it administers the C/RM plan that you put together. Unless the development project is very, very large (and changes are flowing fast and furious), the CCB can meet on an "as-necessary" basis. That the CCB actually hears every change that anyone proposes for the project, however, is imperative.

Anyone proposing a change for review by the board needs to write an official Change Request form for that change. An example of a Change Request form is shown in Figure 10-4. I also include this form as a template (Change Request Form.dot) on the *Software Project Management Kit For Dummies* CD.

If the change originated from a bug report, reference it here

Enter unique ID number here   Make sure this section is complete!

Change Request (CR) Form

Request Date			

CR#

Bug Report #	Call ID#	CMS Task#	Comments/Reference Information

Requested by: _____
CR requested for release(s): _____
Why is a CR being requested? _____
Why can't this fix wait for the
next release? _____

Who is the CR for? Check all that apply:
☐   Customers who: _____
☐   These specific customers: _____
☐   Restrictions: _____
For example, "Customers who: have Product ABC" or "Restricted to: customers who haven't installed CRxxx".

Estimated effort to create the CR (hours): _____

This CR will be incorporated into the next
release. Is there any reason it should not
be? Please state your reasons: _____

Discuss with development team

Figure 10-4: A Change Request form.

The CCB considers each change request on its own merits and compares it against the original project documents. The board then makes a determination of what to do. The CCB can reach any of the following four potential decisions in relation to any given change request:

- **Approval:** The board can choose to adopt the change in the project. Board-approved changes are then prioritized by the development project managers, who assign resources to design, develop, test, and package the changes which will be targeted for a future target release.

- **Deferral:** The board determines that the change has merit but that making it is certain to adversely affect the current project's scope, schedule, or resources. The board tables the change until some future date or software version.

- **Field Fix:** The board determines that the change has merit but only limited applicability. It approves your making the change off-site in a particular customer's implementation of the software but not in the general release.

- **Refusal:** The board rejects the change, determining that it doesn't warrant any future consideration. The board can either make public the basis of its refusal or keep its reasons to itself, depending on the common practice in your organization.

Handling Project Changes

You can take the following four proactive steps to handle project risks and changes: First, find out the project's status from your team members and project sponsor during your weekly project status meetings.

Second, evaluate the effect and cause of the change. Third, modify the plan and schedule to account for the change. Fourth, notify all involved parties of any project changes and reallocation of resources. I cover each of these steps in the following sections.

Getting the project status

Your project sponsor expects project status reports from you on at least a weekly basis. I recommend that you expect the same from your development team members. As a follow-up to the written reports, I also recommend that you hold weekly status meetings with your project team.

General issues that you may want to add to the agendas of your status meeting can include the following questions:

- ✔ Is the team following the prescribed development processes and procedures?
- ✔ Are any issues impeding the work in progress from meeting the planned project goals and objectives?
- ✔ Is the team completing the project tasks on schedule?
- ✔ Do any modules contain any high-urgency or severe bugs?
- ✔ Do you need to address any training issues among team members?

As you monitor the project through these meetings, you get a sense of how it's proceeding. Your team members need to claim both responsibility and accountability for their work. The formal status meetings and status reports are the vehicles through which you can manage responsibility and demand accountability. Nobody ever said that the job of a project manager is easy!

Evaluating the effect and cause of change

You may face a project change during the development cycle that's just waiting to crop up and cause your project to fail. For example, your competitor announces a new feature that your software project does not include. Your sales and marketing groups get the idea to lobby your project sponsor to sneak this new feature into your project scope. I advise you to handle these unplanned change requests carefully.

Blindly accepting huge scope creep changes is a sure way to introduce risks that your project's release date will slip, resources will be overallocated, or workmanship will be shoddy. It's okay to say no to changes, especially when the fate of your project is on the line! If possible, diplomatically "push back" to sales and marketing the responsibility for up-front planning that enables you to add features to future releases.

Particularly in large and complex software projects, a vital part of the project is that each development team member identify the particular risks associated with the tasks that you assign to them.

Two of the major responsibilities of your CCB are figuring out the cause of a change and determining how that change may affect the project as a whole. The board may want to consider many different elements of the proposed change, and each change request requires different deliberations.

In some cases, examining changes to past projects that your organization has undertaken may prove instructive. By understanding such past problems, you can better respond to similar challenges to your own project.

Modifying the scope, schedule, or resources

Suppose that, at the end of the day, after your project team's status meeting, you suddenly realize that you're over the budget that your project sponsor allotted you by $50,000! If that realization doesn't provide enough aggravation for you, you also discover that the total effort estimates for your project exceed your project sponsor's original schedule by more than 1,000 business hours! See Chapter 6 for a detailed discussion on modifying your project's scope, schedule, and resources.

No need to panic yet! After all, you go though this same process (negotiation, compromise, and retrenching) early in the project cycle, so by this point, it's not unfamiliar to you. In Chapter 3, in fact, I describe how you can use the Project Optimization Matrix to determine what possible wiggle room you can find in your project. You can use this same tool to again determine a course of action.

As I describe in Chapter 3, you can change only one of three aspects of your project: scope, schedule, or resources. You need to determine which one needs to "give" so that you can keep your project on course. Talk with your project sponsor and others on your development team to provide the most reasonable solution to addressing any changes creeping into your project.

There's one benefit of figuring out what you need to change later in a project cycle rather than earlier in the cycle. If the changes that require modification of your project's scope, schedule, or resources lie outside the project's original scope, you can diplomatically transfer responsibility to the project sponsor and sales/marketing to implement changes in future releases.

Notifying all concerned parties of change

Whenever you make a change to your project's scope, resources, or time, you absolutely must communicate with the project sponsor, development team, and any other project stakeholders concerning these changes. You want to make your notification somewhat formal in nature, sending everyone a memo and making the appropriate changes to your project's tracking software. You can announce the changes in any of your regularly scheduled status meetings, too, as you deem necessary.

Choosing a Course of Action

After the CCB approves a project change, you can take any of four alternative courses of action in dealing with the change so that your project doesn't slip too far from the yellow-brick road. One way to speed up completion of your project before a change affects it is to reorganize your Work Breakdown Structure so that your staff completes tasks simultaneously rather than sequentially. That way, critical tasks are completed before any changes can delay their completion. If your staff is large enough and not already overburdened with other tasks, such a course of action is quite acceptable. Typically, this course is most effective if you choose to implement it early in the development process. For more information on the WBS process, critical path, and multitasking, see Chapter 3.

A second technique to adjust for schedule changes is to alter the start and finish times of non–mission-critical tasks — providing that your customer approves of such changes, of course. As project manager, you become very good at determining whether an activity's start and finish times are critical to the success of the project.

You can sometimes even shorten a task's duration to speed up the completion of the overall project. Chapter 6 tells you how to shorten a task's duration.

The third approach is to throw more resources at critical activities that may be delayed by changes. As project manager, you probably have some discretion in taking this approach, provided that you stay within the resource limits available to you for the project. The trick to allocating extra resources is making sure that you don't create problems in other areas, such as ignoring other tasks for the sake of finishing one task. Over time, the tasks that you're ignoring may develop their own problems.

A fourth approach is to diplomatically push for some of the features to be scheduled for a future release, which seems to be a good face-saving approach.

Finally, if all else fails, you can decide to remove an activity from the critical path. You need to weigh the relative time and resources that you gain by removing the task versus any potential losses in the new software product's functionality and the resulting effect on the customer's wish list.

The Risk Priority Matrix, as shown in Figure 10-5, describes the four-step change/risk management process.

	Risk Category	Impossible Probable 0<*P<0.4	Probable 0.4<*P<1.0	Frequent 0.7<*P<1.0	Risk Aversion Options
Risk Severity	Software Performance	Software Supportability	Project Cost	Schedule Delay	
Show-Stopper	X	X	X	X	Eliminate critical path task(s) if possible.
Critical	X	X	X	X	Increase resources to speed up project completion.
Marginal	X		X	X	Delay start/finish times of non-critical path tasks
Low		X	X	X	Eliminate deliverable(s)

*P is the range in probabilities of a given risk's occurrence over the full duration of the project.

Figure 10-5: The Risk Priority Matrix.

Using Microsoft Project for Tracking and Controlling Change

Too many project managers overlook how useful tracking information is in their software projects. Throughout this book, I continually ask whether you have any project history files to which you can refer. I'm talking here not only about Microsoft Project files, but also about other items that you may use for tracking project information, including Requirements Documents, customer sales contracts, Work Breakdown Structures, Gantt Charts, test plans/cases, and all the documents that you include in your documentation plan.

Chapters 2 through 11 help you create these and other documents for your software project. By tracking a project's history, these documents help project managers accurately plan future software projects and minimize unforeseen changes.

You're probably wondering exactly how tracking such information helps you after you finish building your software project plan. Well, as project manager, your planning never stops. Project is a great tool for planning, tracking, and controlling your current or future projects. Looking at old Project files can tell you a lot, including how to estimate the scope, resources, and schedule for your current project.

Building the baseline project plan in Microsoft Project is unquestionably a big step toward managing a successful software project, but it's only the first step. You have to track your plan against your team's actual performance on the project, too. Sound difficult? It's quite simple, really, because Project puts valuable tracking information on your project's progress right at your fingertips!

Project gives you three project-tracking views: the baseline project plan, current information on the status of each task's progress, and whether they are on or behind schedule or complete. Project warns you when tasks have fallen behind schedule. Part of controlling project change is letting Project help you keep an eye on your tasks' status before they get out of control!

You can explore Microsoft Project's tools for tracking your current progress and use the program to make schedule updates on project progress, split tasks, and apply the power of the Gantt table to your tracking chores. To use Microsoft Project for tracking progress and making schedule updates, check out the information in Chapter 6.

Part V
Releases, Support, and Implementation

The 5th Wave   By Rich Tennant

I told Russell he should data model before we go any further.

Miss Claudia Schiffer, please.

In this part . . .

In Part V, I try my best to raise your awareness of the importance of the post–GA release implementation phase. Releasing the software to the customers provides only a partial solution to their problems. One of the factors that separate the men from the boys in Silicon Valley is a software vendor's customer reference base. Good customer references are generated by successful implementations (deployments) of your software at your customer sites.

Equally important after the GA release is the importance of providing your customer base world-class customer support. Having happy customers is terrific, but it's not enough. You have to delight them with extra niceties, such as free consulting services, tote bags, Cuban cigars, you name it.

Chapter 11

Releasing and Supporting the Software

● ●

In This Chapter

▶ Creating a product that you can deliver to market

▶ Putting together a great Customer Support Plan

▶ Release notes

▶ Documentation (hard copy, online, and Help files)

▶ Training (Instructor Lead Training, web-based training, and CD-based CBT)

▶ Getting into the grove with service packs and new releases

● ●

*A*fter your software has been certified as a GA (generally available) release candidate by your software quality assurance (SQA) testing group, your next major milestone is to launch your software's first release. Numerous software projects fail to make their debut because of a lack of effective configuration management, inadequate testing, and/or poor customer support. If you effectively apply the information in this book, however, your project is unlikely to become one of them.

In this chapter, your development team faces the big challenge of bringing your newborn software product from mere vaporware to a GA release. I describe how to get everything ready for market, set up a customer support plan, and design processes that enable customers to report various issues involving the product.

Creating a Deliverable Product

At some point, you actually do finish your software. I know . . . in the early days of the project, you may not think that day is ever going to arrive. But how do you know exactly when you *do* finish?

In Chapter 9, I take a close look at the personnel who determine when your software really is ready for release: your SQA engineers. After you send them your software for its system tests, they're running the show. They're the ones who conduct the system tests, keep the beta tests running, and cycle back to the programmers and analysts any problems that they find. Quite simply, after the SQA engineers run out of problems that need fixing, the software is ready for market.

But wait! Isn't it a truism the no software is ever totally bug free? Well, yes, which is why that statement *is* a truism. You probably know by now, however, that software can suffer from several different types of bugs. The primary concern of your SQA engineers is to get rid of every major and significant minor bug that they can find. They don't, after all, want the software to crash and burn at the customer's site. Thus, after they manage to expunge every bug that they find above the level of piddly and nit-picky from the program, you can be certain that it's probably ready for release.

Circulating the release checklist

A *release checklist* is a great tool for assuring that everyone along the development life cycle does their jobs and that no one skips any steps. Each major player on your team signs off on the checklist, verifying that you reached and accomplished all the major milestones, including: SQA, product development, technical publications, configuration management, customer support, and marketing.

You can begin creating your own release checklist by using the template (Release Checklist.dot) on the *Software Project Management Kit For Dummies* CD. Figures 11-1 and 11-2 show an example of this checklist.

You have no hard or fast rules as to what you need to put on the release checklist. It needs, of course, to reflect all the steps that you go through in your project, as well as all its major players. You can probably create the release checklist early in the development cycle, although you don't actually use it until near the very end.

After you complete the release checklist, it becomes a fixture in the permanent project history. The medium for storing project histories may be in the format of Word, Microsoft Project and other electronic file format, a sophisticated document management system such as Lotus Notes or Documentum, or simply a binder containing a hard copy of the release checklist and other project documents.

[Project Name]
Release Checklist

Software Quality Assurance

Complete	Incomplete	Tasks
☐	☐	Tested alpha release build
☐	☐	Tested beta release build
☐	☐	Reported all bugs in Change Control System
☐	☐	Tested all approved Change Requests
☐	☐	Completed SQA system testing
☐	☐	Resolved all critical bugs in Change Control System
☐	☐	Tested install of software
☐	☐	Executed Customer Acceptance Test Procedure
☐	☐	Tested installation instructions

Product Development

Complete	Incomplete	Tasks
☐	☐	Resolved all critical Change Requests
☐	☐	Completed unit testing of all modules
☐	☐	Completed integration testing of all module combinations

Technical Publications

Complete	Incomplete	Tasks
☐	☐	Completed unit testing of all documentation
☐	☐	Completed all documentation

Figure 11-1:
A release
checklist.
Page 1 of 2.

Ancillary components

Even if your software is ready for release, you still need to scurry about and get the ancillary product components in place. *Ancillary product components* are those components of your product that are in addition to the actual software, such as documentation, warranty information, and so on.

Configuration Management

Complete	Incomplete	Tasks
☐	☐	Configured modules for unit testing
☐	☐	Configured modules for integration testing
☐	☐	Configured alpha release build for SQA testing
☐	☐	Configured beta release build for SQA testing
☐	☐	Configured final GA release candidate build
☐	☐	Created final product master

Customer Support

Complete	Incomplete	Tasks
☐	☐	Tested install of software
☐	☐	Tested installation instructions
☐	☐	Executed Customer Acceptance Test Procedure

Product Marketing

Complete	Incomplete	Tasks
☐	☐	Approved customer announcement of software release

Approvals

_____   _____
SQA Engineer (must sign first)   Date

_____   _____
Customer Services   Date

_____   _____
Product Development (Project Manager)   Date

_____   _____
Technical Publications Mgr.   Date

_____   _____
Software Quality Assurance Mgr.   Date

_____   _____
Product Marketing Mgr.   Date

_____   _____
Configuration Manager   Date

Figure 11-2: A release checklist. Page 2 of 2.

Around release time, it's a good idea to start asking questions about packaging all the components of your release, such as: Do you have the printed version of the program documentation, for example, and/or a final electronic version? What about warranty cards, registration cards, marketing materials, and so on?

The number and variety of ancillary components obviously depend on the target market for your software. If you're developing software for the Web, for example, you can create everything electronically. If you're developing software for a limited number of customers, you may not have many components. If you're developing your program for the retail market, you're probably including a broad and varied range of ancillary components.

The bottom line is that you need to develop all these components in parallel with the software itself, and you need to finalize them all by the time you finish the software itself. Pull the components together and make sure that you now have a final product in the same form that you first envisioned so many months ago.

Selecting a delivery vehicle

Another important consideration in finishing up your project is selecting a *delivery vehicle* for your software. In all likelihood, your marketing department probably makes this decision long before you even become grand poobah of the team. On the off chance that *you're* the marketing department (as well as grand poobah), however, you need to concern yourself with how to deliver your software to its intended market.

You can generally deliver software in one of the following three ways:

- ✔ **Personal delivery:** If you're developing software for a single customer or a limited number of customers, you probably hand-deliver the software and personally install it on your customers' systems.

- ✔ **Physical media:** If you're trusting your customers to install the software themselves, you may want to use some sort of *physical media*. This type of delivery vehicle can run the gamut from floppy disk through DVD. Perhaps the most popular method of physical delivery these days is CD-ROM. Besides being quite capacious (great word, huh?), this medium offers the added benefit of read-only status, which means that your customer can't accidentally erase the files you send!

- ✔ **Electronic:** More and more of the world is connecting to the Web. You can easily set up a Web site or an FTP site so that your customers can download your software directly. Satisfying your customers' urges for immediate gratification this way is way cool.

After your software is ready from a quality standpoint, you may still need to whip it into a deliverable form. You may, for example, need to create a master CD that contains the final product and then send that CD off to a third-party vendor for mass replication.

Make sure that your SQA engineers test the final FTP download file or CD to make sure that everything installs correctly and that all components are included in the final build file or on the CD. This final testing may add just a bit more time to the release schedule, but that's better than ending up with a warehouse full of defective product.

Providing World-Class Customer Support

You finally release the 1.0 version of your software on New Year's Eve, five whole minutes before midnight — the drop-dead time. No doubt your staff was burning the proverbial candle from both ends to make this deadline. You're nice enough to send them on an all-expense paid ski trip, where they're all sipping champagne celebrating New Year's Day.

Now, you suddenly realize that they sent the code out the door perhaps a little prematurely to half a dozen customers in the sales pipeline. You hear that your customer-support department's hotline is ringing off the hook, while the support engineers scramble to track customer bug reports.

SQA tries to run duplicable test cases on reported bugs but can't find a frozen test environment for version 1.0. The development team's using all the servers for the future 2.0, 3.0, and 4.0 releases, so they have no time to install the archaic 1.0 release.

Sound like a bad nightmare? Yes, such a situation certainly can be. Your job, however, is to make sure that you provide the necessary materials to your customer-support department and the SQA team to enable them to do their jobs correctly.

Your first step is to create a *Customer Support Plan*. You want this plan to lay out all the specifics of support that your particular project requires after you deliver it to the customers. Figures 11-2 through 11-9 show a sample Customer Support Plan that you can use as a template for your own plan to support your product at the customer site.

Page 1 is a cover page

MISSION: Customer Support

Our commitment is to provide our customers and implementation partners with the best customer support package in the industry, while providing built-in incentives to minimize operation costs.

Short Term Strategy

Customer Support's short-term strategy is two-fold. First, the Customer Support staff will place special emphasis on providing personalized, live telephone support to our customers, with the objective of getting six (6) "live," referenceable customers. Second, Customer Support will assume a liaison role in coordinating optimal solutions for our customers, in concert with our project teams and implementation partners, throughout the project implementation and production cycle.

Your short-term strategy should lead into your long-term strategy

Long Term Strategy

To assist customers with their implementation projects, problem resolution, information requests, and product knowledge, our company will continue to develop and perfect Customer Support proactive Web-based tools for the "virtual" customer support center. These include a hypermedia knowledge base, support models, customer personalized Web pages, project histories, software downloads, FAQs, and a customer USENET Forum.

Web-based customer support tools will empower customers to answer their own questions and meet their own needs online, without even having to pick up the telephone. A self-service customer support approach will significantly accelerate customers' product knowledge, as well as enable Customer Support staff to focus on identifying and resolving issues of greater severity. Such an approach provides quality solutions with shortened response times and minimizes operation costs.

Figure 11-3: A sample Customer Support Plan. Page 2 of 7.

Customer Support Operations Plan

Customer Support's strategy will be carried out by implementing a two-phase operations plan. Phase I will establish skeletal Customer Support, and Phase II will provide customers with the self-service Web tools needed for proactive issue resolution.

Phase I: Establish Customer Support Center

The goal is to establish a Customer Support Center to support production down issues. This is to be accomplished by November 31, 2000. The tasks involved include the following:

1. Formulate Operations Plan

2. Assign dedicated telephone number

3. Assign Customer Support e-mail address

4. Complete first draft of Customer Support Web page

5. Establish customer and partner interaction metrics

6. Develop work flow and escalation process

7. Establish key metrics of customer satisfaction and operation costs

8. Hire and train technical support staff

Create a phased plan for

Formulate Operations Plan

This task was accomplished October 31, 2000.

Assign dedicated telephone number

This task was accomplished November 10, 2000.

Assign Customer Support e-mail address

This task was accomplished October 29, 2000. This address is a temporary repository of customer tickets.

Complete first draft of Customer Support Web page

This was accomplished October 27, 2000 and reviewed by Marketing. The page will be added to the company Web site by November 15, 2000.

Establish Customer & Partner Interaction Metrics

This task was accomplished October 24, 2000.

Figure 11-4: A sample Customer Support Plan. Page 3 of 7.

Contact Options

Customers can report their support issues to Customer Support via:

- **E-mail** at Support@YourCompany.com

- **Online** with 24-hour access to Customer Support's comprehensive Customer Support Center at www.Support.YourCompany.com

- **Fax** at 921-555-1347

- **Phone** at 921-555-1340

Hotline Specifics

Customer Support staff will be backed by the expertise of skilled technicians 24 hours a day, 7 days per week, holidays and weekends.

- **Live support** will be provided from 6 AM to 6 PM PST, Monday through Friday.

- **After-Hours Pager Support** will be provided between the hours of 6 PM and 6 AM for Priority 1 and certain serious transitional implementation-production situations only.

Response Time Matrix

To ensure that customers' needs are addressed in a timely manner, Customer Support personnel will prioritize issues according to the following escalation matrix:

Always include a response-time matrix!

Priority	Problem Description	Response Time
1	CRITICAL – Production system down. Causing interruption in business processing. Needs immediate response.	1–4 hours
2	SERIOUSLY IMPAIRED – Production system slow-down.	1 business day
3	NORMAL – Development or Implementation problem.	2 business days
4	LOW – Information request.	1–3 business days

Implementation Partner Support

Support for issues reported by partners assisting customers on site, with base product installations and implementations, will be coordinated by Customer Support staff in concert with the designated Implementation Manager (IM). See Code Customizations Support section for limitations on support.

Code Customizations Support

For customers that are on maintenance, Customer Support will support all customizations that have been developed exclusively through certified developers and/or consultants, and are ultimately included in a future release of the product. Base product support includes fixes, enhancements, and new releases.

Figure 11-5: A sample Customer Support Plan. Page 4 of 7.

However, support varies under the following circumstances:

- Customizations added exclusively to customer's version of a product, that are performed by on-site consultants, but are NOT included in a future maintenance or release of the product, are supported on a non-billable basis only to the point of system acceptance. The customer will assume all support for these customizations beginning from post-acceptance testing going forward. Additional support after acceptance testing is available on a billable basis and subject to the availability of resources, which will include fixes and enhancements.

- Customizations added exclusively by customer or implementation partner to customer's version of our products, or to base code, are supported only on a billable basis and subject to the availability of Customer Service consulting services.

Develop Work Flow and Escalation Process

This task was accomplished October 24, 2000.

General Ticket classifications

- Code approved Change Requests

- Documentation errors

- Product how-to, questions

- General product information and sales lead questions

- Customer Support Web site access issues

Support Roles and Responsibilities

- Primary Customer Contact (PCC): Each customer will have up to three PCC's responsible for reporting issues to Customer Support.

- Implementation Partner (IP): Third-party certified partner at customer site, who assists in implementation.

- Customer Support: Customer Support Center staff that coordinate support for resolution of issues.

- Implementation Manager (IM): Project manager assigned to a specific customer implementation project.

Work Flow and Escalation Flowchart

Temporarily, until formal Customer Support and defect tracking systems are installed, much of the ticket and defect tracking will be performed via email and Excel spreadsheet.

Figure 11-6: A sample Customer Support Plan. Page 5 of 7.

Establish Key Metrics of Customer Satisfaction and Operation Costs

This task was accomplished October 24, 2000.

Specific measurements and goals

- Measure response time from initial customer report to resolution, according to criteria in Response Time Matrix.
- Measure volume of reported issues by (1) Contact Option, (2) Priority, (3) Customer, (4) Product Group, and (5) time of day/night.
- Measure periodic customer support operating costs incurred by customer in labor hours offset by license revenue.
- Cost as % of revenue and/or cost per client engagement
- Customer retention and repurchase rates
  - % of customer sites serving as references; new business from customer referrals
  - % of incidents solved without personal contact (by problem category)
  - % of incidents resolved on first call; calls/issues
  - Issues per client/project/installation/module
  - Average and longest time to close incidents
- Telephone service level (average and longest hold times, abandon rates)
- Call lengths
- Email and other response times; # emails per incident
- Employee turnover
- Training hours per employee (initial + ongoing)
- Time to resolve escalation outside support
- Speed to reduce most-common problem types

Conduct periodic surveys via Web Site, telephone interviews, and customer site visits, regarding level of quality of customer support provided.

Hire and Train Technical Support Staff

- Train Customer Support staff on YourCompany.com products (accomplished November 3, 2000)
- Recruit, hire and train initial Technical Support Engineer by January 31, 2001.
- Evaluate staffing levels based on above Customer Satisfaction metrics on quarterly basis.
- Recruit, hire and train additional Customer Support Engineers, one additional engineer each quarter, if metric justified.

Figure 11-7: A sample Customer Support Plan. Page 6 of 7.

Phase II: Identify and Implement Web-Based Customer Support Center and Tools

The goal is to implement the Customer Support system. The tasks involved are as follows:

1. Evaluate and Purchase Customer Support System by December 15, 2000.

2. Arrange for Customer Support system demos by December 31, 2000

3. Install Customer Support System by January 31, 2001.

4. Train Customer Support staff on Customer Support System by March 31, 2001.

Future: Customer Support Offerings Still in Development

Personalized Customer Web Pages and Software Downloads

Personalized customer web pages are a great way to showcase Your Companysoft.com products as well as customize customer support. Personalized home pages will be maintained as a repository of customers' historical data, which will assist customers significantly with their installation of Your Companysoft.com products through the post-implementation process. Downloadable software fixes and customized enhancements, specific to the customer's environment, will also be available immediately through "push" technologies.

Support Model Web Page for Customizations

To assist customers with their Your Companysoft.com customizations, Support Model includes a comprehensive library of shared customer customizations. This page is hyperlinked to the Customer Support Center home page.

YourCompany.Com Online Customer Forum and FAQs (USENET)

- **Forum:** Customers can ask questions and share information in real time with other customers and YourCompany.com developers through an interactive forum via YourCompany.com's board.

- **Bulletin Board of FAQs:** Customers can readily obtain answers to FAQs and post questions and answers to each others' complex product adaptation issues, that are not readily answerable or would otherwise involve billable consulting support.

Figure 11-8: A sample Customer Support Plan. Page 7 of 7.

The marketing department can also use your Customer Support Plan to assist in sales of your software. As you can imagine, many potential customers may have a strong interest in knowing how you intend to support the software that they purchase from you. A good Customer Support Plan can become the deciding factor between a sale and no sale.

Reporting issues to customer support

After you release your software, it becomes generally available (GA) to all customers. As soon as a customer finds any problems or has any questions concerning your software, that customer's going to get on the horn or send an e-mail to your customer-support organization.

Reporting issues to customer support can take any number of different forms. You may want to set up a Web site that includes a "problem report," such as the New Case form used in the Customer Self-Service Web example throughout this kit, that automatically routes to the customer support subject matter expert to handle the customer's specific issue.

You can also send a form to a customer in a word-processing document format and then ask the customer to fill it in. The people at your customer support call center can also type reports that they receive directly into a database for later resolution.

Regardless of how you decide to handle the incoming issue reports, you need to track them. You need some sort of form, electronic or hard copy, that enables you to gather and retain the information you need.

The type of information that you need to gather for an issue report varies, depending on the type of product you're supporting. If you're supporting an accounting package, you may need information on debits and credits and transactions. If you're supporting a scientific calculator, you may need information on digits and units. How you tailor the issue-report form is up to your and your organization's needs. Figure 11-9 shows an example of a simple issue report that may suffice for some organizations.

The sample customer issue report shown in Figure 11-3 is available as a template (Customer Issue Report.dot) on the *Software Project Management Kit For Dummies* CD. Also, check out the Access database and Web-form prototype for the Customer Self-Service Web on the CD-ROM, referred to in Chapter 7. There is also a trial version of TRACK help-desk software from Soffront, Inc. on the CD.

After the issue report is on paper (or in the database), good customer service becomes an issue of competently managing the resolution of the customer issues that have been reported and providing intelligent answers to your customers.

Many different products for call tracking are currently on the market. You can often use these programs for setting up and logging all your issue reports. You may want to make a search on the Web for call-tracking software and research which one may prove best for your company's needs. For starters, a trial version of the TRACK help-desk software from Soffront, Inc. is included on the CD. Other vendors include: Vantive, Remedy, Bendata, and many others.

YourCompany.com
Customer Issue Report

Company:	
Contact:	
Title:	
E-mail:	
Phone:	
Fax:	
Date:	

Problem Description [Ask Questions/Define Problem: WHAT, WHEN, WHY, HOW problem and error message occurred. Latest change to system, etc.]:

Release [1.0, 1.1, 2.0, 2.1, etc.]:

Liscensed Products/Problem Module [Choose from Marketing's product list]:

Platforms:
 Operating System [NT 4.0, Sun Solaris 2.5.1, HP-UX 10.1, etc.]:

 Web Server [Netscape Commerce/Enterprise Server 3.0, Microsoft IIS 3.0, O'Reilly WebSite, other CGI-compliant HTTP server (e.g. Apache, etc.)]:

 ODBC Drivers [NT – Oracle 2.5.3.1.0, Sun Solaris – Intersolv 3.0 (3.01), HP-UX – Intersolv 3.0, Sybase – Intersolv 3.x, Informix – Intersolv 3.x]:

 DBMS Server [Oracle 7.3.4, Microsoft SQL Server 6.5, Sybase 11.1, Informix 7.2, or any other ANSI-compliant ODBC-accessible database]:

 Hardware:

Priority:
 ☐ 1 - Critical - Production down (resolved within 8 business hours)
 ☐ 2 - Seriously Impaired - system slow-down (resolved within 1–3 business days)
 ☐ 3 - Normal - Development/implementation (resolved within 1 business week)
 ☐ 4 - Low - Information request (resolved within 1 business week)

Solution [How to fix problem; work-around (if known)]:

Information below this line for internal use only

CR#		Response Time:
Outside Assistance: ☐ Y ☐ N		Resolution Time:

Figure 11-9: A sample issue-report form.

Turning materials over to customer support

After your software goes GA, you need your customer support department on the bandwagon. Simply making your customer support personnel aware of what's coming, however, isn't the end of the line for you. You also need to equip them with everything that they need for success in supporting your product.

You therefore need to provide your customer support team members with several copies of your finished software. More than that, however, you need to give them time to digest and understand the software. How many times are you frustrated by calling a customer-service rep who seems to know less about the company's software than you do? You need to offer your reps training and provide them access to the software experts in your department.

You need to provide resources to assist customer support in setting up sufficient test environments to support your customer base. Just after the GA released software goes out the door, as part of the Release Checklist, customer support will test the download and installation of the software on their server. If they have complications or questions, you need to provide development resources to get their test systems up and running ASAP before the flood of customer calls start coming in.

Such a statement may sound odd to you, but in some organizations, the concept may be downright revolutionary. The fact of the matter is, however, that customer support needs to actually *run* the copies of the software that you give them. They need a plain-vanilla computer system that's set up specifically to run your software — a test-bed system for trying to reproduce any potential errors that customers may report.

Didn't plan for this expense in your budget? Don't worry — the answer may prove easy: Many organizations simply transfer the systems that they use for testing over to customer support after you reach the GA point. These computers are normally already set up with your software, so they're ready to go. They even have some test data loaded, such as employee data including user ID numbers, names, addresses, etc., which can prove very handy in working with irate customers on the phone.

You need to give customer support a part in putting together your Customer Support Plan. If you haven't already done so, make sure that your customer-service reps get a copy of the plan and that they understand its ramifications. You also need to update them on any changes that you make to the software scope after you originally write the plan.

Handling bugs and enhancements

Inevitably, after a software release, customers and consultants in the field begin reporting purported bugs and making enhancement requests to customer support. As such reports pop up, your customer-support team needs to know how to handle them.

You ask why I'm telling project managers like you about bugs and enhancements reported from the field? Well, eventually you are going to have to deal with any software change requests by assigning your development resources to provide the software fixes to keep your customers happy!

First, you need to determine whether the report is a bug. If the customer insists that the issue is a bug, customer support will first see whether they can reproduce it in a plain-vanilla system. If so, you do have a bug and need to issue a Change Request from to development to assign a developer the task and target date to code the fix for the customers. (I cover how to handle Change Requests in Chapters 9 and 10.)

If you can't reproduce the bug, you need to get more information from the customer and determine whether the issue is really a misunderstanding of how the software works. This procedure can often prove frustrating as you try to blindly talk with someone on the phone and lead the person through a series of steps. Patience, of course, builds a great customer-support reputation if that fact's really any consolation.

If the report isn't a bug, you need to consider it an *enhancement*. Enhancement requests are a great thing for a company to collect because requests gives you a gauge for what customers are seeking. Enhancements include those features that the version of the software in question does not currently provide. For example, the *Customer Self-Service Web* release 1.0 may not have included the Web conferencing feature that was not scheduled until release 3.0.

How you handle enhancement requests is up to your organization. Some companies enter enhancement requests directly into their in-house change-request tracking systems. Others let them pile up until such time as they're ready to consider upgrading the software. Check with your company to determine its policy in this regard on previous projects.

Churning Out Service Packs and New Releases

After the New Year's ski-trip celebration, the development team staggers back into their pods either on crutches or halfway hanging over their PCs thanks to a night of indulgence on cheap champagne. There they find out that they're scheduled to work on a 2.0.1 service pack and three future releases, all due for delivery yesterday.

A *service pack* is another name for a bug-fix update. A service pack doesn't typically include software enhancements, but primarily a series of high-priority bug fixes reported since the last major release.

All the extra decimal points that marketing unilaterally adds to the release nomenclature may confuse your project team. Last year, your product was known as Release 1.0 but now suddenly is changing to 1.0.0. Then come the 2.0.0, 2.0.1, 3.0.0, and 4.0.0 releases, which introduce a whole new product line that sales is forever promising to the world — all of them suddenly, mysteriously appearing on everyone's plate.

Chapter 12

Implementing Customizations at the Customer Site

*I*n the six phases that I discuss in the preceding chapters, the focus is on developing a software project from a software vendor's standpoint throughout the development cycle. This chapter covers the implementation phase — the final phase of the development cycle. This phase describes what happens after your customers receive your software as a GA (Generally Available) release.

Your customer's implementation project is a completely new project that begins right after the general availability release of your software is complete. The implementation project repeats, with slight variations, the seven phases of software development that your project team goes through to prepare for the GA release.

The implementation project at the customer site involves customizations to your product that often go far beyond the functionality of the plain-vanilla product. A customer implementing the customer self-service Web may want to customize Case Management Reports to contain additional metrics (or statistics) beyond those that come right out-of-the-box. The customer may want many other customizations as well. The customer's request generates a *service creation,* which is a request for customizing your product that your consulting organization generally implements.

In the following sections, I walk you through the seven steps of the implementation (or service creation) of your software at an external customer site.

Identifying Your Role in the Implementation

In most cases, the project manager of a customer-implementation phase is a different person than the project manager who oversees the development of the software. Typically, a software vendors' consulting organization manages its off-site customer-implementation projects.

If you're the project manager who just finished the development of the GA software release that went out to the customer, however, don't think that your job is over. Both you and the customer-implementation project manager have a stake in the number of customers who successfully implement your new software.

Forgetting that your customers are your bread and butter is sometimes all too easy. Don't overlook the seventh phase of a project — the customer implementations — in which your customer-support people expect you to provide all the support that you can as they handle all the calls from customers and consultants out in the field.

Successful software organizations depend on their various departments working together as a team throughout every phase and level of the organization. Doing whatever is necessary to make customers happy should take precedence over fighting turf wars between departments. So, resist the temptation to walk away from your particular project after development is complete.

Happy customers pass on more references to other potential customers, which means more revenue and long-term maintenance dollars for your company. More customer references and dollars means that your startup company is one step closer to going public (IPO) or, if you're already a public company, that your stock is going to soar to higher grounds.

Keep in close contact with the consulting arm of your organization when it's out at the customer site and support the customer-implementation project manager. This individual takes the handoff from you to complete the seventh and final phase of the software project. The roles of the project managers generally break down as follows:

- **Implementation project manager:** During the implementation phase, this person takes charge — going to customer sites to identify their needs, gathering information, and overseeing the customization project's scope, schedule, and resources.

> ✔ **Software project manager:** Just because the GA release is out the door doesn't mean that you're off the hook! During the implementation phase, the manager of the GA software release acts as the lead expert and consultant to the implementation manager about what the software can and can't do. Also, with the help of the project sponsor, the GA release project manager helps the implementation project manager decide which customer requests fit within the scope of the implementation project and what may be a reasonable time frame to implement the changes.

In small software startups — companies that haven't yet offered their stock to the public — internal development managers and their teams often end up flying around the country, rolling out customer implementations and rushing to put out fires so that customers stay happy.

Implementations That Delight the Customer

You can treat the implementation phase as a rehashing of the previous six phases of your software development project. Yikes, another project! Wasn't one enough? Well, sometimes your revenue stream can be greatly enhanced by customizing your software to meet the needs of particular customers. Personal service can mean the difference between a lasting relationship with a customer and your customer deciding that your competitor's product may be a better fit for their needs.

The gap between an off-site customer implementation and the GA software release results from certain customer requirements going far beyond the scope of the original software product. Customers may request a spin-off version of your product. Suppose, for example, that you sell a client-server network version of an e-mail system. Some customers may then request that you create a version that's scalable across a wide-area network.

When the decision to create a custom implementation has been made by your senior managers, the process is a macrocosm of the steps you undergo to reach this point. Figure 12-1 shows a process flowchart of the workflow steps that a software implementation involves.

The typical steps to completing a software implementation include the following:

1. **Gather the customer's customization requirements and perform a gap analysis between the plain-vanilla software and any customizations that the customer wants.**

2. **Develop the implementation project plan.**

3. **Design the customizations and conversion programs.**

4. **Develop the code.**

5. **Test and fix the code.**

6. **Train the users.**

7. **Roll out the system into production.**

I cover each of these steps in the balance of this chapter.

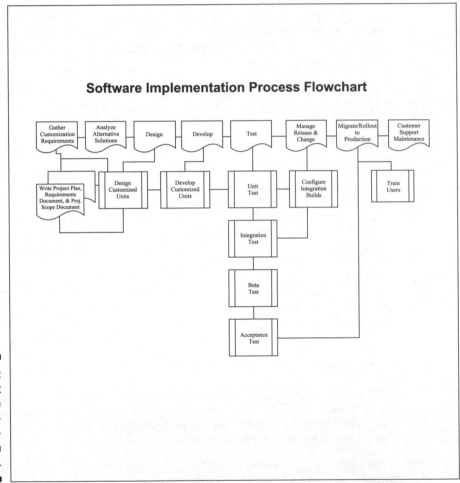

Figure 12-1:
A flowchart
for the
software-
implemen-
tation
process.

Gathering the Customer's Requirements

Suppose that your role changes from software-development project manager to implementation project manager at a customer site. You're now heading up a team of consultants and customer-team members who are responsible for installing, implementing, migrating, and customizing your company's software to meet the customers' specific set of requirements.

Before your implementation team sets foot on the customer site, your sales team gets a signed contract for the purchase of your software. The next step is for you, the project implementation manager, to sell your consulting service package to an executive at the customer site who's willing to sponsor the rollout of your software there.

You always have those customers who want to independently roll out third-party software add-ons to your base software products. Your job, therefore, is to present a compelling case that your consulting package adds value to the product itself. A common approach is to explain up front that your consulting team is on site only temporarily, just long enough to get the customer up and running live with the software. During the full development cycle of the implementation project, the customer's internal project team is both assisting and managing the project.

After you sell your customer's executive team on the idea of paying the big bucks for your consulting service package, your implementation team can take the next flight out to the customer site to begin gathering your customer's customization requirements and technical environment.

Many of the tasks that you must face in gathering requirements for an implementation are the same as those you face while developing the software. (You work on the requirements gathering phase for the original software in Chapters 2 and 3 of this book.) You must, for example, concern yourself with the following tasks:

- Justifying the project (Chapter 2)
- Submitting and approving the Request for Proposal (RFP) (Chapter 2)
- Getting approval (Chapter 2)
- Identifying the project sponsor and project manager (Chapter 2)
- Getting your implementation team in place (Chapter 2)
- Gathering the customer's customization requirements and then performing a gap analysis between the plain-vanilla software and any customizations that the customer wants (Chapter 2)
- Defining the customer's technical environment
- Preparing the Requirements Document (RD) (Chapter 2)
- Creating the Project Scope Document (PSD) (Chapter 3)

But wait! Being the eagle-eyed project manager that you are, you immediately spot two tasks that you've never seen before: Performing a gap analysis and defining the customer's technical environment are unique to an implementation project.

Although I leave you to draw on information that you can glean from Chapters 2 and 3 in conjunction with the templates on the CD-ROM in this kit for most of these tasks, the following two sections enlighten you concerning two new and unique tasks.

Performing a gap analysis

You already know your company's software, right? (If not, you're in way over your head right now. Sorry, Bucko.) What you're finding out at this point is what your customer *wants* your software to do. The difference between what your software does off the shelf and what your customer wants it to do (through any customizations) is known as *the gap*.

Many project managers and consultants fall into the gap and lose their professional lives. How far does your project have to come to meet customer needs? Not far if the original Requirements Document was well thought out and executed. The gap is a dangerous area that you must traverse carefully. Analyzing the gap, therefore, is critical to your success.

In performing a gap analysis, you list all the features that you must add to your software so that it can fulfill the expectations of your customer. Remember that your customers expect your software to fit the ways that they do business and are reluctant to change how they work to fit your software.

Be careful that you know the limitations of your software so that you can reset the customer's expectations to what customizations are reasonable given the project budget and schedule constraints. This approach keeps you from falling into the trap of overcommitting and underdelivering. With this basic expectation firmly in mind, you can start to see why the gap is a dangerous place.

No one understands the software's strengths and limitations better than the software project manager who worked through the original development of the product. This person is among the main informational resources to the implementation project manager.

As you perform your gap analysis, listing detailed information about customer expectations is critical. Simply saying that the customer needs a data-input screen, for example, isn't enough detail. Your software probably already includes a data-input screen; what you need to know is what type of data-input screen actually lives up to the client's expectations. What proprietary information does the customer want to put in place? What information does the customer not care about storing? Should the look and feel mimic another application that the customer's workers are familiar with to cut down on training time?

You want to list each feature that the customer requires of your software and then list what your software actually does in this area — if it does anything at all. If possible, include screen shots or screen layouts of both the customer's existing system and the new system you're implementing. Indicate exactly what you need to change for the customer's implementation.

Performing a gap analysis can prove arduous and demanding, depending on the size of the implementation project. Meeting the needs of the client, however, is essential. After you finish the gap analysis, you have in your hands the basis of a new Requirements Document. You can find out how to create an RD in Chapter 2.

By using the *Software Project Management Kit For Dummies* CD, you can easily adapt the Requirements Document template (Requirements Document.dot) that I present in Chapter 2 to your needs for the implementation project.

Defining the customer's environment

A continual challenge for project implementation teams is the wide variance in customer environments. The one-size-fits-all approach to software selection seldom applies to large and medium enterprise-wide software implementations.

In preparing for your development environment and for the rollout of your software at the customer site, I recommended that you conduct a thorough capacity planning study. During this capacity planning study, you evaluate the customer's current technical environment so that you can make accurate recommendations for any hardware or software upgrades that the customer needs.

The accuracy of your capacity planning recommendations primarily depends on the extent of the historical data tracking that you conduct on your implementation projects. The more implementations you do (and keep accurate records of), the more accurate your recommendations become.

The following list describes two basic steps to developing your customer's capacity planning study:

✔ **Inventory existing hardware and software:** You want to take an inventory of what network and computer configurations your customer currently uses. You're looking at: whether the customer's network is a 10baseT or 100baseT, and so on; how many NT or UNIX servers, Web servers, and database servers are on the network; and the processor type, clock speed, memory (RAM), and hard-disk capacity for each.

Obviously, the more bandwidth that your customer has and the faster the computers run on the network, the better your implementation will run. But in some cases, your customer may need to purchase new equipment just to get started. Try to strike a balance between making hardware recommendations that ensure that your application runs well and recommendations that elicit customer sticker shock.

Gather as much infrastructure information as possible — as early in the implementation as possible. Telling a customer halfway through the implementation that obtaining acceptable performance requires them to significantly change their IT structure may not sit well.

✔ **Review previous capacity planning project histories (if any):** If your software company's been around for a while, you can probably dig up some historical records on previous customer implementations of your software products.

✔ To perform accurate capacity planning, you need empirically solid data. Before rolling out an implementation of the Customer Self-Service Web software at a customer site, for example, you want to look at previous project implementations — and especially historical estimates of the following:

• **Network-bandwidth capacity:** You can look over project histories for software implementations similar to the one you're conducting at the current customer site. You can look at what the recommended requirements were for other customers' network-bandwidth capacity configurations, including network 10baseT, 100baseT, or other Hubs; the number of NT or UNIX servers; and the servers' processor types, clock speeds, memory (RAM) capacities, and hard-disk capacities.

In applying this approach of capacity-planning estimation to the Customer Self-Service Web project example, the objective of the network bandwidth-capacity estimate may be to determine the number of pages that the Web server can deliver through the network interface per second.

• **User-load capacity.** User-load capacity planning estimates the total possible number of user transactions that the customer can run in a given interval. The *estimation period* identifies a time interval, such as a typical business day's activity, for which you want to estimate or, preferably, calculate results.

In applying this approach to capacity-planning estimation to the Customer Self-Service Web project example, the objective of the user-load capacity planning estimator is to estimate the total number of Web pages that a typical user visits during a single session on the Customer Self-Service Web site to complete a given transaction.

In adding a new case record via the New Case Form, for example, you find that the average user may visit a sequence of five Web pages. Given this parameter, you can then estimate the average number of user transactions. Assuming that each user performs a single transaction during the interval, you can further estimate the maximum number of users that the site can serve at one time.

- **Hardware-memory (RAM) capacity:** Basing your figures on the maximum user-load capacity estimates (see the preceding bullet), you now can estimate the main memory requirements for the Web server and database server. The Web server must run an operating system (Windows NT or UNIX) plus the Web-server software and still maintain room for the database-client software.

  The database server machine also must run several software components. Each component has a fixed memory requirement, as well as one that varies as the number of connected users or as the number of database connections varies. In estimating the total memory requirements, you also take into account the total number of concurrent users that you calculate in the network bandwidth-capacity estimate.

- **Budget estimates:** Your project history records may also help you and the customer in budgeting your capacity plan to purchase the optimal hardware and software mix to best suit the needs of your customer's software-implementation project.

For more information on capacity planning and networking, please refer to *Networking For Dummies*, 2nd Edition by Doug Lowe (published by IDG Books Worldwide, Inc.).

Develop the Implementation Project Plan

After you gather the customer's software requirements and complete the Requirements Document for the implementation phase of the project, you need to hold the implementation planning meetings. These meetings include the following:

- ✔ Implementation kickoff meeting
- ✔ Implementation-plan brainstorming meeting
- ✔ WBS (Work Breakdown Structure) meeting

As you conduct these meetings, you start to pull together the materials that you need for your implementation project plan. The following sections describe these meetings in more detail.

Implementation kickoff meeting

As implementation project manager, you coordinate the scheduling and agenda for the *implementation kickoff meeting* with your customer's executive sponsor and core project team. This meeting serves the same general purpose as the project kickoff meeting that I describe in Chapter 3. This kickoff meeting, however, does offer a few subtle differences from the earlier one. The main agenda items for this meeting now include the following:

- Presenting the Requirements Document
- Conducting a project question-and-answer session
- Identifying the project name
- Introducing the project sponsor
- Introducing the project manager
- Presenting the team members' roles and assignments
- Drafting a preliminary Project Scope Document
- Agreeing on a meeting schedule

If you're the implementation project manager for an off-site customer location, you need to be aware that that the same process applies to this type of kickoff meeting as to the earlier one — only the players and roles vary slightly. Instead of the product manager gathering the requirements and writing and presenting the Requirements Document, you, as implementation project manager, assume these responsibilities.

Instead of an internal management executive from your software company serving as project sponsor, a top executive representative of your customer fills this role during the implementation phase. And finally, your implementation team may consist of both internal employees of your company and customer team members, and often even third-party consultants.

Implementation plan brainstorming meeting

Your second implementation team meeting is the *implementation plan brainstorming meeting*. Ideally, you set up a conference room containing large white boards or easels. I recommend handing out a stack of sticky notes to each of your team members to enable them to jot down any requirements, objectives, and tasks that they may think up during the meeting. You then post all the sticky notes to the board in six to ten high-level task categories.

The focus of this meeting is to give your implementation team the opportunity to analyze the Requirements Document and brainstorm ideas to help define the scope, objectives, and tasks for the Project Scope Document and the preliminary project plan.

At the close of the meeting, your team needs to walk away with the following deliverables:

- ✔ A statement of the primary goals and objectives of the implementation
- ✔ A refined Project Scope Document
- ✔ A decision on which requirement to include and exclude from the project
- ✔ A preliminary project schedule
- ✔ An estimate of required resources
- ✔ A preliminary Change/Risk Management plan

Notice that, essentially, no difference exists between these items and those that I develop in Chapter 2 of this book. In other words, the Project Scope Document for the implementation team serves the same purpose as the PSD for your earlier development team. The only difference, of course, is the focus of these deliverables — here you're focused solely on a single implementation of your software for a specific customer.

Work Breakdown Structure meeting

Your third implementation team meeting is the Work Breakdown Structure meeting. Here is where you divide up the work to do (as the RD and the PSD define it) among your team members. This meeting may run relatively short or quite long, depending on the size of the implementation project.

By the time you reach the implementation phase of a project, you're probably an old hand at conducting a WBS meeting. (If not, see Chapter 3.) As my grandfather used to say, "Work is work." Whether you're implementing or developing the project doesn't really matter; you still need to divvy up the work among the workers.

As I describe in Chapter 3 in reference to the software project manager, your job as implementation manager is to make sure that you assign the best resources to the right tasks, without overburdening any individual member. Focus on well defined tasks and try to develop durations for each of the tasks.

In working with an implementation team, you face a bit more risk in making work assignments than you do with a development team. You probably understand the character and capabilities of the development team members. You probably don't have such an understanding of team members that come from your customer site and from consulting firms, and this is a significant challenge to implementations.

Being a good implementation-project manager, therefore, requires extremely good listening skills and tact. You have to be able to determine which team members have the technical expertise and drive to get the job done, and you have to avoid offending people in your assignments. If you assign tasks to team members who aren't competent in that area of expertise, you risk the possibility that the tasks may never reach completion or may be incorrectly corrected, which can, in turn, delay the completion of the entire implementation project.

As implementation project manager, you need to develop a rapport with managers at the customer site because these folks know the strengths and weaknesses of their own people and can therefore help you immeasurably.

Remember that managers at the customer site are accustomed to being in charge of their people, which may put you in a tough spot as manager of the implementation project. Make sure that customer-site managers are fully on-board with the implementation and know how important their input is to the success of the operation. Make doubly sure that your team treats team members from the customer site with the utmost respect. Your team's mission isn't to critique the IT setup of the customer site.

As you plan the migration or integration, you also want to take into consideration any organizational effect that the event may have. Technology often forces people to change, and one of the benefits your customer may try to achieve through your new system is a reduction in personnel. The people that such a decision affects don't work in a vacuum, however, and the awareness of such change may cause hostility or distrust on the parts of many people. Be aware that human resources issues such as these can affect your migration or integration plans, and even the performance and cohesiveness of your implementation team.

You also face the possibility that you (along with your consulting team) aren't even in charge of the implementation process and answer to the customer's appointed project manager. This situation really isn't so different than when you're in charge. In both instances, listening carefully and being tactful are paramount to the success of the project. You may even give your customer a copy of this kit to help them through the process.

With all your implementation tasks in hand, you can start to put them in order. The implementation-brainstorming meeting, therefore, needs to focus on which tasks to carry out in which order. Figure out whether you can handle any of the tasks in parallel and whether the start and end times of any tasks can overlap. The tasks that are dependent on each other determine the critical path of the implementation. For further details on the WBS meeting, I recommend taking a good look at Chapter 3.

You may find using the old whiteboard-and-sticky-note approach to ordering your tasks helpful. Write each task on its own sticky note and place it on the white board. Then start moving the tasks around until they're in the optimal order by task priority and dependency in the overall WBS task network.

After you finish creating the WBS, make sure that you enter it into a program such as Microsoft Excel. Doing so enables you to make changes to the order of your tasks and to get senior management's sign off before you move the entire project into Microsoft Project.

Creating the implementation plan

After completing the first three meetings, you're ready to begin building your implementation plan document. Essentially, you accomplish this task by pulling together the documents that you create to this point in the process, as the following list describes (including references to previous sections in this chapter):

- ✔ A list of the implementation team members and their skills (see the section "Implementation kickoff meeting," earlier in this chapter).

- ✔ An analysis of the customer's environment (see the section "Defining the Customer's Environment," earlier in this chapter).

- ✔ The Requirements Document (see the section "Implementation kickoff meeting," earlier in this chapter).

- ✔ The Project Scope Document (see the sections "Implementation kickoff meeting" and "Implementation plan brainstorming meeting," earlier in this chapter).

- ✔ The Work Breakdown Structure (see the section "Work Breakdown Structure meeting," earlier in this chapter)

- ✔ Your estimate of the resources that you need (see the section "Implementation-plan brainstorming meeting," earlier in this chapter).

- ✔ The Change/Risk Management plan (see the section "Implementation plan brainstorming meeting," earlier in this chapter).

These documents become your implementation plan. After you get them in place, get everyone on the project to sign off on the package. With signatures in hand, you're ready to get things rolling!

If you need help on starting any of these documents, refer to Chapters 2 and 3 and the list of templates on the CD-ROM at the end of each chapter that you can use as a basis for your own implementation-project documents.

Designing the Customizations and Conversion Programs

At the time that you first design your software (which I discuss in Chapter 7), you labor over getting just the right mix of features within the available time frame. You're looking to ensure in the process that the interface and other elements are applicable to a wide range of customers.

In the implementation phase, the goal is to revisit the design and, this time, adjust it for a single customer. Although that adjustment may mean considerable work, you also find an upside in the procedure — you don't need to worry about your software being all things to all people. Instead, you can focus on the needs of your specific customer (as I define in the section "Performing a Gap Analysis" earlier in this chapter) and make sure that your design reflects those needs.

So much for the customizations — but that's not all that you need to design. You need to refer again to that gap you analyze at the beginning of your implementation project. After you define this gap, you know a starting point and an ending point for the software — a point A and point B, if you will. You now need a way to get from point A to point B. Customizing the software to reflect point B is easy enough, but you may also need to convert existing data so it's still accessible after you reach point B.

You may, therefore, need to design a number of conversion programs for the customer. Again, you need to know the current state of the data and the customer's desired ending state of the data; then you must create the programs to change the data from one state to the other.

I recommended that you conduct several meetings with your implementation team to hammer out the configuration and conversion design details. Focus on the same deliverables that I describe in Chapter 7 but, this time, from the customer's perspective.

The deliverables include designing the customizations and the conversion programs and creating all the design documents that you know and love: an Entity Relationship Diagram, a Data Flow Diagram, Functional Specifications, and Detailed Design Specifications, which I cover in detail in Chapter 7.

You can start with the same design documents that you create for your in-house software project. Simply modify them to reflect the specific needs of your customer.

Developing the Code

During the design phase, your implementation team performs the high-level and detailed design of the software solution to the customer's problem, as you define that problem in the initial gathering phase and later analysis phase. Now you start to create the code for the solution according to your designs.

Unless the implementation project you're undertaking is huge, developing the actual code is relatively easy if you compare this task with your original development efforts. Granted, you may need to modify several of the existing modules, and you may need to create several new modules. The hard work, however, is complete, and now you're simply looking at customizing an existing product.

You may, however, run into a gotcha while developing this code. If the programmers you use for the coding are on your customer's payroll instead of on yours, they may not use the same standards of development that you use in first creating the software. You can make a strong case for using your own programmers for the customization, using the reasons in the following list:

- ✔ Your programmers know the original code and don't need to go through a learning cycle.
- ✔ Your programmers follow the same coding standards that you use for the original code.
- ✔ If your programmers experience problems, they have direct access to others in your organization.
- ✔ Your programmers know what you, as implementation manager, expect.
- ✔ Your programmers are answerable to you and not to a different boss.

For the reasons in the preceding list, I highly recommend that you use your own programmers if possible. Doing so can make your job quite a bit easier.

Testing and Fixing the Code

By this point, you may have gathered that I'm a firm proponent of testing your code. (That's why I dedicate a long chapter — Chapter 9 — to the topic.) You need to take the same rigorous approach to testing your code during an implementation project as you do during a regular software-development project.

You need, therefore, to conduct all the same tests that you conduct during development, with the exception of beta tests. Because you're not releasing this version of the software to the general public, beta tests don't serve any real point. Instead, you want to focus all your testing energies on making sure that, after customization, the software works exactly as you anticipate during the design phase.

Focus your testing during this phase on the following types of tests (for which Chapter 9 covers all aspects in detail):

✔ **Unit testing:** Test each customized module as you complete it, as well as each brand-new module. Do this testing before you integrate any software.

✔ **Integration testing:** After you start combining modules into builds, test each build thoroughly. Pay particular attention to regression testing, because you know how the original software fared in these tests.

✔ **System testing:** As you start system testing, make sure that those implementation team members who work for your customer understand that this is just the system testing and not the final testing. In other words, they need to know to still expect bugs at this stage.

As you test your software, make sure that you keep meticulous notes on any errors that you encounter and how you remedy them. Testing and correcting errors generally don't take as long during this phase as they do at the time that you first develop the software.

Make sure that the test cases you develop for the implementation project are not mirror images of those that you use for in-house testing. You can start with the in-house tests as a jumping-off point, but your customers probably have special data requirements that warrant special test cases for their particular situations.

The reason I'm warning you not to rely exclusively on the in-house tests but to turn to out-of-house tests is that you're now testing a software product with significant customizations from the off-the-shelf version that you originally delivered. So you need to look at each customization to develop designer test cases that exercise all the new functions and then regress the original off-the-shelf functions to make sure that they all still work correctly.

Training Everyone (Even Your Grandmother!)

Training the customer's system administrators and users is critical for a successful software implementation rollout at a customer site. This stage of the process is where you can involve the documentation writers and trainers from your company in the implementation project.

Any training that you conduct really needs to start well before the actual day that you go live with the new system. The obvious reason for starting so early in your training efforts is that the users need to know how to use the system on the very day that you install it.

Putting a phased training plan into place is generally a good idea. For most cases, the phased approach that I describe in the following list works best:

- **Train the administrators:** These people are technically responsible for the new system. Your trainers need to train them in every aspect of how to configure and use the software. You may also want to get them familiar with the behind-the-scenes design documents (that is, the Entity Relationship Diagram, a Data Flow Diagram, Functional Specifications, and Detailed Design Specifications) for the software.

- **Train the trainers:** The purpose of this training is to develop in-house trainers for the customer. These people are the ones who remain on-site after you leave and are responsible for ongoing training. Your in-house trainers and the customer site administrators that you train can work together to train the customer's training staff.

- **Train the users:** The users and the customer's technical support staff are the last people you train, and the customer's trainers and administrators conduct this training. Your own trainers, however, remain on-site for at least the first cycle of training to make sure that everything goes smoothly. Keep in mind, too, that trainers sometimes ignore tech support personnel, although these people are the ones who always end up training the user community after all the formal training is complete. Making sure that the customer's tech support staff receives sufficient training in your product is important to a successful implementation.

As you conduct training, do so at a location distinctly apart from the normal work areas of those you're training. If someone can track them down with a phone message, they're sure to do so, which has a disruptive effect on everyone involved in the training. I suggest an off-site conference center in which you can create an atmosphere conducive to effective training.

Your trainers need to prepare training materials for each of the three groups they're going to train. Each group has specific needs and a unique perspective on the software that these materials must address. If you take the time to develop quality training materials, the implementation of your software can go that much smoother. Effective training materials may include the following items:

- Handouts
- Manuals
- Workbooks
- Video courseware
- Computer-based training courses

The standard documentation that you develop for your GA software are probably insufficient for customized needs. Make sure that your technical writers develop a documentation plan that takes into consideration the changes that you're making to the software. This new documentation is also a great marketing tool as customers love to see their own names on the cover of a new set of plans.

The *Software Project Management Kit For Dummies* CD includes a Training Preparation Checklist document that you can put into your project binder and use to check off necessary high-level training needs. The document is shown in Figure 12-2.

[Project Name]
Training Preparation Checklist

Complete	Training Preparation
☐	Identify courseware and equipment requirements
☐	Develop courseware
☐	Develop trainer evaluation form
☐	Train the trainers
☐	Prepare schedule
☐	Identify and reserve locations
☐	Schedule sessions
☐	Train the System Administrators
☐	Train the Users
☐	Measure and Improve Quality of Training
☐	Distribute trainer evaluation forms
☐	Customers evaluate trainers
☐	Measure results
☐	Execute training improvement plan

Figure 12-2:
The Training Preparation Checklist.

Rolling Out the System

No, this heading doesn't reflect some polka refrain *Roll out the system — we'll have a barrel of fun!* A system rollout, however, can be fun. It can also be embarrassing and painful. The deciding factor is how well you do your work to this point. You should go into the rollout with the confidence that only thorough testing can provide.

After all the development is complete and testing proves the validity of the coding, the time arrives to finally throw the switch and make the change. Your customer either migrates from the old system to the new at this point or integrates the new system with the old. This day is probably one of much trepidation for your customer. Your testing, however, is likely to go a long way toward minimizing any fears the customer may have.

Plan to make the migration or integration during a time in which the customer isn't experiencing a busy workload. You may want to make the switch overnight, for example, or on a weekend. Doing so enables you to get everything in place before work starts in earnest on the following business day.

In some cases, simply "throwing a switch" and going from one system to another doesn't make sense. Instead, the customer may want to run parallel systems for a time to verify that all the kinks are out of the new system. In effect, having two systems — old and new — online at the same time provides a safety net for the customer. If your customer wants to proceed in this manner, you need to know the plan very early in the design phase of the implementation project, which I cover in the section "Gathering the Customer's Requirements," earlier in this chapter.

Part VI
The Part of Tens

The 5th Wave — By Rich Tennant

"I'm always amazed at the technological advances made at ad agencies and PR firms."

In this part . . .

1was watching David Letterman's top ten reasons for not trusting your project schedule when I wrote this part. Okay, so it's not the project schedule's fault, it's the project manager!

Check out these two ten-or-so long lists for quick and dirty project management tips. Chapter 13 provides ten tips for effective project management. Chapter 14 answers the hard questions that are on project managers' top ten FAQs list.

Chapter 13

Ten Tips for Effective Software Project Management

*A*s project manager, you can employ a number of proven methodologies, tools, and processes to promote the success of your software project. The most important maxim I want to leave you with is that effective project management is a team sport. A project manager doesn't make successful projects alone, but only through the collective effort of your project team.

Just for you bottom-line-on-top project managers, this chapter provides an executive summary of the top ten tips for effectively managing software projects, taken from the many methodologies, tools, and processes that are presented in this kit. If your development team doesn't look at any other part of this book, I strongly recommend taking a few minutes out of your busy schedule to check this chapter out.

Where appropriate, tips include references to chapters and CD-ROM templates that you can refer to in your free time. (You know — those blissful minutes you're eating lunch, in the restroom, or stuck in rush-hour traffic.)

Happy software project management!

Do Your Homework

The recurring theme in software project management is planning. Planning is doing your homework. And, yes, your fifth-grade math teacher's unstated belief that you can never do enough homework is correct. Don't be tempted into diving headlong into a project without answering the hard questions about scheduling and costs or looking at what products the competition already has out on the market.

The success of the Yahoo!s and Amazon.coms is a result of smart project managers doing their homework. They put together great business plans, took a close look at their competition, added new products and features, set aggressive project schedules, and estimated the costs for the resources to successfully execute the project plans. The result was overnight success.

Table 13-1 lists the templates on the *Software Project Management Kit For Dummies* CD that may be helpful in analyzing the competition, market factors, comparing project candidate returns of investment, scheduling, and estimating your project's costs.

Table 13-1 Useful Templates for Gathering Customer Requirements

Chapter	Template
2	Cost-Benefit Summary.dot
2	Customer Requirements Survey.dot
2	Project Candidate ROI analysis.xlt
2	Requirements Document.dot

Do the Up-Front Work

There's a lot of preparation work that goes into kicking off a successful software project, including putting together a dynamite project team, gathering and analyzing the software requirements, and creating a Project Scope Document.

The selection of your project team is the single most important component in preparing your software project plan. Recruiting highly qualified and committed staff is crucial to your project's success. The fact that you were selected for this software project is a vote from senior management that you have a special skill set to get the job done. Now's your chance to use your people skills to search out the cream of the crop.

The Development Team Skill Matrix introduced in Chapter 2 can help you ensure that all the requisite skills necessary to ensure your project's success are available on your project team.

Another key issue you need to focus on up front (before throwing tons of dollars and resources at your software project) is exactly what *problem* your customers are trying to solve. That may sound rather pessimistic, but if you forget to look closely enough at the problem, your software may never become part of the *solution*.

Further details on gathering your customer's software requirements can be found in Chapter 2.

The Project Scope Document is a great tool to get a jump start on your software project by setting the parameters for the nature and amount of work involved with your software project. The PSD serves as the development team's response to marketing and the customer requirements defined in the Requirements Document. It's helpful to think of the PSD as the mission statement that outlines the primary project goals. Creating this document often becomes a wake-up call for what features fall into the must-have category, the important-but-you-can-live-without category, and the add-on-nicety category. For further details on writing a PSD, refer to Chapter 3.

The *Software Project Management Kit For Dummies* CD contains a Project Scope Document that may be helpful in deciding the scope of your project.

Develop Consensus

As project manager, you're often the liaison and developmental diplomat between marketing and your project team, sales, tech support, and the customer. Information flows through you as your project's single point contact. One of your primary functions is to foster consensus among all stakeholders of your project.

Because of your pivotal position, you need to be aware of the importance of being open, accessible, and communicative. Your development team counts on you not only for leadership, but also to be their champion to the "powers that be." Your customers and/or company organization expect you to lead your development team to deliver a product they expect and need. Not only are you faced with the seemingly impossible challenge of trying to deliver the product on schedule, but also at the level of quality that sales and marketing have sold to the customers.

Be Realistic

An old maxim states that those who fail to plan should plan to fail. Don't fall into that old trap — make sure you develop a rock-solid project plan that can see you through the entire software development cycle. But even the best plan can't fit an elephant into an acorn. One of the most difficult tasks for a new project manager is identifying when a schedule is impossible to meet. You want to wow your bosses by delivering every cool feature in an amazingly short time without cutting corners in testing. Well, I have news — sometimes, it just isn't gonna happen.

Finding out what's realistic requires careful research. You want to base your plan on accurate estimates and metrics based on historical data from similar projects in your organization. Set accurate benchmarks and try to avoid the mistakes that others have made.

Every project plan contains three components:

- ✔ **Scope:** The work or tasks required to complete the project in accordance with the goals and objectives set forth for the project
- ✔ **Schedule:** A timeline with the estimated duration required to finish each of the project tasks
- ✔ **Resources:** The people, equipment, money, and facilities necessary to complete the work according to the project schedule

Your mission is to play a give-and-take game between these interdependent components to come out with a plan that provides the right mix that can allow you to finish the project when you say that you will. Table 13-2 lists some templates to help you build a realistic project plan for your software. For further details on developing a software project plan, refer to Chapters 3 through 5.

Table 13-2	Useful Templates for Creating a Project Plan
Chapter	*Template File*
3	Project Optimization Matrix.dot
3	Work Breakdown Structure.dot
5	Human Resources Estimation Worksheet.dot

Optimize Your Schedule as the Project Changes

Although you strive to minimize any major changes in your project plan by the time you're ready to begin development, you should expect the unexpected. As proposed changes arise, you constantly participate in the negotiation process with your project sponsor, marketing, and your customer over the usual issues: scope, schedule, and resources.

Microsoft Project can assist you in optimizing your project plan in two important ways:

✔ Adjust your project scope by modifying tasks on the critical path

✔ Change your project's schedule by playing with time, reallocating resources, and reducing costs

For further details on project scheduling, tracking, and controlling, you can refer to Chapters 4, 5, 6, and 10. There are many example files in these chapters which provide guidance on how you can use Microsoft Project in your planning and tracking efforts.

Keep People Informed

Successful software project managers are effective communicators. Remember the maxim: Overcommunication is better than no communication. One of your critically important functions is to ensure that all project team members are on the same page. Keeping everyone informed allows you to handle changes on the fly with the least possible negative effect on the scope, schedule, and resources of your project.

In the new networked world, a number of mediums can help you keep your project's stakeholders constantly informed. You can communicate in person, via video conferencing, over the telephone, through e-mail, using a Web site — take your choice.

Plan to hold a weekly status meeting with your project team and to submit a weekly status report to your project sponsor, at the minimum. Ideally, you can reserve a room for your status meeting at the same time and place every week, preferably in a central location so that everyone can physically attend. You can pipe in your off-site team members via speaker phone or video conferencing.

Prior to your weekly status meetings, put together a word-processing document or spreadsheet of open project issues, a summary bug report, and so on — and e-mail the document to your project sponsor and team members. The document serves as both a status report and as an agenda for your weekly status meetings, which can take the following format:

- ✔ **Overall Project Status:** A high-level executive summary focused at your project sponsor. Don't bore your sponsor with details that he or she doesn't need to know. Serve up the beef of where the project stands. This leaves them the choice of leaving or staying around for all the details.

- ✔ **Major Accomplishments:** A high-level listing of milestones and tasks accomplished both collectively or individually.

- ✔ **Old Action Items (generated from last week's meeting):** During the status meeting, each team member should provide a quick status report on their action items and the deliverables for which they are responsible in the overall success of the project.

- ✔ **Open Issues:** A detailed listing of issues that affect the project that have not been previously addressed by the prior week's Action Items list.

- ✔ **New Action Items (for next week):** Assign tasks to individual team members with specific deadlines set. They will provide a status report at the next weekly project status meeting.

With a minimal amount of effort, you can set up an intranet project Web site where you can publish your status reports by attaching your status reports or converting them to HTML format. Microsoft Project 2000 also has a Web server that enables your team to access the latest and greatest project plan and schedule.

Be Responsive

Much of your job as project manager will be playing the role of primary contact and informant. Not only do you have to be a Reaganesque great communicator, but you also have to respond to queries from your team members. You can never predict the number of visits to your office, telephone calls, voice mails, e-mails, faxes, or mail you may receive during the course of a project. Don't feel guilty for not getting back to everyone immediately, but get back to everyone in good time, each according to the priority of the issue as it affects your project.

As project leader, you may have such a great number of unsolicited queries. Here are a few tips below that can to help you deal with information overload:

✔ **Prioritize unexpected office visits, telephone calls, and voice mails as High, Medium, or Low.** Be sure to record each issue in a central place, such as a Franklin Planner so that you respond within an appropriate time frame.

✔ **Reset peoples' expectations for Medium and Low priority queries.** Provide an approximate time frame for your response.

✔ **Don't answer every phone call.** Let some calls go to voice mail, check all messages at a certain time, and then respond according to the priority of the message. Don't be afraid to put your phone in Do-Not-Disturb mode during the period of the day when you work most effectively.

✔ **Redirect or delegate queries when appropriate.** Refer people to other resources, such as subject matter experts, internal documents, corporate intranet, external Websites, and so on.

Be Proactive about Deadlines

By definition, every project has deadlines. Stay on top of these dates and remind the people responsible that a deadline is approaching. Doing so may keep you from having to remind them that a deadline has passed. Remember: It's better to be proactive than reactive.

The more that you can anticipate and factor into your project plan, the more likely that your plan will become reality. The objective of the proactive approach is to spend a lot of time up front during the gather requirements and analysis phases of the software development cycle, so your team can accurately estimate your project's components including scope and scheduled deadlines, and allocate resources appropriately.

The last thing you want to happen is for a team member to wait until the last minute to complete a task or to forget about the task altogether. For example, if a project team member is responsible for completing a task on the critical path and has insufficient lead time or is completely clueless about this task, the entire project schedule can be thrown off schedule.

Microsoft Project and other tools will serve an important scheduling function to help keep your team apprised of upcoming deadlines. Project 2000 (included on the CD-ROM in the back of this book) includes a Web server feature so that you can make your project schedule available to all stakeholders via a browser.

Fix the Problem, Not the Blame

Handling mistakes is a real art. Ever since the beginning of time, people have been either blaming everyone but themselves for mistakes or thinking of every excuse under the sun to dodge responsibility. What your project team needs most of all is an expert on the proper handling of mistakes — someone who can ensure that the same bloopers don't keep raising their ugly heads project after project.

The best project managers ignore tattletales who make a career of playing office politics, trusting their team members to resolve the mistakes on their own. However, some blunders can't be resolved by the offender. That's when your help comes into play. Here are some tips on handling mistakes tailored especially for software project managers:

- ✔ Maintain an open-door policy, encouraging values such as honesty, constructive criticism, and creative problem solving.

- ✔ Reward team members for taking responsibility for mistakes and assist them in figuring out solutions.

- ✔ Set an example for your team by taking responsibility not only for your own mistakes, but also by taking the heat for your team members.

- ✔ Discourage tattletales by making them responsible for being a part of the solution, rather than a part of the problem.

- ✔ Hold a postmortem meeting at the end of every project to review what went right, lessons learned, and mistakes that you can improve on going forward.

Stay Positive

As project manager, you're in the limelight — whether you like it or not. You're on stage as a role model for your team, playing the parts of mentor, mediator, and confidant. You are constantly shaping the attitudes and actions of your development team, and you need to remember that everything you do and say shapes how your team views the project and its chance of success.

You're both the bearer of good tidings and bad news. Suppose, for example — and this is a true story — that you're told halfway into a project that your budget or schedule just got cut in half, but you still have the same scope. How do you react? Do you pick a fight with your project sponsor at the local bar, or do you begin a win-win negotiation process?

At the end of the day, how do you break the news of the shortened schedule and budget to your team? Do you complain, or do you try to smooth over a sticky situation?

Sure, you want to go to your team and complain that your boss doesn't listen to you or understand the needs of the project team. Sure, you want to pass around a voodoo doll and stick the first pin in it.

But your dad was right: Attitude *is* everything. If you start a complain-a-thon, then you're telling your team to focus on the negative aspects of the situation. But your team doesn't need help here. They'll naturally look at the negative aspects. What they may have trouble seeing, however, are the positive aspects of the situation. When the chips are down, your team looks to you for guidance. Okay, you may have trouble finding a positive side in the example that I provide, but what about saying that if any group of people can make the impossible possible, it's the group of people that are in the room with you right at that moment. Then you could start a brainstorming session about what steps can do just that.

At the end of the day, you have to make the best of tough situations — or find yourself another line of work.

The value of mistakes

Bill Gates and the rest of the senior management team at Microsoft foster *the value of freely making mistakes.* By feeling free to make mistakes, employees are willing to take more risks, which fosters greater creative software solutions and results in higher bottom-line revenues, so the theory goes.

Microsoft burned millions on the OS2 project in partnership with IBM, which fizzled out as the multitasking Windows operating system of the future. A couple of years later, Microsoft dusted off the OS2 code and was able to reuse much of it to develop Windows NT, which has been slowly gobbling up client/server marketshare since. However, Microsoft's value of freely making mistakes is no substitute for good software product planning and development.

Chapter 14

Ten Frequently Asked Questions

During your exciting adventures in software project management, you never have a dull moment. You and your project team inevitably come up with many questions along the way. In this chapter, I provide a number of frequently asked questions specific to software projects to which you can refer whenever you're not sure what course of action to take.

What Are Successful Software Project Managers Made Of?

To be successful as a software project manager, you will be drawing on a number of skills. Notice that I listed soft skills ahead of the hard (technical) skills. Your effective management of software projects isn't just about your ability to write and read software code, or how many cool bars and graphs you can make in Microsoft Project.

Surprisingly enough, your level of technical expertise is among the less-important skills on the list compared to your interpersonal and organization skills. The skills that good project managers share include:

- **Interpersonal and communicative skills:** Effective software project managers are people-oriented. They are also effective communicators. Good project managers are approachable and go out of their way to regularly make contact with their entire team. As effective communicators, they not only ask the right questions but also listen and readily admit that they don't have all the answers. They aren't afraid to defer the answers and tasks from themselves to the appropriate subject experts.

- **Diplomacy:** Much of your role as a project manager is cultivating and applying your people skills to diplomacy. You have to try to keep everyone happy as the liaison between your project team and your customer constituencies. Honing your diplomacy skills can be critical to minimizing interpersonal conflicts, competing concerns, and other sore spots that arise during the course of your project.

  Keeping sticky situations under control when unforeseen project risks arise takes a special person with the right mindset. In the midst of challenges, the project manager's ability to exude calm keeps a team focused and confident. Although some people are gifted with special diplomatic talents, diplomacy is a skill that you can develop, too.

- **Vision and leadership:** Good software project managers are visionaries focused on the project's mission who can provide the kind of leadership that their project team needs to carry implement that vision. For more information on vision and leadership, check out *Leadership For Dummies* by Marshall Loeb and Stephen Kindell and published by IDG Books Worldwide, Inc.

- **Relentless passion for success:** Software project managers aren't easily defeated by the various obstacles in their paths. Good project managers see challenges as opportunities. They keep the project moving forward toward success. They plan, but they take calculated risks, too. When those risks don't pan out, they learn from their mistakes, improve, and move on.

- **Recruiting:** One of the prerequisites of effective software project managers is the ability to recruit a solid project team. You're looking, of course, for the most technically brilliant developers and engineers for your team. But, just as technical skills and experience are important, so is each individual team member's ability to get along, communicate effectively, and work as a team with other team members.

During your recruitment process, keep in mind the importance of both technical and interpersonal skill sets. Soliciting the input of your team members about adding a new team member is also a good idea. If you're interviewing potential employees for your project teams, preparing a solid list of questions that include real life what-if scenarios is a good idea.

✔ **Mentoring:** Good software project managers are good teachers. When team members stop by your cubicle, they know that no matter how busy you may be, you're always eager to lend a hand. Try your best to include a generous portion of dollars in your budget for training on Java or some other new technologies that your project may require.

✔ **Analytical and problem-solving skills:** Every project has its challenges. Challenges are often problems that you and your project team need to resolve. Here's where your ability to define and analyze the problem to find the optimal solution comes into play. Every software project has the changes of balancing scope, schedule, and resources.

Project managers generally have good analytical and problem-solving skills. Not everyone is a born problem-solving and analytical genius, however. You can work to build these skills as new challenges arise. Remember that challenges can become opportunities. Work through each opportunity logically and methodically, critically analyzing the issues, and then evaluate the alternatives until you finally arrive at a creative solution.

✔ **Knowledge of software project-management tools:** Knowledge and expertise with software project management tools — including project planning and scheduling tools such as Microsoft Project, requirements and design document templates, and processes — will be very useful on the job. Although, don't feel you must be an expert with the tools to be effective in managing your software project. Project management tools are just that: tools. Tools and processes are something you can learn too. So, don't worry, be happy!

✔ **Software engineering/development technical expertise:** Wow! You were probably wondering when I was going to get to the technicalities. It goes without saying that the more technical knowledge you have in programming and the software engineering/development life cycle, the better off you are and the better your team is likely to accept your leadership. In general, however, in conducting most of the tasks you perform as project manager, you act as a generalist rather than as a technical specialist.

On occasion, you may be involved in a code walkthrough, or you may be assisting your team in debugging some detailed code problem that requires technical acumen. However, at the end of the day, the project managers with solid interpersonal and organizational skills, who can articulate a clear and inspiring vision, have the highest chance of success.

You need technical expertise to create a software project. Nothing can change that fact, and any technical expertise you have can only help the project. But if you don't happen to have 20 years of programming experience, you can also rely on other team members to provide this expertise.

I can't overemphasize the importance of trying to be a hands-on project manager. Hands-on project managers are involved with the design specs and the code while interacting on a daily basis in the development trenches. While it's important to be a high-level generalist in managing the overall project, don't lose touch with the technical specifics of the tasks and people. Keep in touch, but at the same time don't lose track of the forest (the project's big picture) by getting lost in the trees (the technical details).

How Do I Invent a Billion-Dollar Software Project?

Everyone's trying to get a piece of the IPO pie. An *IPO* is the initial public offering of a company's stock being traded over the stock exchanges. IPOs are not a new concept; they've been around since the first publicly traded companies. It wasn't until the recent explosion of the Internet and high-tech startup get-rich-quick craze that companies like America Online, Yahoo!, and Amazon.com of the brave new Cyberworld managed to capture the public's attention.

The key to the success of these Internet startup companies, software vendors, and service providers in general is the ability to invent software products and service offerings that have never been done before. Or, if the ideas aren't entirely new, then they are at least differentiated enough to sell.

Two distinct types of software vendors exist: license software vendors and service providers. In selecting your new software project idea, you need to first figure out which category your project falls under. The following list can help:

- ✔ **License software vendors:** This group of software vendors is in the market of developing and selling software applications for off-site use by its customers. License software falls into one of two primary classifications:

  - **Shrink-wrapped applications:** These software products are packaged for the everyday business or home users, such as Microsoft Project. Such applications are shrink-wrapped in plastic and attractively packaged. These one-size-fits-all solutions are distributed through mass-market distribution channels and sold at an affordable price.

  - **Enterprise applications:** These software products aren't sold through mass-market distribution channels for everyday users, but are developed for larger customer audiences, such as the Fortune 2000 corporations. Enterprise applications can be very expensive and generally require customization for particular customers.

✔ **Service providers:** These firms provide software services to their customers instead of licensing their products. The two primary classifications of software service providers are:

- **Application service providers (ASPs):** ASPs, also known as service bureaus or outsourcing providers, aren't a new business model. Service bureaus have offered legacy mainframe software application services (such as timesharing, payroll services, and benefits administration services to large companies) since the 1970s as alternatives for companies that didn't want to spend millions on in-house licensed enterprise software applications.

  Over a period of seven years, ASPs offering myriad services over the Internet have exploded. Online malls and business-to-business e-commerce sites (such as Concur.com) provide online procurement of products and services ranging from personal computers to pet food, auctions, bookstores, weather, airplane tickets, expense management, and human resource administration. Numerous World Wide Web search engines such as Yahoo! offer free phone, fax, e-mail, active messaging, chat rooms, Web boards, and many other services.

- **Internet Service Providers (ISPs):** ISPs aren't a new concept, either. Just as the concept of service bureaus has been around since the mainframe days, Internet providers have been providing Internet bandwidth and customized services for some time now. The ISPs that are hitting it big, such as America Online, are constantly providing new services and a sense of community for their customers.

Even though you may invent a hot e-idea that nobody else has thought of, before your company invests substantial time and resources into a software project, your firm's management needs to know that the product has a good chance of providing a high return on investment.

After you think of a number of software product or online service ideas, refer to Chapter 2 for the steps I recommend you do to justify your software project.

What Can Your Customers Do for You?

Ask not what your customers can do for you; ask what you can do for your customers. With apologies to John Kennedy, these words probably describe your general feeling regarding your relationship with your customers. During the process of developing, testing, and fixing bugs and enhancements, you may be tempted to focus exclusively on meeting your customers' requirements and solving their problems.

The software development cycle, however, makes it a two-way street! Try to keep in mind that you're not alone in your battle to provide the best possible product suite for your customers. Your customers can act as your allies.

You can depend upon your customers to assist you in several tasks, including:

✔ Completing customer surveys for future software and product requirements

✔ Providing funding and staff resources for new software projects and enhancements

✔ Participating as a live beta test site to provide early feedback to your project team concerning software defects and enhancement requests.

So please, don't forget to ask your customers for their help! It's in their best interest to participate actively throughout your software project's development cycle.

You Mean I Have to Plan Ahead?

As a software project manager, you should plan ahead on your software project just as Bobby Fisher used to think ten moves ahead in his chess matches.

After you define your customers' software requirements and identify the software product, you're ready to begin developing your project plan. You can find out all about gathering your customers' requirements and product selection/justification process in Chapter 2.

Your software project plan will include the following components:

✔ **Statement of scope, goals, and objectives:** The SOS is a detailed but succinct statement outlining the project's goals and deliverables that serves as the thesis statement of the Project Scope Document. For more information, refer to Chapter 3.

A sample Project Scope Document and a template for creating a Project Scope document that includes a sample Statement of Scope appears on the *Software Project Management Kit For Dummies* CD.

✔ **Budget:** Preparing a budget for your software project is one of your primary responsibilities as project manager. You should include estimates for your project team staffing costs, personal computers, software, training, and so on in your budget. For more information, refer to Chapter 3.

✔ **Work breakdown structure:** Your project team can look forward to a lengthy WBS meeting where you divide up the work of your software project into milestones, summary tasks, and dependent tasks. You can then enter your preliminary WBS into an Excel spreadsheet. After finalizing your WBS, you can then enter the tasks into Microsoft Project. For more information, check out Chapter 3.

A sample WBS Excel spreadsheet template and Microsoft Project file (CSSW5.mpp) are provided on the *Software Project Management Kit For Dummies* CD.

✔ **Task network including the PERT and critical path:** A sample PERT Chart Task Network is provided on the *Software Project Management Kit For Dummies* CD.

✔ **Task durations and cost estimates:** Using proven software cost schedule estimation tools, you can accurately estimate your project parameter, which enables you to assign the optimal number of resources to your project with a reasonable degree of certainty.

On the *Software Project Management Kit For Dummies* CD, you can find trial versions of Marotz Software's Cost Xpert and Strategy Xpert software tools that you can use for your project's cost schedule estimates. You can also find a Baseline Software Project Schedule for Microsoft Project (CSSW5.mpp), a Resource Assignments Cost Estimation Worksheet, and a Human Resources Estimation Worksheet. For more information, flip to Chapter 5.

✔ **Schedule:** In your Microsoft Project file, you will be able to schedule the tasks of your project along a timeline, using the Gantt Chart view. For additional information, you can refer to Chapter 6.

A sample Gantt Chart in Microsoft Project file (CSSW6.mpp) appears on the *Software Project Management Kit For Dummies* CD.

Can't We (Our Project Team) All Just Get Along?

Reginald Denny maintained the all-American team spirit during the Rodney King riots after he was almost beaten unconscious when he barely uttered the words: "Can't we all just get along?" Believing that your project team members will always get along peachy keen is deluding yourself. Project teams have their rivalries and human frailties, which can sometimes lead to conflicts that can drag the entire team down, sometimes even causing a project to fail.

A large part of your job as project manager is to observe your project team during its day-in/day-out operations. From the moment of your project kickoff meeting, you have the opportunity to observe the interactions and dynamics of your project team members.

Here are some tips to consider in effectively avoiding and/or resolving your project team's conflicts:

- Work to select team members who have compatible chemistries.

- Create an open door communication atmosphere, which fosters teamwork and morale.

- Provide your team with a clear Project Scope Document and objectives in writing to eliminate any ambiguity and lack of focus.

- Assign tasks fairly and appropriately.

- Provide positive feedback for a job well done to all team members.

- Schedule frequent team-building and social activities.

- Provide necessary technical training and mentoring to meet the needs of your team to meet the project objectives.

- Maintain a neutral position in resolving conflicts between team members.

- Exercise effective listening skills before recommending conflict resolution measures.

- Empathize with your team members — put yourself in their shoes.

- Volunteer for tasks that can potentially cause conflict between team members.

- Reassign team members as appropriate to minimize interpersonal conflicts.

- Foster a healthy amount of competition between team members as long as it contributes to the overall success of the project!

In sum, as project manager, you have a unique opportunity to be a good role model and foster teamwork and a positive spirit among your project team members. Even during the most intense conflicts between members, you're the glue that maintains the cohesion and collaborative focus necessary to produce a successful software project.

Should I Cut Project Scope, Schedule, or Resources?

The three main variables of every project are scope (tasks), resources (budget), and schedule (time). You, as project manager, must balance the total amount of scope of the project against the your budgetary and scheduling constraints. Of time, budget, and quality, you often must pick your favorite two.

Your project team can use the Project Optimization Matrix to weigh the importance of your project's scope, resources, and schedule, and for making project plan adjustments in response to project changes. The POM is a useful tool because it helps you see what possible wiggle room you may have in your project's scope, resources, or schedule. Depending on the project goals and mood of your project sponsor, this amount of wiggle room can vary significantly.

For example, you can't increase the scope of your project without either increasing the available time or adding to the project's resource pool (possibly by hiring temps). Likewise, you can't push the project out the door ahead of schedule without cutting features or increasing the budget — you have to add resources to the project (or both). You have to reach compromises with your project sponsor about where the priorities for your project lie.

You can use Microsoft Project to assist you in optimizing your project plan by: adjusting project scope by modifying tasks on the critical path; changing your schedule by playing with time; reallocating resources; and reducing costs. After optimizing your project plan, the plan's baseline estimates change. For the remaining duration of the project, you use the baseline estimates to track actual progress of your project. Refer to Chapter 6 for the full scoop on this topic.

The *Software Project Management Kit For Dummies* CD contains a Project Optimization Matrix template (Project Optimization Matrix.dot), which is a great starting point for developing your POM. There is also a Microsoft Project baseline template (CSSW6.mpp) that has been optimized.

How Do I Control Costs?

In a perfect world, your up-front project planning keeps you under budget throughout the development cycle. The reality, as you may guess, is that most projects are underbudgeted. Here are some of the courses of action you can take to keep your project's costs from running out of control:

- **Make accurate estimates and stand by them.** You need two important prerequisites for accurate project estimates: solid empirical data and good estimation tools. Enter historical project data whenever possible into your Microsoft Project baseline plan. When you don't have historical data, then use an estimation product, such as Cost Xpert, to provide real-world cost data.

- **Control costs using Microsoft Project.** Continually monitor your project's costs to see where you stand from a budgetary perspective. Microsoft Project provides a number of features that allow you to identify cost discrepancies and inaccurate estimates, helping you to reduce your project's costs.

If you want to do further research on how to control your project costs, check out *Microsoft Project 2000 For Dummies* by Martin Doucette and published by IDG Books Worldwide, Inc.

Why Is the Customer's Problem So Important to Understand?

The pivotal question you and your project team need to focus on throughout the requirements phase is to really understand exactly what problem your customers are trying to solve. That may sound pessimistic, but if you forget to look closely enough at the problem, your software project may not ever become a part of the solution.

What the software industry refers to as the "problem" is the actual or perceived product needs or requirements of your customers and target market. Some of the activities that go into understanding the customer's actual problem include:

- ✔ Interviewing your customers on-site
- ✔ Surveying your customers
- ✔ Getting feedback from user group forums
- ✔ Researching market trends and literature
- ✔ Analyzing the competition
- ✔ Conducting internal company-wide new product idea brainstorming sessions

For additional information concerning the gathering requirements phase, refer to Chapter 2.

How to Say No to Unreasonable Deadlines?

Sometimes one of the most difficult things in life is having the nerve to say "No". As a software project manager, you're constantly up against project deadlines. Saying no to unreasonable deadlines may make you unpopular, especially to your project sponsor, the marketing department, your executive management team — and to the company's shareholders if the company doesn't make its numbers for the quarter. But you and the powers that be must decide what is more important: customers getting quality products (perhaps a little late), or taking a temporary hit to your company's stock price.

If you do say no to a deadline, you'd better have good reason. The best time to voice your opinion on deadlines is while you're still planning your project, preferably well before the project start date. An important deliverable that will come out of your project plan will be an estimated project schedule that includes an overall project start and finish date plus detailed task durations and start/finish dates.

On the other hand, if a schedule isn't going to happen, then you're actually doing everyone a favor by identifying the fact early in the process rather than later.

How Often Should I Update My Project's Tracking Information?

As a general rule, software project managers keep a pulse on the status of their projects on a daily basis. Frequent tracking of your software projects is important for two reasons. First, tracking provides important feedback to management on your current project's status. Second, tracking information provides the necessary historical data that future projects can rely on in making accurate estimates to ensure future successes.

In Chapter 6, I provide the details on how to track the progress of your software project using Microsoft Project.

You can also open the CSSW6.mpp project file from the *Software Project Management Kit For Dummies* CD (in the Chapter 6 examples folder) if you want.

For a more in-depth look at Microsoft Project's tracking features, check out *Microsoft Project 2000 For Dummies* by Martin Doucette, published by IDG Books Worldwide, Inc.

Part VII
Appendixes

The 5th Wave   By Rich Tennant

FIRED
YOU

"NIFTY CHART, FRANK, BUT NOT ENTIRELY NECESSARY."

In this part . . .

*H*ere is where you come to find out which human organs are being offered on eBay this week. Nah, just kidding . . . if that were the case, then this part would be titled "Spleens."

Two appendixes can be found in *Software Project Management Kit For Dummies* for your reading enjoyment. Appendix A is a glossary of important software development and project management terms. Appendix B gives you the full scoop on how to install and use the wealth of templates and tools contained on the CD-ROM accompanying this book.

Appendix A

Glossary

● ●

*A*ctual: The characteristics of a task that has already begun, including start/end dates, cost, and the amount of work competed.

Alias: A Structured Query Language (SQL) short nickname or alternative name for a table or column in the data model.

Analysis phase: This is the second phase of the software project-development cycle where the project team looks carefully at the software's requested features identified during the gathering requirements phase with an eye toward what issues each may create in the actual coding of the software.

Applications programs: The type of software that programmers develop for use by end users. Examples of applications include spreadsheet, word-processing, and accounting programs. Application programs are distinguished from operating system programs, such as Windows NT or Unix.

Architecture: The software architecture includes the data model (database) structure, user interfaces, workflow, and the interactions of the various components. Software architecture is concerned not only with structure and behavior of the program, but also with the usage, functionality, performance, robustness, reuse, and the look-and-feel user interface design issues that go into developing a software project. Think of the architecture as the detailed blueprint design of your software project.

Automated test scripts: Automated test scripts are programs that are coded to test specific aspects of a software product based on predefined test cases. The objective of automated test scripts is to replace manual test cases, which will save time in the overall testing effort. Examples include testing the installation process, software functionality, security, error messages, online documentation and examples defined in the test plan, functional specifications, detailed design specifications, and requirements document. Please also see *test cases* and *test plan*.

Back end: That part of a relational database management system that interacts directly with the database. Examples of RDBMS include Oracle, Sybase, MS-SQL Server, Informix, and DB2.

Baseline: The finalized project plan (for example, in Microsoft Project) including the estimated task durations and costs before the project start date. Once your project begins, the baseline is used for tracking your project's progress against the project's actual progress. Also called the baseline plan.

Bug: See *defect*.

Build: An executable version of the program, usually for a specific part of the system. Development proceeds through a succession of builds before releasing the general availability (GA) release to the customers.

Change Control Board (CCB): Appointed representatives from the software organization who evaluate change requests throughout the software project's development cycle. The CCB will approve, defer, or reject CRs for the proposed changes to the requirements and design documentation, project's scope, documentation, and so on. The CCB also has the authority to assign resources to resolve CRs that are targeted for future releases or service packs. The CCB then notifies all interested individuals of the resolution of each CR. Also, please see *Change/Risk Management (C/RM)* plan and *Change Control*.

Change control process: The process of controlling software project changes involving all aspects of the project throughout the development life cycle. Also, please see *Change Control Board (CCB)*.

Change Management System: The practice of recording all defects (bugs) and enhancement requests found in the executable software and other work products and monitoring them throughout the project.

Change request (CR): A method of requesting a proposed change to a software project according to the defined change control process. Typically, CRs are either software or documentation defects or enhancement requests. CRs can be document- or form-based. The requester enters a description of the change requested and a business case that justifies the change. Also, please see *Change Control Board (CCB)*. Please also see *Defect and Enhancement*.

Change/Risk Management (C/RM) plan: The document that describes how software change control is to be conducted on a specific project. Also, please see *Change Control Board (CCB)*.

Column: A component of a table in the data model (database) that holds a single attribute of the table. Sometimes referred to as a *field*.

Component: A substantial part of the software product that combined with other components makes up all the program. A component usually comprises one or more modules. Also, see *Module*.

Configuration management: The task of defining and maintaining configurations and versions of the structural elements of software such as objects, modules, components, and builds. Configuration management includes baselining, version control, release control, status control, and storage control of the various elements.

Constraint: (1) In the project management world: a condition that limits the start or the finish of a task, or a condition that affects the duration of a task in some manner. (2) In the database (RDBMS) world: a data restriction defined on the data in the database.

Control: The power to decide on a project's initial scope, resources, schedule, or other aspects of the project and the power to make changes to those aspects.

Critical path: A network of tasks that must be completed on or ahead of schedule for a project to be completed on time. Please also refer to *critical path method (CPM)* and *program evaluation review technique (PERT)*.

Critical path method (CPM): A project management methodology for creating the critical path task network of dependencies in the project schedule that must be completed for a project to succeed. Please also refer to *critical path* and *program evaluation review technique (PERT)*.

Customer: The target audience for whom the software project is being developed. There are two sources of software customers: internal and external. Customers of information systems (IS) organizations working on software projects for in-house use are the company's *internal* end users. The customers for software vendors developing and selling shrink-wrapped software and enterprise applications are *external* customers.

Database: A collection of information organized in some uniform manner.

Defect: A bug that has been identified somewhere in the software, documentation, or development process.

Deliverable: A project task that is required to be completed according to the project plan (schedule).

Demoting: To lower the status of a task to a subtask in a task outline structure.

Design phase: The third phase of the software develoment cycle when you really begin to solve (conceptually, at least) the technical problems that you face in making your project a reality. In this phase, the relationship of the code, database, user interface, and classes begin to take shape in the minds of the project team.

Detailed Design Specifications: Just as the functional specifications provide a high-level view of the project, the *Detailed Design Specifications* document lays out the detailed blueprint of how you intend to develop the project. The design specifications include every major design document that you create (including the functional specifications) but provides detailed — and, in some cases, step-by-step — information on how you intend to implement the specifications.

Develop phase: This is the software project phase that follows the design of the data model, user interface, prototype, Documentation Plan, Functional Specifications, Detailed Design Specifications, and Software Quality Assurance test plan. This is the phase when your team actually begins coding, writing the documentation, and developing the SQA test cases, entrance criteria, and automations. If your analysis and design efforts are superb, actually developing the software is usually a relatively easy task.

Developer: A software project team member participating on your software project as a programmer or engineer who designs and develops the software.

Documentation Plan: This plan provides an overview of the software product you're documenting, the recommended documentation processes and procedures, and a list of document deliverables for the project. The technical publications manager or the technical writer on the project writes the *documentation plan*.

Domain: The set of possible values that you can assign to a particular database element.

Duration: The method of measuring the time estimated or required to complete a task or group of tasks. Durations can be measured in minutes, hours, days, weeks, and so on.

End user: The ultimate user of the software. The end user of a word processing program could be a secretary or technical writer. The end user of a debugger program could be a software developer.

Exit conditions: Criteria that are required to be started, completed, or in place before a design, development, or test activity can be completed.

Foreign Key: A column or combination of columns in a database table that references the primary key of another table in the database. See also *primary key*.

Functional Specifications document: From a high-level standpoint, this document provides a definitive overview of the necessary components and functionality of the project. This deliverable incorporates many of the documents that you prepare to this point, gathering them into one place for easy reference.

Gantt Chart: A graphical representation of a project task's relationships and duration. The length of a bar in a Gantt chart represents the duration of a particular task. Lines between bars represent a relationship between the tasks.

Gather requirements phase: The phase of the software development cycle during which requirements involved in defining the customer's problems are explored and developed.

Implementation phase: This phase is what I call the dividing line because it delineates the end of your GA software-release project and the beginning of yet a new software project at the customer site. The implementation phase encompasses many of the previous phases — only this time, they're not for the general product but to meet the specific needs of your customer's off-site installation and customizations.

Integration: The combination of multiple software modules into a functional larger unit. Integration involves compiling and linking part of a system's components together into one or more executables (which are also components). This concept is also commonly referred to as *system integration.*

Integration testing: Testing the interaction of newly combined software modules that have been individually tested via unit testing.

Leveling: The project management process of extending task durations in order to lower the utilization of a given resource or resources.

Linked tasks: Tasks connected in some kind of relationship.

Manage release and change phase: The release manager is responsible for properly configuring each software unit, module, and integration version of the software to include all the latest fixes and enhancements to the code. Release management depends on the testing phase. In other words, you can't manage releases until the releases are ready, and you can't release anything until it passes testing.

Metadata: Data about the structure of the data in a database.

Milestone: A task that indicates a beginning, a completion, or a significant event in a project. In Microsoft Project, milestones have a duration of 0d (zero days). These are important project checkpoints when management makes important business decisions concerning the future of the project. Milestones are important times for celebration, such as meeting certain predefined objectives for a certain phase of the project, thus enabling management to decide whether to continue to the next phase.

Module: Software code that encompasses one or more functions. A compoent is made up of one or more modules.

Object-oriented design (OOD): A software design process that makes use of object-oriented programming concepts.

Object-oriented programming (OOP): A method of computer programming that focuses on building computer programs from collections of objects (storage programs that combine the data and the methods for manipulating the data together into a single structure). Object-oriented programs differ from procedural programs in that you think of the program in terms of the interaction of objects rather than the logical set of steps that complete a given task. Object-oriented programs tend to be more modular and reusable than procedural programs. Programming languages that support object-oriented programming include C++, Visual Basic, Java, and Smalltalk.

Outline: A structured format in the Gantt Chart review containing higher-level summary tasks and lower-level subtasks.

PERT chart: A network chart depicting relationships among tasks. Tasks appear as boxes, or nodes. Task relationships are illustrated by connecting lines. In Microsoft Project 2000, a PERT chart is called a Network Diagram.

Phase: A project time period where the project team performs specialized tasks, such as the gather requirements, analysis, design, develop, test, manage release and change, and implement phases.

Predecessor: A task that has a start and end date before that of another task.

Primary key: A column or combination of columns in a database table that uniquely identifies each row in the table. See also *foreign key*.

Program: The code portion of software, or a collection of integrated modules or components.

Program evaluation review technique (PERT): A project management scheduling tool used for determining the total estimated project duration along a task network of dependencies. Also see *critical path* and *critical path method (CPM)*.

Programming: The general process of software development, especially construction activities.

Project Scope Document (PSD): The name applied to the combination of a resource document and the Statement of Scope document. Also commonly referred to as the Statement of Work.

Project plan: A plan that outlines an overall "road map" for a project, covering the schedule, major milestone dates and criteria, and the breakdown of the phases into iterations.

Promote: In an outlined project, to move a subtask to a higher level. Promoting is performed by decreasing the indent (sometimes called outdenting).

Prototype: A proof-of-concept model of your software product. Because the development of the actual software typically takes months or decades, developing demo prototypes is critical.

RDBMS: An acronym for relational database management system. A type of database in which information is organized into tables. A relationship between information in one table can be established with information in another table.

Record: A representation of some physical or conceptual object in a relational database management system (RDBMS).

Regression test: This type of testing involves a thorough battery of tests designed to uncover detrimental effects of adding new code to the functionality of previously tested code. This is a common practice after new code fixes have been reconfigured into a new software build, used to make sure nothing else got broken.

Relation: A two-dimensional array of rows and columns, containing uniquely valued entries and no duplicate rows. Please also refer to *RDBMS*.

Release: A fully functioning software product that is to be delivered to a customer. The term release and delivery are sometimes used interchangeably. For example, the GA release is the general availability release delivered to the customers. There are also alpha and beta releases, as well as point and maintenance releases.

Release checklist: A list of prerequisite activities that must be completed in order to release a software product. Various representatives in the development cycle will sign the checklist showing their agreement that a software release is ready to be released to the customer. In some situations, a representative may refuse to sign the release checklist in the event that some critical activity has not been completed to his satisfaction.

Request for Proposal (RFP): A document that addresses two primary topics: the Project Scope Document or Statement of Work, and the instructions to bidders (vendors).

Requirements Document: A document deliverable that becomes the main input to the analysis phase. The RD is your main blueprint for the high-level description of the project that includes a summary of the problem to solve, the objectives of the project, the major features of the product, a documentation plan, a support plan, and licensing issues.

Resource pool: A list of resources available for assignment to a task or group of tasks for multiple projects.

Reuse: The degree to which previously developed software code components can be also used in another component. Reuse of code is a great way to avoid duplication of effort and to help keep your development costs under control.

Risk: A project variable that endangers or eliminates success for a project. Risks can include a project experiencing undesirable events such as schedule delays, cost overruns, or outright cancellation.

Schedule: The timeline on which a project is to be completed.

Software development life cycle: The software development process is often divided into phases that roughly identify the project's current status in relation to the project life as a whole. Although opinion differs as to the optimum way to divide a software project, the approach I take in this book involves seven phases: gather requirements, analysis, design, develop, test, manage release and change, and implement.

Software integration plan: The sequence of steps that developers must follow when they combine newly developed code with code that has already been integrated.

Software quality assurance (SQA): A planned and systematic pattern of activities that verify that a system has the desired characteristics.

Specifications: The software "requirements" that are referred to in the various design documents, including Requirements Document, Functional Specifications, and Detailed Design Specifications.

SQL: An acronym for structured query language, an industry standard data language designed to create, manipulate, and control relational database management systems (RDBMS).

Statement of Scope (SOS): A short, thesis-like description of the scope of a project. This should be the first part of your Project Scope Document (PSD).

Statement of work (SOW): A document that is originally part of the Request for Proposal document, or also referred to as the Project Scope Document. The statement of work includes information, such as the Statement of Scope, the work to be performed by the vendor, the work schedule, metrics that measure the work for acceptance, and the working relationship between the vendor and your organization. The SOW becomes a major part of the eventual contract between the vendor and your organization.

Subtask: A task indented under a summary task.

Successor: A task that follows another task.

Summary task: A task that comprises a summary of the duration, cost, and work of a group of subtasks.

System integration: See *integration*.

System test: A test of a product in a total systems environment with other software and hardware product combinations. A portion of the test should be conducted in a real customer environment.

Table: A collection of related records in a relational database management system (RDBMS).

Task: One of the planned activities of a software project.

Test phase: Testing isn't so much a phase as a mindset. You find yourself conducting many tests, usually in tandem with the actual development process. Thus the fine line between Phase 4 (development) and Phase 5 (testing) often blurs. This blurring is fine; you just need to understand that a line really is there.

Test cases: A description of inputs, execution instructions, and expected results, which are created for the purpose of verifying whether a specific software feature works as designed or a specific requirement has passed or failed the test.

Test plan (spec): A document that describes who's doing the testing, what needs to be tested, and the expected results.

Tracking: Monitoring the status of a software project by regularly comparing actual results to planned results, such as comparing the actual schedule and budget with the planned schedule and budget, or the actual functionality present with the required functionality.

Unit test: The isolated testing of each flow path of code within each module.

User-friendly: The intuitive feel that enables users to quickly get up and running on your software. Also referred to as *ease of use*.

User interface (UI): The functions of a product that allow a user to interact with that product; also called man-machine interface. Examples: operator commands, user screens, and messages.

User manual: A document that is used both as end-user documentation and as a specification of the software requirements.

Variance: The difference between your baseline plan and the actual project performance.

Work breakdown structure (WBS): A hierarchical structure used to organize tasks for reporting schedules and tracking costs. With Microsoft Project, you can use the outline feature, use tasks IDs, or assign a WBS code to each task in the task detail form.

Workflow: The business rules defining the data flow and processing of your software's transactions, including the inputs, processes, and outputs graphically described in the Data Flow Diagram.

Appendix B

About the CD

· ·

*L*ook at all the goodies you can find on the *Software Project Management Kit for Dummies* CD-ROM:

- ✔ Over 40 software project management templates
- ✔ Trial version of Microsoft Project 2000
- ✔ Trial versions of *Cost Xpert v2.1* and *Strategy Xpert* from The Cost Xpert Group, a division of Marotz, Inc.
- ✔ Trial versions of TRACK Defects, TRACK Help Desk, TRACKWeb, TRACK Web, TRACK Rules, and TRACKKB from Soffront Software Inc.

System Requirements

Make sure that your computer meets the minimum system requirements listed below. If your computer doesn't match up to most of these requirements, you may have problems using the contents of the CD.

- ✔ A PC with a 486 or faster processor, or a Mac OS computer with a 68040 or faster processor.
- ✔ Microsoft Windows 95 or later.
- ✔ Microsoft Office 95 or later: Templates appear on the CD for use with Microsoft Word, Microsoft Excel, Microsoft Access, and Microsoft Powerpoint.
- ✔ At least 16MB of total RAM installed on your computer. For best performance, we recommend at least 32MB of RAM installed.
- ✔ At least 300MB of hard drive space available to install all the software from this CD. (You need less space if you don't install every program.)
- ✔ A CD-ROM drive — double-speed (2x) or faster.
- ✔ A monitor capable of displaying at least 256 colors or grayscale.
- ✔ For Internet access, a modem with a speed of at least 14,400 bps or a network connection.

If you need more information on the basics, check out *PCs For Dummies,* 7th Edition by Dan Gookin; or *Windows 98 For Dummies* or *Windows 95 For Dummies,* 2nd Edition, both by Andy Rathbone (all published by IDG Books Worldwide, Inc.).

Using the CD with Microsoft Windows

To install the items from the CD to your hard drive, follow these steps.

1. **Insert the CD into your computer's CD-ROM drive.**

2. **Click Start⇨Run.**

3. **In the dialog box that appears, type** D:\START.HTM

   Replace *D* with the proper drive letter if your CD-ROM drive uses a different letter.

   If you don't know which drive letter corresponds to your CD-ROM, look for the CD-ROM icon in My Computer and note the drive letter beneath it.

4. **Click OK.**

5. **Read through the license agreement, nod your head, and then click the Accept button if you want to use the CD — after you click Accept, you'll jump to the Main Menu.**

6. **To navigate within the interface, simply click on any topic of interest to take you to an explanation of the files on the CD and how to use or install them.**

7. **To install the software from the CD, simply click on the software name.**

   You can eject the CD now. Carefully place it back in the plastic jacket of the book for safekeeping.

What You'll Find

The *Software Project Management Kit For Dummies* CD-ROM is an integral part of this kit. Here's a summary of the software on this CD arranged by category. The CD interface helps you install software easily under Microsoft Windows. (If you have no idea what I'm talking about when I say "CD interface," flip back a page or two to find the section, "Using the CD with Microsoft Windows.")

Software Project Management Templates

Included on the *Software Project Management Kit For Dummies* CD are templates and sample documents that I designed to give you a head start in creating the documents necessary to plan and manage your software project. The documents fall into the following categories:

- **Word for Windows 95 documents.** Use this version of the documents with Microsoft Word 95 or later. After you install these templates, they appear on your hard disk in the following folder: `C:\SPMKIT\W95TEMPLATES`.

- **Microsoft Project 2000 files.** Use this version of the documents with your trial version of Microsoft Project 2000, which is also included on the CD. After you install these templates, they appear on your hard disk in the following folder: `C:\SPMKIT\P2000PROJECT`.

- **Microsoft Access and Internet Explorer 5 files.** The sample prototype uses the Microsoft Access database and Internet Explorer as the HTML front end. After installing this prototype, it appears on your hard disk in the following folder: `C:\SMPKIT\PROTOTYPE`.

- **Microsoft PowerPoint file.** The single PowerPoint file is the sample storyboard. Find this in the following folder: `C:\SMPKIT\POWERPOINT`.

- **Excel 4.0 files.** Use this version of the documents if you use Microsoft Excel 4.0 or later as your spreadsheet. After you install these templates, they appear on your hard disk in the following folder: `C:\SPMKIT\E4TEMPLATES`.

Software Project Management Tools

Here's a summary of the software on the CD. The CD interface helps you install software easily. (If you have no idea what I'm talking about when I say "CD interface," flip back a page or two to find the section, "How to Use the CD Using Microsoft Windows.")

Microsoft Project 2000

The CD contains a trial version of the latest version of the popular project management software from Microsoft. Project gives you all the tools you need to plan and track software projects, from simple to complex. Project also enables you to view and complete the Project plan templates contained on the CD, which you can tailor to your own particular software projects. While this book contains a good introduction to Microsoft Project, if you need a more in-depth analysis, check out *Microsoft Project 2000 For Dummies* by Marty Doucette, published by IDG Books Worldwide, Inc. You can also access Microsoft's Web site at `www.microsoft.com` for information about obtaining an unlimited version of Microsoft Project 2000.

Cost Xpert and Strategy Xpert

The folks at The Cost Xpert Group (a division of Marotz Software, Inc.) bring you trial versions of two programs that ease the critical task of accurately estimating costs and schedules for your software projects:

✔ **Cost Xpert** is a great cost estimating tool that performs metrics oriented estimates, including Lines-of-Code, function points, GUI metrics, and object metrics. With a database of real-world costs from 8,000 live software projects, you won't be estimating blind when you create your plan!

✔ **Strategy Xpert** automatically guides you through the process of prioritizing your management decisions to optimally align your project's and organization's strategic objectives. You can find out more information and register to receive a complimentary online newsletter at the Cost Xpert Group Web site www.costxpert.com.

TRACK Suite by Soffront Software

You can find trial versions of Soffront Software's outstanding fully Web-enabled TRACK software application suite on the CD. This fabulous product can serve you from the beginning of the design process until well after the product ships. The TRACK suite includes:

✔ **TRACK Defects:** This product is a database that you can use to track software defects, enhancements, code changes, test cycles, product releases, system configurations, and much more.

✔ **TRACK Help Desk:** This product aids a software help desk with problem management, problem resolution, asset inventory management, change request management, and more.

✔ **TRACKWeb:** This product provides a Web interface for database administration, information submission and retrieval, query, and report functions for the entire TRACK application suite.

✔ **TRACK Rules:** This product is a flexible rules definition system that enables a system administrator to define complex conditions that trigger automatic event activation.

✔ **TRACKKB:** This tool learns product and service information from expert support personnel, thus creating an available pool of wisdom for users who need to quickly find answers to their questions.

You can find out more about the TRACK product suite at the Soffront Web site at www.soffront.com.

Templates at a Glance

Table B-1 summarizes the templates on the CD-ROM.

Table B-1	Templates at a Glance	
Template Name	*Type*	*Description*
Change Request Form	Microsoft Word Template	Form that documents requests for defect fixes or product enhancements
Cost-Benefit Summary	Microsoft Word Template and Document Sample	Form to use internally or at a customer site to decide whether a particular product meets their needs
CRM Plan	Microsoft Word Template	Form that documents your Change/Risk Management plan for the project
Customer Acceptance Test Procedure	Microsoft Word Template	Template to use to document the acceptance criteria at the customer site
Customer Issue Report	Microsoft Word Template	Customer service form to log problems at a customer site
Customer Require-ments Survey (and sample)	Microsoft Word Template and Document sample	Survey to use at trade shows to gauge the needs of cus-tomers and the problems that they need to solve
Customer Support Plan	Microsoft Word Document	Sample document outlining a short- and long-term support-structure implementation plan for a customer
Customer Training Plan	Microsoft Word Template	High-level checklist of steps to creating an effective training plan
Data Dictionary Sample	Microsoft Word Document	Sample data dictionary for the Customer Self-Service Web project
Data Flow Diagram (DFD)	Microsoft Word Document	Sample model of the data logic for the Customer Self-Service Web project

(continued)

Table B-1 *(continued)*

Template Name	Type	Description
Data Model Sample	Microsoft Word Document	Sample model of the database tables and fields for the Customer Self-Service Web project
Detailed Design Specifications	Microsoft Word Template	Template to create the detailed technical specifications for use in the creation of the software project
Development Team Skill Matrix	Microsoft Word Template and Document Sample	Template to use to fill in your design team
Documentation Plan	Microsoft Word Template and Document Sample	Plan to create documentation for your software project
Entity Relational Diagram (ERD)	Microsoft Word Document	Sample of the relationships between tables for the Customer Self-Service Web project
Functional Specifications	Microsoft Word Template	Template to create the technical specifications of the project for use by the management team and customer
Human Resources Estimation Worksheet	Microsoft Word Template and Document Samples	Template to use in estimating the cost of the resources in your project
Implementation Project Plan	Microsoft Word Template and Document sample	Template to use in creating the plan for customizing software for a particular customer
Microsoft Project Files	CSSW1.mpp–CSSW6.mpp	Six files to get you started in estimating, scheduling, and tracking a software project with your trial version of Microsoft Project 2000
PERT Chart Task Network	Microsoft Word Document	Overview of the Network Diagram for the project

Template Name	Type	Description
Project Candidate ROI Analysis	Microsoft Excel Template	Template to identify the software project that will provide the greatest return on investment
Project Optimization Matrix	Microsoft Word Template and Document Sample	Document that helps you prioritize scope, schedule, and resources of your project
Project Scope Document (PSD)	Microsoft Word Template and Document Sample	Template you use to get managerial sign off on features that are within the scope of the project within the given time frame
Project Status Report	Microsoft Excel Template	Template that you can use in reporting the status of your project
Prototype Sample	Microsoft Access Database with HTML pages	Sample early-version prototype for the Customer Self-Service Web project
Release Checklist	Microsoft Word Template	Checklist of important tasks prior to releasing software to a customer
Release Notes	Microsoft Word Document	Document that explains the process of creating release notes for a software project
Request For Proposal (RFP)	Microsoft Word Document	Document that explains the process and necessary information to include in a document upon which the initial go/no go decision is made for a project
Requirements Document (RD)	Microsoft Word Template and Document Sample	Document that helps the team define the problem and possible solutions for the software project

(continued)

Table B-1 *(continued)*

Template Name	Type	Description
Software Project Management Checklist.doc	Microsoft Word Document	Document that provides an overview of the deliverables for a software project using the seven-step development process
Storyboard Sample	Microsoft PowerPoint Document	Sample of an early UI sample for the Customer Self-Service Web project
SQA System Test Case	Microsoft Word Template and Document Sample	Template for outlining the procedures for exercising a software function
SQA System Test Plan Sample	Microsoft Excel Document	Sample of a complete test plan for the Customer Self-Service Web project
Training Preparation Checklist	Microsoft Word Template	Checklist of training tasks for a customer training program
Work Breakdown Structure (WBS)	Microsoft Excel Template and Document Sample	Document that contains the tasks outlined in this book to use in creating a project's task network and duration estimates

If You've Got Problems (Of the CD Kind)

I tried my best to compile programs that work on most computers with the minimum system requirements. Alas, your computer may differ, and some programs may not work properly for some reason.

The two likeliest problems are that you don't have enough memory (RAM) for the programs you want to use, or that you have other programs running that are affecting installation or running of a program. If you get error messages such as insufficient memory, try one or more of these methods and then try using the software again:

✔ **Turn off any anti-virus software that you have on your computer.** Installers sometimes mimic virus activity and may make your computer incorrectly believe that it is being infected by a virus.

- ✔ **Close all running programs.** The more programs you're running, the less memory is available to other programs. Installers also typically update files and programs; if you keep other programs running, installation may not work properly.

- ✔ **In Windows, close the CD interface and run demos or installations directly from Windows Explorer.** The interface itself can tie up system memory, or even conflict with certain kinds of interactive demos. Use Windows Explorer to browse the files on the CD and launch installers or demos.

- ✔ **Have your local computer store add more RAM to your computer.** This is, admittedly, a drastic and somewhat expensive step. However, if you have a Windows 95 PC, adding more memory can really help the speed of your computer and enable more programs to run at the same time.

If you still have trouble installing the items from the CD, please call the Customer Service phone number: 800-762-2974 (outside the U.S.: 317-572-3994). You can also contact Technical Support at www.wiley.com/techsupport.

Index

• D •

• *S* •

Notes

Notes

Notes

Notes

Wiley Publishing, Inc.
End-User License Agreement

READ THIS. You should carefully read these terms and conditions before opening the software packet(s) included with this book "Book". This is a license agreement "Agreement" between you and Wiley Publishing, Inc. "WPI". By opening the accompanying software packet(s), you acknowledge that you have read and accept the following terms and conditions. If you do not agree and do not want to be bound by such terms and conditions, promptly return the Book and the unopened software packet(s) to the place you obtained them for a full refund.

1. **License Grant.** WPI grants to you (either an individual or entity) a nonexclusive license to use one copy of the enclosed software program(s) (collectively, the "Software" solely for your own personal or business purposes on a single computer (whether a standard computer or a workstation component of a multi-user network). The Software is in use on a computer when it is loaded into temporary memory (RAM) or installed into permanent memory (hard disk, CD-ROM, or other storage device). WPI reserves all rights not expressly granted herein.

2. **Ownership.** WPI is the owner of all right, title, and interest, including copyright, in and to the compilation of the Software recorded on the disk(s) or CD-ROM "Software Media". Copyright to the individual programs recorded on the Software Media is owned by the author or other authorized copyright owner of each program. Ownership of the Software and all proprietary rights relating thereto remain with WPI and its licensers.

3. **Restrictions On Use and Transfer.**

   (a) You may only (i) make one copy of the Software for backup or archival purposes, or (ii) transfer the Software to a single hard disk, provided that you keep the original for backup or archival purposes. You may not (i) rent or lease the Software, (ii) copy or reproduce the Software through a LAN or other network system or through any computer subscriber system or bulletin- board system, or (iii) modify, adapt, or create derivative works based on the Software.

   (b) You may not reverse engineer, decompile, or disassemble the Software. You may transfer the Software and user documentation on a permanent basis, provided that the transferee agrees to accept the terms and conditions of this Agreement and you retain no copies. If the Software is an update or has been updated, any transfer must include the most recent update and all prior versions.

4. **Restrictions on Use of Individual Programs.** You must follow the individual requirements and restrictions detailed for each individual program in the "About the CD" appendix of this Book. These limitations are also contained in the individual license agreements recorded on the Software Media. These limitations may include a requirement that after using the program for a specified period of time, the user must pay a registration fee or discontinue use. By opening the Software packet(s), you will be agreeing to abide by the licenses and restrictions for these individual programs that are detailed in the "About the CD" appendix and on the Software Media. None of the material on this Software Media or listed in this Book may ever be redistributed, in original or modified form, for commercial purposes.

5. **Limited Warranty.**

   (a) WPI warrants that the Software and Software Media are free from defects in materials and workmanship under normal use for a period of sixty (60) days from the date of purchase of this Book. If WPI receives notification within the warranty period of defects in materials or workmanship, WPI will replace the defective Software Media.

   (b) WPI AND THE AUTHOR OF THE BOOK DISCLAIM ALL OTHER WARRANTIES, EXPRESS OR IMPLIED, INCLUDING WITHOUT LIMITATION IMPLIED WARRANTIES OF MERCHANTABIL-ITY AND FITNESS FOR A PARTICULAR PURPOSE, WITH RESPECT TO THE SOFTWARE, THE PROGRAMS, THE SOURCE CODE CONTAINED THEREIN, AND/OR THE TECHNIQUES DESCRIBED IN THIS BOOK. WPI DOES NOT WARRANT THAT THE FUNCTIONS CON-TAINED IN THE SOFTWARE WILL MEET YOUR REQUIREMENTS OR THAT THE OPERATION OF THE SOFTWARE WILL BE ERROR FREE.

   (c) This limited warranty gives you specific legal rights, and you may have other rights that vary from jurisdiction to jurisdiction.

6. **Remedies.**

   (a) WPI's entire liability and your exclusive remedy for defects in materials and workman-ship shall be limited to replacement of the Software Media, which may be returned to WPI with a copy of your receipt at the following address: Software Media Fulfillment Department, Attn.: *Software Project Management Kit For Dummies,* Wiley Publishing, Inc., 10475 Crosspoint Blvd., Indianapolis, IN 46256, or call 1-800-762-2974. Please allow four to six weeks for delivery. This Limited Warranty is void if failure of the Software Media has resulted from accident, abuse, or misapplication. Any replacement Software Media will be warranted for the remainder of the original warranty period or thirty (30) days, whichever is longer.

   (b) In no event shall WPI or the author be liable for any damages whatsoever (including without limitation damages for loss of business profits, business interruption, loss of business information, or any other pecuniary loss) arising from the use of or inability to use the Book or the Software, even if WPI has been advised of the possibility of such damages.

   (c) Because some jurisdictions do not allow the exclusion or limitation of liability for conse-quential or incidental damages, the above limitation or exclusion may not apply to you.

7. **U.S. Government Restricted Rights.** Use, duplication, or disclosure of the Software for or on behalf of the United States of America, its agencies and/or instrumentalities "U.S. Government" is subject to restrictions as stated in paragraph (c)(1)(ii) of the Rights in Technical Data and Computer Software clause of DFARS 252.227-7013, or subparagraphs (c) (1) and (2) of the Commercial Computer Software - Restricted Rights clause at FAR 52.227-19, and in similar clauses in the NASA FAR supplement, as applicable.

8. **General.** This Agreement constitutes the entire understanding of the parties and revokes and supersedes all prior agreements, oral or written, between them and may not be modified or amended except in a writing signed by both parties hereto that specifically refers to this Agreement. This Agreement shall take precedence over any other documents that may be in conflict herewith. If any one or more provisions contained in this Agreement are held by any court or tribunal to be invalid, illegal, or otherwise unenforceable, each and every other provi-sion shall remain in full force and effect.

FOR DUMMIES®

The easy way to get more done and have more fun

PERSONAL FINANCE

0-7645-5231-7

0-7645-2431-3

0-7645-5331-3

Also available:

Estate Planning For Dummies
(0-7645 5501-4)
401(k)s For Dummies
(0-7645-5468-9)
Frugal Living For Dummies
(0-7645-5403-4)
Microsoft Money "X" For
Dummies
(0-7645-1689-2)
Mutual Funds For Dummies
(0-7645-5329-1)

Personal Bankruptcy For
Dummies
(0-7645-5498-0)
Quicken "X" For Dummies
(0-7645-1666-3)
Stock Investing For Dummies
(0-7645-5411-5)
Taxes For Dummies 2003
(0-7645-5475-1)

BUSINESS & CAREERS

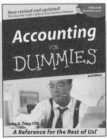

0-7645-5314-3

0-7645-5307-0

0-7645-5471-9

Also available:

Business Plans Kit For
Dummies
(0-7645-5365-8)
Consulting For Dummies
(0-7645-5034-9)
Cool Careers For Dummies
(0-7645-5345-3)
Human Resources Kit For
Dummies
(0-7645-5131-0)
Managing For Dummies
(1-5688-4858-7)

QuickBooks All-in-One Desk
Reference For Dummies
(0-7645-1963-8)
Selling For Dummies
(0-7645-5363-1)
Small Business Kit For
Dummies
(0-7645-5093-4)
Starting an eBay Business For
Dummies
(0-7645-1547-0)

HEALTH, SPORTS & FITNESS

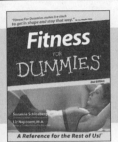

0-7645-5167-1

0-7645-5146-9

0-7645-5154-X

Also available:

Controlling Cholesterol For
Dummies
(0-7645-5440-9)
Dieting For Dummies
(0-7645-5126-4)
High Blood Pressure For
Dummies
(0-7645-5424-7)
Martial Arts For Dummies
(0-7645-5358-5)
Menopause For Dummies
(0-7645-5458-1)

Nutrition For Dummies
(0-7645-5180-9)
Power Yoga For Dummies
(0-7645-5342-9)
Thyroid For Dummies
(0-7645-5385-2)
Weight Training For Dummies
(0-7645-5168-X)
Yoga For Dummies
(0-7645-5117-5)

Available wherever books are sold.
Go to www.dummies.com or call 1-877-762-2974 to order direct.

 WILEY

FOR DUMMIES®

A world of resources to help you grow

HOME, GARDEN & HOBBIES

0-7645-5295-3

0-7645-5130-2

0-7645-5106-X

Also available:

Auto Repair For Dummies
(0-7645-5089-6)

Chess For Dummies
(0-7645-5003-9)

Home Maintenance For
Dummies
(0-7645-5215-5)

Organizing For Dummies
(0-7645-5300-3)

Piano For Dummies
(0-7645-5105-1)

Poker For Dummies
(0-7645-5232-5)

Quilting For Dummies
(0-7645-5118-3)

Rock Guitar For Dummies
(0-7645-5356-9)

Roses For Dummies
(0-7645-5202-3)

Sewing For Dummies
(0-7645-5137-X)

FOOD & WINE

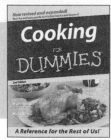

0-7645-5250-3

0-7645-5390-9

0-7645-5114-0

Also available:

Bartending For Dummies
(0-7645-5051-9)

Chinese Cooking For
Dummies
(0-7645-5247-3)

Christmas Cooking For
Dummies
(0-7645-5407-7)

Diabetes Cookbook For
Dummies
(0-7645-5230-9)

Grilling For Dummies
(0-7645-5076-4)

Low-Fat Cooking For
Dummies
(0-7645-5035-7)

Slow Cookers For Dummies
(0-7645-5240-6)

TRAVEL

0-7645-5453-0

0-7645-5438-7

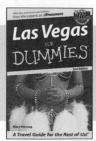

0-7645-5448-4

Also available:

America's National Parks For
Dummies
(0-7645-6204-5)

Caribbean For Dummies
(0-7645-5445-X)

Cruise Vacations For
Dummies 2003
(0-7645-5459-X)

Europe For Dummies
(0-7645-5456-5)

Ireland For Dummies
(0-7645-6199-5)

France For Dummies
(0-7645-6292-4)

London For Dummies
(0-7645-5416-6)

Mexico's Beach Resorts For
Dummies
(0-7645-6262-2)

Paris For Dummies
(0-7645-5494-8)

RV Vacations For Dummies
(0-7645-5443-3)

Walt Disney World & Orlando
For Dummies
(0-7645-5444-1)

Available wherever books are sold. Go to www.dummies.com or call 1-877-762-2974 to order direct.

FOR DUMMIES®

Plain-English solutions for everyday challenges

COMPUTER BASICS

0-7645-0838-5

0-7645-1663-9

0-7645-1548-9

Also available:

PCs All-in-One Desk Reference For Dummies (0-7645-0791-5)

Pocket PC For Dummies (0-7645-1640-X)

Treo and Visor For Dummies (0-7645-1673-6)

Troubleshooting Your PC For Dummies (0-7645-1669-8)

Upgrading & Fixing PCs For Dummies (0-7645-1665-5)

Windows XP For Dummies (0-7645-0893-8)

Windows XP For Dummies Quick Reference (0-7645-0897-0)

BUSINESS SOFTWARE

0-7645-0822-9

0-7645-0839-3

0-7645-0819-9

Also available:

Excel Data Analysis For Dummies (0-7645-1661-2)

Excel 2002 All-in-One Desk Reference For Dummies (0-7645-1794-5)

Excel 2002 For Dummies Quick Reference (0-7645-0829-6)

GoldMine "X" For Dummies (0-7645-0845-8)

Microsoft CRM For Dummies (0-7645-1698-1)

Microsoft Project 2002 For Dummies (0-7645-1628-0)

Office XP For Dummies (0-7645-0830-X)

Outlook 2002 For Dummies (0-7645-0828-8)

Get smart! Visit www.dummies.com

- **Find listings of even more *For Dummies* titles**

- **Browse online articles**

- **Sign up for Dummies eTips™**

- **Check out *For Dummies* fitness videos and other products**

- **Order from our online bookstore**

Available wherever books are sold. Go to www.dummies.com or call 1-877-762-2974 to order direct.

FOR DUMMIES®

Helping you expand your horizons and realize your potential

INTERNET

0-7645-0894-6

0-7645-1659-0

0-7645-1642-6

Also available:

America Online 7.0 For Dummies
(0-7645-1624-8)

Genealogy Online For Dummies
(0-7645-0807-5)

The Internet All-in-One Desk Reference For Dummies
(0-7645-1659-0)

Internet Explorer 6 For Dummies
(0-7645-1344-3)

The Internet For Dummies Quick Reference
(0-7645-1645-0)

Internet Privacy For Dummies
(0-7645-0846-6)

Researching Online For Dummies
(0-7645-0546-7)

Starting an Online Business For Dummies
(0-7645-1655-8)

DIGITAL MEDIA

0-7645-1664-7

0-7645-1675-2

0-7645-0806-7

Also available:

CD and DVD Recording For Dummies
(0-7645-1627-2)

Digital Photography All-in-One Desk Reference For Dummies
(0-7645-1800-3)

Digital Photography For Dummies Quick Reference
(0-7645-0750-8)

Home Recording for Musicians For Dummies
(0-7645-1634-5)

MP3 For Dummies
(0-7645-0858-X)

Paint Shop Pro "X" For Dummies
(0-7645-2440-2)

Photo Retouching & Restoration For Dummies
(0-7645-1662-0)

Scanners For Dummies
(0-7645-0783-4)

GRAPHICS

0-7645-0817-2

0-7645-1651-5

0-7645-0895-4

Also available:

Adobe Acrobat 5 PDF For Dummies
(0-7645-1652-3)

Fireworks 4 For Dummies
(0-7645-0804-0)

Illustrator 10 For Dummies
(0-7645-3636-2)

QuarkXPress 5 For Dummies
(0-7645-0643-9)

Visio 2000 For Dummies
(0-7645-0635-8)

Available wherever books are sold. Go to www.dummies.com or call 1-877-762-2974 to order direct.

FOR DUMMIES®

The advice and explanations you need to succeed

SELF-HELP, SPIRITUALITY & RELIGION

0-7645-5302-X

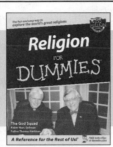

0-7645-5418-2

0-7645-5264-3

Also available:

The Bible For Dummies
(0-7645-5296-1)

Buddhism For Dummies
(0-7645-5359-3)

Christian Prayer For Dummies
(0-7645-5500-6)

Dating For Dummies
(0-7645-5072-1)

Judaism For Dummies
(0-7645-5299-6)

Potty Training For Dummies
(0-7645-5417-4)

Pregnancy For Dummies
(0-7645-5074-8)

Rekindling Romance For Dummies
(0-7645-5303-8)

Spirituality For Dummies
(0-7645-5298-8)

Weddings For Dummies
(0-7645-5055-1)

PETS

0-7645-5255-4

0-7645-5286-4

0-7645-5275-9

Also available:

Labrador Retrievers For Dummies
(0-7645-5281-3)

Aquariums For Dummies
(0-7645-5156-6)

Birds For Dummies
(0-7645-5139-6)

Dogs For Dummies
(0-7645-5274-0)

Ferrets For Dummies
(0-7645-5259-7)

German Shepherds For Dummies
(0-7645-5280-5)

Golden Retrievers For Dummies
(0-7645-5267-8)

Horses For Dummies
(0-7645-5138-8)

Jack Russell Terriers For Dummies
(0-7645-5268-6)

Puppies Raising & Training Diary For Dummies
(0-7645-0876-8)

EDUCATION & TEST PREPARATION

0-7645-5194-9

0-7645-5325-9

0-7645-5210-4

Also available:

Chemistry For Dummies
(0-7645-5430-1)

English Grammar For Dummies
(0-7645-5322-4)

French For Dummies
(0-7645-5193-0)

The GMAT For Dummies
(0-7645-5251-1)

Inglés Para Dummies
(0-7645-5427-1)

Italian For Dummies
(0-7645-5196-5)

Research Papers For Dummies
(0-7645-5426-3)

The SAT I For Dummies
(0-7645-5472-7)

U.S. History For Dummies
(0-7645-5249-X)

World History For Dummies
(0-7645-5242-2)

Available wherever books are sold. Go to www.dummies.com or call 1-877-762-2974 to order direct.

Installation Instructions

To install the items from the CD to your hard drive, follow these steps.

1. **Insert the CD into your computer's CD-ROM drive.**

2. **Click Start⇨Run.**

3. **In the dialog box that appears, type** D:\START.HTM

   Replace *D* with the proper drive letter if your CD-ROM drive uses a different letter.

   If you don't know which drive letter corresponds to your CD-ROM, look for the CD-ROM icon in My Computer and note the drive letter beneath it.

4. **Click OK.**

5. **Read through the license agreement, nod your head, and then click the Accept button if you want to use the CD — after you click Accept, you'll jump to the Main Menu.**

6. **To navigate within the interface, simply click on any topic of interest to take you to an explanation of the files on the CD and how to use or install them.**

7. **To install the software from the CD, simply click on the software name.**

   When you finish, eject the CD and carefully place it back in the plastic jacket of the book for safekeeping.